PROPHETS AND PEOPLES

PROPHETS and PEOPLES

Studies in Nineteenth Century Nationalism

By HANS KOHN

OCTAGON BOOKS

A Division of Hippocrene Books, Inc.

New York   1983

OCTAGON BOOKS
A DIVISION OF HIPPOCRENE BOOKS, INC.

Library of Congress Cataloging in Publication Data

Kohn, Hans, 1891-1971.
    Prophets and peoples.

        Reprint of the ed. published by Macmillan, New York. This book grew
    out of five lectures delivered in July, 1945, as the Norman Walt Harris
    Foundation lectures at Northwestern University in Evanston, Illinois."

        Includes bibliographical references.
        1. Nationalism.   I. Title.
JC311.K568   1975   320.5′4′094   75-4697
ISBN 0-88254-842-5

PREFACE

This book grew out of five lectures delivered in July, 1945, as the Norman Wait Harris Foundation Lectures at Northwestern University in Evanston, Illinois. Their purpose was to explain the character of Europe's leading nations as a background for an understanding of their policies in modern times. The lectures have been amplified and annotated for publication.

The many courtesies extended by the University and the Norman Wait Harris Lecture Committee made my stay in Evanston memorably pleasant. My special gratitude goes to my former colleague, Ray Allen Billington, now Professor of History at Northwestern University, and to Mrs. Billington for their gracious hospitality.

Mrs. Vincent Erikson has assisted me in a most conscientious and efficient manner by typing the manuscript and preparing it for publication. Parts of it appeared in *The Review of Politics* and *The Journal of the History of Ideas*.

H. K.

Northampton, Massachusetts
Autumn, 1945

CONTENTS

Introduction

The recent Past contains the key to the present time. All forms of thought that influence it come before us in their turn, and we have to describe the ruling currents, to interpret the sovereign forces that still govern and divide the world . . .

By Universal History I understand that which is distinct from the combined history of all countries, which is not a rope of sand, but a continuous development, and is not a burden on the memory, but an illumination of the soul. It moves in a succession to which the nations are subsidiary. Their story will be told, not for their own sake, but in reference and subordination to a higher series, according to the time and the degree in which they contribute to the common fortunes of mankind.

—ACTON, *letter as Editor of the "Cambridge Modern History."*

In the meantime I would recommend to you as guides in this controversy truth, charity, diligence, and reverence, which indeed may be called the four cardinal virtues of all controversies, be they what they may.

—GLADSTONE, *December 5, 1879.*

INTRODUCTION

THE age of nationalism saw for the first time the peoples, aroused to national consciousness, as the decisive actors of history. They found their spokesmen in national prophets who became the voice and the conscience of their people, interpreting its history or mission and shaping its character and personality. They were historians or journalists, statesmen or creative writers, orators or social scientists. In most cases they combined several of these vocations; always they developed a philosophy of history and society, in the center of which stood their own nation and the principle which was to sum up its idea and faith. In that sense Shelley in his "Ode to Liberty"—

> And England's prophets hailed thee as their queen
> In songs whose music can not pass away—

greeted his fellow poets as the prophetic singers of national symbols, and Woodrow Wilson, referring to Lincoln and Jefferson yet thinking also of himself, defined the role of prophetic statesmen when he said: "A great nation is led by a man in whose ears the voices of the nation do not sound accidental and discordant but reveal to him a single vision, so that he can speak what no man else knows, the common meaning of the common voice." [1]

Each of the men designated as "national prophet" expressed the genius of his people or at least an important and representative aspect of it. Each one was recognized and acclaimed in his own time as a national spokesman. They have not been selected here because they were the greatest or wisest men in their own fields or in their own time—there were many wiser

men than Michelet or Mazzini, Treitschke or Dostoevsky; only
Mill can really be called wise—but because each of them made
a highly significant contribution to the understanding of nationalism and helped to shape the age of nationalism. It would
be a dangerous mistake to assume that any one of them represents the whole image of his nation and its trends. For a national character is a highly complex phenomenon with many
cross-currents of thought and aspirations and with all the human breadth of individual variations. Yet throughout the ever-
flowing change of time and events and the ever-broadening
diversity of occupations and classes, and above all the unfathomable variety of individual characters, there is, at least over
centuries or decades, a very definite constancy and consistency
in national character, a national "idea." "National prophets"
express such ideas in their words and often in their lives and
call for better realization of the ideas; these ideas thus become
the normative form and goal of national life. In the age of
nationalism the people identify themselves more and more with
their national ideas which, in a process of constant interaction,
shape and strengthen the national character. The seemingly
uniform pattern of nationalism includes a great diversity and
even contrariety of national ideas which a closer study of their
history projects into bold relief.

Modern nationalism originated in the seventeenth and eighteenth centuries in northwestern Europe and its American set-
tlements.[2] It became a general European movement in the nineteenth century. In the middle of the century England and
France had long found their national organization and symbols; in the center of the continent Italy and Germany were
at work to give form and content to their national existence;
while on its eastern border Russia groped her way to enter the
comity of European nations. These five nations were the great
powers of the second half of the century: [3] a century in which
European civilization led and shaped the world through—and

to—the very form of social cohesion which it had found in nationalism. Its leadership resulted in nationalism becoming in the twentieth century the common form of life all over the earth; at the same time the developments in science and communication brought about an ever greater similarity of the social pattern on the five continents. Many have believed that one humanity with a common cultural design is emerging in this one world. In reality, however, the age of nationalism has made the divisions of mankind more pronounced and has spread the consciousness of antagonistic aspirations to wider multitudes of men than ever before. The closer contact between various cultures and their growing rootedness in the minds and morals of the masses have not only deepened conflicts between nations but have produced cultural tensions which invest the national struggles with the halo of a semireligious crusade. Wars between nations have become wars between national ideas, in which not only the well-being or existence of a nation but the validity and potency of fundamental principles of social conduct and of ethical values appear at stake.

Each new nation looked for its justification to its national heritage—often re-interpreted to suit the supposed needs of the situation—and strove for its glorification. Out of the myths of the past and the dreams of the future, national prophets have often created an ideal fatherland which, though it had little historical or political reality, influenced the shape of things to come and endowed international conflicts with emotional and religious fervor. As the early modern nations were born in an age and under the symbols of reason and liberty, the later nationalisms, in conflict with and in differentiation from the older ones, often tended to reject the Western values. Sometimes they proclaimed their alleged superiority by belittling or burying the free state and the free individual of modern society. The wars of 1870, 1914 and 1939 were for the

Germans, whose nationalism had been awakened by the French Revolution, not simply wars of national defense or for national aggrandizement, but conflicts between the German idea and the allegedly irreconcilable idea of the Western nations. Similarly, many Russians, who had been aroused to modern nationhood by contact with Germany and the West, turned against Western influences, this time including the Germans with the West, and sought justification for their national aspirations in a largely legendary reconstruction of their past that opposed Slavic to Western (or German) ideas.

This process has been in no way confined to Europe. When Macaulay in 1835 presented his Memorandum on education in India, contact between the civilizations of Europe and Asia had for centuries been slight and superficial. In this Memorandum he proposed to promote English education and English ideals for India. The reform following on the Memorandum created a new India, and its effects were felt all over Asia. Through contact with England a generation of Indian intellectuals imbued with English ideas of freedom, justice and human dignity grew up. Under the impact of English ideas and in imitation of English political methods they formed, in 1885, with the help of English liberals, the Indian National Congress, the first representative organization of public opinion in Asiatic lands. The intellectual and moral stir in India, known as the Indian national movement, was entirely a product of India's cultural contact with Britain. The application of English ideas to Indian life awakened an Indian desire for nationhood and led to an agitation against the continuation of British domination over India. Soon this Indian nationalism objected not only to Britain's political control but to her cultural influence. In order to be "truly" Indian, it felt the need of sharp differentiation from England and the West. It began to look to the past for its inspiration. Originally an insistence upon the right to demand constitutional liberties under the new rule of law, it now proclaimed a moral obligation to protect ancient religious and tribal customs from foreign influence, and in particular from an imitation of English liberalism. Legends of the past and dreams of the future combined to create a vision of India's peculiar and unique task in the service of mankind. A mission was discovered for India: Indian religious spiritualism and metaphysical profundity were to save Europe from Western materialism, a craving for physical (superficial) comfort, and competitive strife. This goal was set before Indian youth, sometimes with extravagant exuberance: "You shall help to create a nation, to spiritualize an epoch, to Aryanize the world. And that nation is your own, that epoch belongs to you and your children, and that world is no mere tract of land, but the whole earth with its teeming millions."

II

The age of nationalism brought to Europe a sense of conscious and growing differentiation. The great voices of former ages—Aquinas, Erasmus, Voltaire—spoke for Christendom or Europe; Bentham, Rousseau and Kant were concerned with mankind; but in the nineteenth century the European society and the European mind lost the oneness of the preceding age and dissolved into conflicting groups and culture patterns. Yet even in the age of nationalism an underlying unity survived: though Europe no longer spoke with one voice, the polyphony of its leading national voices carried on a dialectic conversation in which a new European personality was revealing itself. Though nationalism presents itself in a great diversity of forms and aspirations—the same name does not imply the same values and attitudes—yet as a result of so many centuries the common heritage of Western civilization, of Athens, Jerusalem and Rome, has persisted, a heritage which Russia more and more began to share in the nineteenth century.[4]

The age of nationalism stressed national pasts and traditions against the rationalism of the eighteenth century with its emphasis on the common sense of civilization. This historical perspective has enriched man's understanding of himself, for history is the unalterable background of human life. Yet it carries with it a strange and sometimes pernicious fascination. For it is no less dangerous to forgo historical perspective and to regard Anglo-American liberties, German national socialism, or Russian lawless autocracy as accidental or ephemeral events or stages without deep roots in national history, than to regard historical and time-bound conditions as carrying with them the permanency of divine institutions or natural laws, above the changes wrought by the flow of time and the contact of cultures.[5]

Many examples of recent experience show the danger of fascination with the past, with memories of the Roman or the Byzantine Empire, of ancient migrations of Germanic tribes, of historical frontiers of Slav settlement. Poland's misfortune has been partly caused by the identification of the ethnic Poland of the age of nationalism with the seventeenth-century Polish commonwealth in its supranational vast territories. Bulgarians have fought and lost three wars because the dream of San Stefano and of the medieval empire of Tsar Simeon, whose name the present boy king bears, obsessed them. General Franco's followers in Spain have set their hearts not upon the thorough modernization and liberalization of their country in a spirit of rational tolerance but upon the resurrection of the glories of the Golden Century, of the great Catholic empire of the Hispanidad which irretrievably broke down before the modern liberal world which they so deeply and haughtily despise. No romantic dreams can undo the story which led from the dispersion of the Invincible Armada by England in 1588 to the destruction of the Spanish fleet 310 years later by the United States.[6]

The British and American peoples, in their eighteenth-century optimism and their trust in common sense, often miss the impact of history because they have short memories. Other nations miss the opportunities of life because they have too long memories and lose themselves in the tragic implications of "destiny." They remember too vividly, almost as a present-day reality, what happened hundreds or even thousands of years ago, embellishing it by national legends and reinterpreting it by the present alleged national needs. To cope with present conflicts, men must draw understanding from the past, from the deep resources of history; but nothing is more dangerous than the wish to fix mankind into the molds of the past and to have nations haunted by its ghosts.

In the age of nationalism some nations have claimed for themselves a "mission" here on earth: the divine right of kings was replaced by the divine right of nations. Messianic dreams with the nation as their center put the nation into immediate and independent relations with the Absolute. (Of the "national prophets" considered here, only Mill was without such dangerous delusions.) In actuality the nations in the age of nationalism have fulfilled functions, a task which demands their integration into an interdependent community of nations. Such a community with its roots in a common cultural heritage has been growing up in modern Europe. Mill, Michelet and Mazzini, though not Treitschke or Dostoevsky, were good Europeans. In 1916, during the great war, Romain Rolland, a good European himself, predicted that "in the near future, the union of the nations of Western Europe will form the new fatherland. It itself will be only a stage on the road which leads to the greater fatherland: Europe." [7] These words have lost nothing of their urgency in the aftermath of an even greater war.

Europe has always been characterized by a great diversity within its loose unity, by its wealth of individual growth and free interplay. It has resisted every attempt to impose, for its ideological salvation or its economic welfare, uniformity and "order." It has found its greatness in the manifold exercise of freedom. The small continent has never bowed for long to dictation nor has it ever acknowledged the right or precedence of bigness. Its heart beats as strongly in Switzerland as in France, in Holland as in England. Europe's smaller nations have been and will remain equally important in the growth and in the cross-fertilization of its civilization. Their "national prophets" were often outstanding as good Europeans. Differences of origin have disappeared before the unity of the spirit. Men like Thomas G. Masaryk, born where Czech and Slovak peasants intermingle, and Asher Ginsberg, brought up in a Jewish ghetto in Russia, were, in the sobriety of their moral realism, in their unsparing search for truth, and in their respect for human dignity, of the same race as Mill.

Many of the social, intellectual and political problems which troubled the "national prophets" of the nineteenth century confront Europe today. Hopes and anxieties voiced by them, demands and solutions proposed by them, still fill the minds and hearts of twentieth-century Europe. Today, in the uncertainties and confusion of the aftermath of the two great wars, Europe scans the horizon of the future more anxiously than ever before. The continent which guards vigilantly its vitality of spirit and its heritage of freedom, has no cause for despair: "Many are the shapes of the divine; many things the gods accomplish beyond hope; and often the expected is not fulfilled, but a god finds a path unexpected by us." [8]

Chapter One

ENGLAND: J. S. MILL

Those nations have the best chance of escaping a catastrophe
. . . who find a way of opening the most liberal career to the
aspirations of the present without too rudely breaking with all
the traditions of the past.

—JOHN MORLEY.

Je suis, arrivé à l'âge où je suis, à travers bien des événements
différents, une seule cause, celle de la liberté régulière.

—TOCQUEVILLE, *May 1, 1852.*

Freedom was born in the West—to be precise, in your little
island. Everything great is born out of something little—men on
the little Planet, the Earth; our culture in Greece; Christianity in
Palestine; freedom in England. It arose in mediaeval England; from
there it spread all over the world, and now it is again confined
within the limits of the Anglo-Saxon countries. Only there is it
deeply bound up with Christianity. That is why the spiritual destiny of the world is being decided on your little island, the destiny
of Russia also.

—*A Russian scholar to an English friend, 1941.*

1

O F ALL the modern nations England is the oldest. Sometimes the rise of a nation requires decades: that was the case of Italy and Germany. Sometimes it is consummated in one short brilliant moment: that was the case of France. Sometimes it happens in two stages of which one may be compared to actual birth and baptism, the other to confirmation: that was the case of Russia—where Peter's age represented the birth and Stalin's the confirmation—and of England, where both events occurred in the seventeenth century. The English nation was born in the Puritan and confirmed in the Glorious Revolution. The former was filled with the fire and fury of the intolerant hatreds and the passionate struggles which are generally implied in the word "revolution"; the latter was in comparison an almost quiet settlement by compromise and tolerance, devoid of the spectacular luster which men think a necessary attribute of most "glorious" events. Yet the small and still voice of the confirmation took up and followed to realization the trumpet calls of the baptism: the supremacy of law over the king, the preponderance of Parliament in lawmaking, the impartiality of justice, the security of individual rights, the freedom of thought and press, religious tolerance.

But though the Glorious Revolution continued and realized the main promises of the Puritan Revolution it did it in an entirely different spirit. It lifted the new liberties above the welter of fanatical religious and party strife: it made them the common foundation of the whole nation and anchored them as "true and ancient rights of the people of this realm" in its historical tradition. The achievements of the seventeenth-century English revolutions—the dignity of the individual and the free state—have since become the guiding star for the progressive development of all mankind; but only with the English-speaking peoples have they become so firmly a part of national life and character that no serious attempt has ever been made to undermine them. The new order in England, more revolutionary and yet more orderly than anything known before, has shown a unique firmness because it sprang from the national compromise of a settlement, not from the partisan fanaticism of a revolution. It was not imposed by force but was accepted through discussion; it did not liquidate "wicked" opposition, but invited the cooperation of political opponents and respected their personalities and opinions. It created the spirit of reconciliation which democracy demands.[1]

Nations are often determined for a very long time by the forces and ideas which influenced their beginnings. The English inherited from the Puritan Revolution the religious matrix and the spirit of non-conformism, from the Glorious Revolution the habits of toleration and respect for law. The absolutism of monarchy was not exchanged for the despotism of revolution: the Parliament, thanks to the party system a body divided against itself, could never assume dictatorial powers infringing the rights of any individual. Parliament protected political liberties, as common law, the other fruit of the English mind, protected civil rights. In the new security of liberty under law man's manners changed: a hitherto unknown regard for one's fellow man, a refinement and mellowing of feeling, began to transform human relations in the eighteenth century, and even more in the nineteenth. The settlement of 1689 was based upon a new civilized attitude, to live and let live; in its moral atmosphere old fanaticisms disappeared in the exhilarating experience of new unlimited horizons in nature and society. In the years of the Glorious Revolution the Western European mind began its definite transition from the Middle Ages to modern times. "The great work of interpreting nature was performed by the English of that age as it had never before been performed in any age by any nation. The spirit of Francis Bacon was abroad, a spirit admirably compounded of audacity and sobriety. There was a strong persuasion that the whole world was full of secrets of high moment to the happiness of man, and that man had, by his Maker, been entrusted with the key which, rightly used, would give access to them." [2]

The English—in England, in North America and in Australasia—have since pioneered in the spirit of that audacity and sobriety for the expansion of political and social freedom. In this ever-broadening diffusion of culture and comfort to the masses, the spiritual and the material, religious faith and secular life, tradition and progress, rarely became conflicting opposites: while logic threatened to separate them, the spirit of compromise harmonized them. Even in late Victorian England Christianity survived as a living force in a secular age, aristocracy in a commercialized age, monarchy in a radical age. [3] In all the innovations of the industrial mass civilization, the political frame exhibited its stability and flexibility, because with the English-speaking peoples the initiative rested with society, not with the state. The characteristics of the state are enforcement and uniformity, the characteristics of society are voluntary cooperation and variety. In other nations life was held in order and progress achieved by the state, which either dominated or absorbed society or wasted its strength in conflicts with it; in England society and state lived together, one supporting the other, but of the two society showed the far greater vitality and initiative. Free association and public opinion inspired and pioneered in all fields: in economic enterprise and social work, in education and empire-building, as sects in religion and as parties in politics. [4] "Nine-tenths of the internal business which elsewhere devolves on the government," J. S. Mill wrote about England, "is transacted by agencies independent of it." Law and freedom created the spirit of self-reliance and initiative which democracy demands.

With the seventeenth century England assumed leadership in the progress of political life and the growth of civil liberty. But her insularity and empiricism limited the influence of the English mind. The example of English liberty spread through the medium of France. These two Western nations were never in closer cultural interchange, in spite of wars and imperial rivalry, than in the eighteenth century, when so many educated Englishmen travelled in France and Locke's and Newton's philosophy fertilized French enlightenment. Montesquieu, Voltaire and Rousseau were only the most outstanding crests in the wave of Anglomania which swept France. The French eighteenth-century mind illumined English reality with the light of logical clarity and universal rationalism,[5] and radiated it all over Europe. The events of 1792 revived the fire and fury of the Puritan Revolution. But where the religious fanaticism of the seventeenth century had lighted an intra-Christian struggle, now it turned on a battle between Christianity and irreligion. The matrix of the Revolution was no longer religious; in the unitarian character of Catholic countries there was no room for the individual varieties of nonconformism. The French like the Puritan Revolution degenerated into a parliamentary and a military dictatorship. It aroused deep-seated fears and fanned bitter hatreds. But no Glorious Revolution followed: the tensions of 1792 were never reconciled in a national acceptance of the mature fruit of the Revolution. France of the nineteenth century, from the white terror of 1815 to the Dreyfus Affair, remained a potential battleground between revolution and counter-revolution. This ever-present threat to democracy made France, not the English-speaking nations, the model for the European and South American continents where the struggle for liberty, long be-

fore settled in England and North America, began in the nineteenth century. In France the inspiration of the eighteenth
century always made the forces of liberty prevail over those
of authority. But the very tension of religious and social
conflict which weakened French society quickened French
thought, which in its turn stimulated and sharpened developments in England. It combated that complacency which in
the security of liberty and law may lead to spiritual stagnation.

II

England's eighteenth century was placid and tranquil, compared with the turbulence of the preceding century. The ship
of state sailed slowly and smoothly, proud of her stability and
her advanced liberty. But the Glorious Revolution's achieve-
ment of equilibrium between tradition and progress, order and
liberty was becoming endangered by the growing stress on
the more conservative side. To save and revitalize the settlement, a new dynamism was needed; it was introduced by two
movements which though different in their starting points and
attitudes led to the same end: the quickening of liberal progress. On the one hand the Methodist and Evangelical movements revived the religious rigorism and enthusiasm of the
seventeenth century; but this time they did not become destructive: they were kept in bounds by the broad-minded
tolerance which they now encountered; turned into construc-
tive channels, they strengthened, and in many cases awakened,
the spirit of self-reliance and initiative in the lower classes and
taught them the use of free association. Again non-conformist
Christianity, in an atmosphere of social activism and free agitation, inspired many of the humanitarian reforms in which
England soon was to lead the other countries.

On the other hand the Radical and Utilitarian movements,
though English in their emphasis on utility and experience,

showed a strong continental influence in their radical logic, their abstract principles and their demands for clarity and simplification. Jeremy Bentham devoted a very long life to the pursuit of two goals which were both contrary to the main trends of the English tradition: the codification of laws and constitutions, not only for England but for all countries; and the understanding of life through one basic principle which was to be applied in every field of morals and politics. His main concerns were those of the Glorious Revolution: liberty and law. In his wish to make them more effective in the interests of the happiness of the individual and of good government, he became a crusader for rational justice against the abuses of tradition. What he achieved was not a utopia of logical perfection but the gradual reform of law and parliament, and the improvement of social institutions and of the conditions of the poor, which ushered into the nineteenth century a new England and reestablished the equilibrium. Non-conformist piety and experimental rationalism, audacity and sobriety, combined again in the service of practical humanitarianism and individual advancement.

With all its one-sidedness and platitudes, Bentham's principle of the greatest happiness of the greatest number spurred the spirit of practical reform as no other principle could have done at that time. To him the principle of pleasure never meant vulgar hedonism. His personal life, the ceaseless labor of a disinterested sage for the common good, was the noblest testimony to the ideal. "I would have the dearest friend I have," he said, "to know that his interests, if they come into competition with those of the public, are as nothing to me. Thus will I serve my friends—thus would I be served by them. Has a man talents? he owes them to his country in every way in which they can be serviceable." But he thought equally of all other countries, and never claimed for his country any privileges or leadership. Few Englishmen have been as little insular

as Bentham; he concerned himself as much with reform and
progress in France and Russia, in Greece and Spain, in Guate-
mala and Venezuela as in his native land. He looked forward
to "a period when the moral code, grounded on the greatest-
happiness principle, will be the code of nations, teaching them,
in their vast political concerns, to create no useless misery and
to make their patriotism subservient to the demands of benevolence." He regarded the work of Adam Smith as a treatise
upon universal benevolence, "because it has shown that commerce is equally advantageous for all nations—each one profit-
ing in a different manner, according to its natural means; that
nations are associates and not rivals in the great social enterprise." Universal peace and trade, not national glory and
greatness, were his ideals. He opposed military patriotism in
every form, and worked out a plan for a universal and perpetual peace. Because the English constitution seemed to him
to guarantee liberty, he wrote in 1830 that he preferred the
English constitution to every other with the exception of the
United States' government, in which he saw an extension of
English liberty and habits under the conditions of democracy.[6]
He wished to make as many individuals as happy as possible,
but there could be no happiness without the incentive of liberty and the security of law.

A new and more radical note was introduced into Benthamism by James Mill, its foremost disciple. While Bentham came
from a comfortable middle-class family of lawyers, Mill spent
his childhood in a lowly Scotch home where Calvinist morality mingled with earthly poverty. Trained for the Presby-
terian ministry, he soon abandoned the religion of his fathers,
but carried into his new rationalism the austere gloom and the
love of justice of his former faith. Through the hard work of
many years he finally achieved for himself a responsible position at the India Office. He systematized Bentham's rather
incoherent teachings and efforts, and organized the personal

influence of an "impractical" recluse into a school. He enriched the utilitarian doctrine by a new emphasis on economics and economic theory, a field in which he cooperated with Ricardo. Thus he adapted Bentham's eighteenth-century outlook to the needs of a new age. Through his efforts the Utilitarians became a powerful element in the English reform agitation of the 1820's, but they also revealed the severe limitations of their movement: the aridity of its psychology and the class-character of its reforms. Its exclusive stress on reason and self-interest, its preference for property rather than welfare, carried the danger of losing touch with the new emotional forces and social aspirations which began to stir and move men in the age of romanticism and industrialism.

This new dogmatism, into which Benthamism fell fast under James Mill, made a restatement of the relations of individual liberty and the social order necessary. The fundamental principles of the Glorious Revolution remained but they had to be adjusted to the intellectual and moral climate of the nineteenth century. This task fell to John Stuart Mill, the natural and spiritual heir to utilitarianism, who overcame its limitations. He endowed rational and individual liberty with a new warmth and richness by fusing with it the missionary emotionalism of the Evangelical gospel, the spiritual values of the Romantic tradition, and the humane fellowship of the Socialist movement. His work and the progress of time combined in changing the creed of a fighting sect into a representative manifestation of the national mind. After John Mill and through him liberalism in the broad sense of the word became the common basis of all English parties. Within half a century after his death the Liberal Party, which through its reform work under Gladstone and Campbell-Bannerman embodied Mill's spirit into statute and custom, could disappear as a decisive factor on the political stage of England because the conservatives and labor also carried on the liberal heritage.

This common liberal heritage re-created the unity in fundamentals which makes possible the working of democracy under the severest tests. In the years which have passed since Mill's death in 1873 England has gone through greater crises than in any period since the seventeenth century. Twice did the threat of powerful external enemies bring the free institutions of the nation and the peaceful progress of the empire, seemingly so secure when Mill died, to the brink of total disaster. Internally, the drastic change from the complacent heyday of Victorianism was illustrated by economic decline and mass unemployment, general strikes and millions of socialist votes. In the midst of these national storms England's structure remained unshaken. Democracy was steadily expanded, liberty nowhere abandoned, leadership in social reforms maintained. All this was achieved in the spirit of the national settlement of 1689 which was restated by Mill himself when he wrote: "One of the most indispensable requisites in the management of free institutions is conciliation: a readiness to compromise; a willingness to concede something to opponents, and to share good measures so as to be as little offensive as possible to persons of opposite views." To the continuing success of the settlement, however, Mill contributed not only by his teachings, but as much through his personality, of which Morley wrote: "He was unrivalled in the difficult art of conciliating as much support as was possible and alienating as little sympathy as possible for novel and extremely unpopular opinions." [7] That spirit of conciliation continued and strengthened the historical foundations of English nationhood and cemented a national solidarity on the basis of individual liberty and human progress. The England of the seventeenth century had known great prophetic voices: Milton and Cromwell, who in a heroic age had called the English people to the mission and duty of liberty. The humane atmosphere of post-1689 England was hardly favorable to prophets. Instead there were men who quietly yet forcefully restated the English national idea in the light of reason and the understanding of tolerance. Such a man was John Stuart Mill.

III

Mill was born in 1806. His childhood was far from easy or happy: his father made him the object of a famous educational experiment which Mill has described in his autobiography. The boy was to become by rigorous training of the mind the perfect Benthamite. He was excluded from play or pleasure, tender love or childish companions. At the ungodly early age of three he began the study of Greek. At a time when other boys enter school, young Mill had read many Greek and Latin authors in the original language and had become exposed to the workings of a method which may be compared to that of the "One Hundred Great Books." His father took care of the boy's entire education, and it was one which modern educators would hardly call utilitarian. It was a broad liberal education in the traditional classical sense except that religion and·poetry were strictly excluded. It speaks well for Mill that he survived its rigors. Fortunately other influences counteracted the one-sidedness of this stern rationalist discipline; the earliest of these was the close contact with France, where Mill spent his fifteenth year and where he returned for long periods of residence in the latter part of his life. Mill remained one of the best informed Englishmen on France and the continent of his time. Ten years after his first visit to France two experiences became decisive for his development: the discovery of the world of poetry and beauty, and the meeting of his future wife. France, poetry, his wife: these three influences broke the exclusive grip of Benthamism on his mind. He remained faithful to the need of a philosophical and broad understanding. In 1835 he complained that the English, who had once stood at the head of Europe on philosophy, were not interested in thought for its own sake and did not believe that important practical consequences could follow from a study of the principles of human society and the philosophy of civilization. Throughout his life he showed a broad receptivity and a catholicity of interests. But fundamentally he remained, through heritage and early environment, a Calvinist moralist, mellowed through a deep human sympathy and a rare objectivity of thought. Gladstone called him a rationalist saint.

Mill's life was uneventful. He was an official at India House for a number of years, until he was retired at the dissolution of the East India Company. A few months later, his wife's death at Avignon, in 1858, dealt a terrible blow to him. His relationship with her had been one of the happiest and most intimate spiritual companionships known in history. The outward tranquility of his remaining fifteen years, of which he spent a large part near her tomb in southern France, was broken only by the three years when he represented the borough of Westminster in the House of Commons. It was the time in which Parliament discussed the second Reform Bill. In his own estimate, Mill's most important public service there was an amendment to the Bill to strike out the words limiting the franchise to males and thus to admit women to the suffrage on equal footing with men. This was a new and daring proposal, though it had occupied Mill's mind and his discussions with his wife for many years. Surprisingly, Mill could record more than eighty votes in favor of this amendment so dear to his heart. Characteristically, none of his writings is filled with as much passion and even one-sided exaggerations as his essay "On the Subjection of Women," the last book which he published. The passion of its pages may have been the result of the close companionship with his wife, but the reasoning itself was part of Mill's lifelong dedication to the fight against all abuses of power.

For though Mill's life was outwardly uneventful it was a constant and in the end successful struggle for unpopular causes.[8] He was not bent upon institutional reforms alone. He had seen during his life many reforms for which he had contended either effected or in course of being so, but they had produced little real improvement in the intellectual and moral state of the people. "I had learned from experience," he wrote in his *Autobiography*, "that many false opinions may be exchanged for true ones, without in the least altering the habits of mind of which false opinions are the result." In the middle of the nineteenth century the old opinions in religion, morals and politics were becoming discredited while they yet preserved life enough to impede the growth of any better opinions on those subjects. In that transitional period "of weak convictions, paralyzed intellects, and growing laxity of principle which cannot terminate until a renovation has been effected in the basis of belief, all thinking or writing which does not tend to promote such a renovation is of very little value beyond the moment." This renovation of men's thoughts and convictions was the task which Mill set himself.

Mill saw this renovation and free society threatened by two dangers: the selfish interests of individuals and classes who do not care sufficiently for their fellow men, and the threat to individual liberty implied in the growing power of the masses. He saw better than his contemporaries the great task of modern times: the preservation of individual liberty and its harmonization with the demands of solidarity and the needs of the age of the masses. He believed that only education could bring a solution. Men must learn by practice to labor and combine for generous and social purposes. "Interest in the common good is at present so weak a motive because the mind is not accustomed to dwell on it as it dwells from morning till night on things which stand only to personal advantage. Education, habit, and the cultivation of the sentiment, will

make a common man dig or weave for his country, as readily
as fight for it." But an uncontrolled growth of solidarity might
bring with it the equally dangerous tyranny of society over
the individual. Mill feared "lest the inevitable growth of social
equality and of the government of public opinion should impose on mankind an oppressive yoke of uniformity in opinion
and practice," so that all the great progress of liberty achieved
in the last two centuries might be lost. For without respect
for the free individual no free society can exist.

With prophetic insight Mill discerned, in the new world
of nationalism, industrialism and militarism which came into
being during his manhood, the growth of trends which only
the twentieth century brought fully into the open. In his
essay "On Liberty," which he thought likely to survive longer
than anything else he had written, he stressed the importance,
to man and society, of promoting spontaneity and a large variety of types of character, and of giving to human nature full
freedom to expand itself in innumerable and conflicting directions. Faith in individual liberty seemed to him never more
urgently needed than in a period when the powers of government and society over the individual were constantly growing.
For the absolutism of the masses can stunt and dwarf human
nature more efficiently than any royal absolutism ever dreamt
of doing. Mill knew that his warning might be regarded as
superfluous by his contemporaries, who perceived the trends
of the time less acutely than he did. Like all prophets he had
a forewarning of coming disasters; he was convinced that it
would be only in the future that the teachings of his essay
"On Liberty" would assume their real value and urgency.
What seemed to his contemporaries an exaggerated fear appears clearly in the middle of the twentieth century as a
world-wide threat.

Like Bentham, Mill was never concerned for England alone:
he cared less for national greatness than for the expansion of

liberty. Perhaps he knew that the reign of liberty and law was least threatened among Englishmen, of whom he remarked that "in all questions between a government and an individual, the presumption in every Englishman's mind is that the government is in the wrong." Respect for law, tolerance for fellow men and their opinions, distrust of power and its possible abuses, a dislike of violence, have rooted liberty more strongly in England than in other lands. But in the twentieth century individual liberty had to be envisaged in its worldwide social frame. Mill again stated it in prophetic words: "How to unite the greatest individual liberty of action with the common ownership in the raw material of the globe, and an equal participation of all in the benefits of combined labor."

Today the English-speaking peoples are more concerned than in Mill's time with his vision of the one world of free individuals, but they are as unable as he was to state when it would become practicable and by what form of institutions. For though the world is mechanically more one today than it was in Mill's time, actually it is today more sharply divided in fundamentals, for individual liberty and the free state are no longer the generally accepted ideals which they were in the nineteenth century. They are hardly valid today outside the lands whence they derived in the seventeenth and eighteenth centuries.

IV

The settlement of 1689 belonged to the pre-industrial era of landed squires and trading middle classes. Under the different dynamic conditions of the industrialized society of the nineteenth century the old problem of progress and order presented itself in a new form: how to integrate the masses into a system of liberty and how to control the power of the industrial and financial lords. The self-dependent individual had to be protected against the abuse of this potential tyranny, in the face of which he might be held back as much by absence of help as by its excess. Though self-reliance remained the only dignified attitude, assistance to a man discouraged by adverse circumstances might act not as a sedative but as a tonic restoring his dignity and initiative. For even under the most complex conditions these remain the only true ends; though an intelligent despotism may show much greater skill in carrying through vast projects of social improvement than liberty exhibits, only the latter can call forth the best in man and arouse "an energy which is never seen elsewhere, and which may, under favorable circumstances, beget the most amazing benefits." Mill referred to the United States as proof of liberty's ability to diffuse initiative and intelligence among the masses.[9] Social progress needed individual liberty.

For individual liberty implied much more than the absence of interference. It was the condition for making people think and making them better. Through liberty men grew spiritually and were able to acquire new ideas. And ideas, in Mill's conviction, were potent powers in history, shaping the course of mankind as much as social conditions. Political revolutions originated in moral revolutions; but only a free government was not afraid of having people think for themselves and follow new ideas. When England took up Milton's plea in the seventeenth century and decided to risk an unheard of revolutionary step of unforeseeable consequences, the abolition of censorship—perhaps the most portentous single innovation in modern history—which for the first time made a free press and free public opinion possible, she expressed a new trust in human nature, a confidence in the individual and in his abilities. This trust was not Rousseau's faith in the natural goodness of man, the dangerous fiction of the paradisaic nature of primitive man, of the divine character of the people elevated into a mystical entity. It was a rational faith in the educational force of liberty, belief that the enlightened civilization of a free society would improve men by making them less subject to prejudice and caprice and more attentive to reason.

Order and liberty were not mutually exclusive: the former did not lead to absolutism, the latter did not lead to anarchy: in an atmosphere of freedom and compromise individual and society were complementary. In such a regime the moral development of the individual leads toward greater mutuality, the social development of the state leads toward greater liberty. For a free individual should be a thinking man with definite responsibilities of citizenship. Mill thought that the citizen in casting his vote "is under an absolute moral obligation to consider the interests of the public, not his private advantage, and give his vote to the best of his judgment, exactly as he would be bound to do if he were the sole voter, and the election depended on him alone." The vote thus becomes not a right used according to caprice or momentary interests, but a duty like that of the juryman, exercised according to one's best and most conscientious opinion of the public good. A free state is not a mystical entity with its *raison d'état* used to justify a policy of self-interest; it is a mutuality of free individuals whose liberty it protects by a rational justice against political and economic tyranny.

The economic tyranny of an oligarchy of wealth, the political tyranny of the masses, the economic and political tyranny of a totalitarian bureaucracy are developments hardly foreseen in the Victorian age. Press and radio, factories and barracks have multiplied the pressure on the individual. The world has become so crowded, gregarious and noisy that privacy becomes ever more difficult. Mill has warned against these dangers to human liberty. "It is not good for man," he wrote, "to be kept perforce at all times in the presence of his species. A world from which solitude is extirpated is a very poor ideal." Solitude is essential for growth of character and mind; modern society tends to leave little to spontaneous personality. But, as Mill warned, "not by wearing down into uniformity all that is individual in themselves, but by cultivating it and calling it forth, will in the limits imposed by the rights and interests of others, human beings become a noble and beautiful object of contemplation. The despotism of custom is everywhere the standing hindrance to human advancement; the only unfailing and permanent sort of improvement is liberty, since by it there are as many possible independent centers of improvement as there are individuals." What has given the European family of nations leadership in progress? "Not any superior excellence in them, but their remarkable diversity of character and culture. Individuals, classes, nations, have been extremely unlike one another: they have struck out a great variety of paths, each leading to something valuable. Europe is indebted to this plurality of paths for its progressive and many-sided development." But should mankind become for some time unaccustomed to see diversity it might speedily become unable to conceive it. Liberty and progress are not secure possessions. They are fragile and have to be carefully cultivated. They are the product of a continuous educational effort.

In modern mass society, with its natural tendency toward collective mediocrity, only the diversity and intelligence of free individuals will make representative government work. To counteract this tendency it is necessary to insure that intelligent opinions have a chance to obtain by weight of character and strength of argument a greater influence than would belong to them numerically. But democracy cannot be regarded as the ideally best form of government unless it can be so organized that even the most numerous class or opinion shall be unable to reduce minorities to political insignificance, and to direct the course of legislation and administration to its own exclusive interest. "The problem is, to find the means of preventing this abuse, without sacrificing the characteristic advantages of popular government" which in itself is a potent factor in the education of the masses. But a majority unchecked by moderation and forbearance can become as selfish and tyrannical as a monarch, pursued with similar adulation and sycophancy, and subject to the same corrupting effects of power. People who have not the habits and love of liberty are therefore not fitted for representative government. In some cases the passion of military or national glory is so much stronger than the desire for personal independence that the people are ready to sacrifice the latter for the former. "Each one of their number is willing, like the private soldier in an army, to abdicate his personal freedom of action into the hands of his general, provided the army is triumphant and victorious, and he is able to flatter himself that he is one of the conquering host." In other cases subjection to a foreign government, notwithstanding its inevitable evils, can be of greatest advantage to a less advanced people and clear away obstacles to improvement which might have lasted indefinitely if the people had been left unassisted to its native tendencies. Self-government demands a maturity of mind and heart which rarely grows up but in the long cultivation of liberty. Mill had come to understand much better than Bentham the difficulties and dangers to which freedom, by its very nature, is exposed in the conditions of man. He knew that the road was arduous and long; [10] his mature and disciplined mind was not given to the dreams of easy utopias. He was fully conscious of the power of custom and traditions, of the tenacity of prejudice and interest, of man's almost unlimited ability to self-delusion; yet, like Bentham, he carried on his fight, without fail or fear, with audacity and sobriety, to open new paths to human freedom and to increase human happiness. Above all, he, like Bentham, was entirely free of any national self-glorification or self-indulgence.

V

Mill applied the same concern for liberty and standards of morality to the domestic field and to the discussion of international relations. An ever watchful critical sense, common sense in the full meaning of the word, preserved him from falling into the depth of any messianic nationalism or prophetic romanticism. He never expressed hatred or unfair criticism of another nation, he never attributed to England a manifest destiny or a world-embracing mission. He realized England's leadership in liberty; but even there he conceded America's primacy. He admired France and never claimed intellectual preëminence for England. He saw, like most English liberals, England's conspicuous iniquities rather than her not often manifest goodness. At the same time his objectivity did not allow him to share "the predisposition of the English" to be hypercritical of their own government and its actions. He found the English prone "to look unfavorably upon every act by which territory or revenue are acquired from foreign states and to take part with any government, however unworthy, which can make out the merest semblance of a case of injustice against our own country." For all countries he considered individual liberty and human progress more important than the missions or rights of nations and governments. Knowing Indian history well, and living in the period of the great imperial expansion of the United States through Mexican and Indian wars, he never deluded himself into thinking that national independence in itself would lessen injustice or tyranny, or that every acquisition of territory by a free nation would be disastrous for the cause of humanity. On the contrary he pointed out that though "the Romans were not the most clean-handed of conquerors, yet would it have been better for Gaul and Spain, Numidia and Dacia, never to have formed part of the Roman Empire? . . . If the smaller nationality, supposed to be the more advanced in improvement, is able to overcome the greater, as the Macedonians, reinforced by the Greeks, did Asia, and the English India, there is often a gain to civilization." [11]

But wherever he found human dignity threatened or justice denied he protested. He took sharp issue with Carlyle, who had been his friend, when the latter invoked human and divine laws in behalf of Negro slavery. Mill answered him that as regards human laws, "the so-called eternal Act of Parliament is no new law but the old law of the strongest, a law against which the great teachers of mankind have in all ages protested." And as regards divine laws in sanction of slavery Mill stated that "if the gods will this, it is the first duty of human beings to resist such gods. Omnipotent these gods are not, for powers which demand human tyranny and injustice cannot accomplish their purpose unless human beings cooperate." This cooperation with higher powers, divine or secular, in the denial of justice or liberty, he firmly rejected. When in 1865 Edward John Eyre, a distinguished explorer and administrator, suppressed with undue severity Negro insurrection in Jamaica where he was then governor, Mill took the leadership of liberal public opinion in England to demand the criminal prosecution of Eyre, who had been recalled by the government. He thought the speech which he delivered at that occasion in Parliament the best of his speeches in the House. He was convinced that as a result of his efforts lasting for more than two years, colonial governors and other persons in authority would in future have a considerable motive for stopping short of such extremities. Events have justified Mill's confidence.

The readers of Mill's articles on some of the questions of his day will be moved to realize how much these problems are still with us and how forward-looking and farsighted Mill's comments were. The question of English intervention

in the continental struggles for liberty was widely discussed
in the middle of the nineteenth century. Britain was often
accused of acting only for her own narrow interests and interfering only to satisfy her own insatiable greed. Mill tried to
analyze Britain's motives and the reasons for the general distrust of them. In his article "A Few Words on Non-Intervention" [12] he found the Britain of his time "desiring no benefit
to itself" at the expense of other European nations. "A nation
adopting this policy is a novelty; so much so that many are
unable to believe it when they see it." [13] Paradoxically, "it is
this nation which finds itself, in the respect of its foreign policy, held up to obloquy as a type of egoism and selfishness;
as a nation which thinks of nothing but of outwitting its
neighbors. Those most friendly to us think they make a great
concession in admitting that the fault may possibly be less with
the English people, than with the English government and
aristocracy. They believe that we have always other objects
than those we avow; and the most far-fetched suggestion of a
selfish purpose appears to them better entitled to credence than
anything so absolutely incredible as our disinterestedness."
Mill explained this general distrust by English shortcomings,
their shyness and fear of appearing "good," above all the habit
of English statesmen to declare publicly that England would
not interfere in Europe so long as no English interests were
involved. "England is thus exhibited as a country whose most
distinguished men are not ashamed to profess that they will
not move a finger for others" except for England's private
advantage. What England really meant, Mill thought, was
that she would act only when her national safety was threatened; but instead of invoking the common right of self-defense,
English statesmen phrased their position in such a way as to
imply that England would act only for interest and aggrandizement.

Mill understood the urgency of the problems of intervention which have so much occupied the attention of the world lately. Eighty years ago he wrote that "there are few questions which more require to be taken in hand by ethical and political philosophers, with a view to establish some criterion whereby the justifiableness of intervening in the affairs of other countries, and the justifiableness of refraining from intervention, may be brought to a definite and rational test." Unfortunately the problems of the justifiableness of intervention have remained unsolved. Mill himself opposed widespread demands for an English crusade on behalf of liberty on the European continent; he rejected war for an idea, and thought it as little justifiable to force ideas upon other peoples as to compel them to submit in other respects. But even without fighting for liberty and interfering in other nations' inner struggles, England, Mill realized, on account of her freedom remained a standing reproach to despotism everywhere. For that reason he thought she might find herself menaced some day, directly or indirectly, by continental despotism. In such a case she should consider the liberals in all European countries as her natural allies, and regard the war for her national security also as a war of ideas. Should one day such a danger actually arise, England would do well to put herself at the helm of an alliance of free peoples, so strong as to defy the efforts even of a league of autocracies united against her and at the same time against the cause of freedom. "The prize is too glorious not to be snatched sooner or later by some free country; and the time may not be distant when England, if she does not take this heroic part because of its heroism, will be compelled to take it from consideration for her own safety."

The question of intervention was soon afterward discussed in England in connection with the American civil war. The Southern states declaring for independence invoked the right of self-determination so dear to liberals. Many people in England sided with the South, some out of sympathy for its resistance to the powerful North which tried to force the South against its will into imperial union. Mill strongly protested against the widespread sympathy for the South, the defender of self-determination.[14] English liberals accused him of inconsistency. Did not the North, in resisting the separation of the South, commit the same wrong which England committed in opposing the original separation of the thirteen colonies? Mill answered those liberals who favored dissolution of other people's empires, that it is wonderful "how easy and liberal, and complying, people can be in other people's concerns." He reminded those Englishmen who were so concerned about American imperialism and the sacred right of self-determined rule, of Ireland or India or the Ionian Islands—not foreseeing that one year later England would voluntarily cede the Ionian Islands to Greece, an unprecedented step in the attitude of empires and nations, setting the example which she applied later in Egypt and Iraq and which the United States is following in the Philippine Islands.

Mill not only declared emphatically for the right of the North to oppose the self-determination of the South. He warned against all the proposals for a negotiated peace, which increased in numbers and urgency as this greatest and most savage of all nineteenth century wars demanded ever greater sacrifices. But Mill rejected peace-at-any-price. "War, in a good cause, is not the greatest evil which a nation can suffer," he wrote in regard to America. "War is an ugly thing, but not the ugliest of things; the decayed and degraded state of moral and patriotic feeling which thinks nothing worth a war is worse. As long as justice and injustice have not terminated their ever-renewing fight for ascendancy in the affairs of mankind, human beings must be willing, when need is, to do battle for the one against the other." [15] The victory of the North seemed to him essential for the cause of individual liberty; the freedom of man was of higher importance than the rights and independence of states.

VI

Though Mill rejected the absolute application of the principle of national self-determination, he can be regarded as one of the fathers of this modern doctrine. In identifying nationality and state and demanding the right to independence for the nation-state, he expressed in a famous chapter of his "Considerations on Representative Government" the prevalent opinion of nineteenth-century liberalism which so strongly influenced Woodrow Wilson. He believed that "it is in general a necessary condition of free institutions that the boundaries of governments should coincide in the main with those of nationalities." His critical penetration did not warn him of the great dangers which self-determination based on nationality might involve for human liberty. He lived before it became evident how the fight for national independence tends to consume all energies and to divert them from the struggle for human liberty, how nations after having gained their independence often do not use it to foster liberty nor to respect the independence and liberties of other men and groups. The struggle for national independence leads easily to a stress upon exclusive features and rights, to a passionate appeal to the past and to praise of true or fictitious national glories and concerns, with disregard for the claims of individuality and of humanity alike. Nor has the independence of nationalities increased mutual benevolence or shown itself to be necessarily a factor conducive to peace; it has rather lent greater emotional warmth to the appeal of war and intensified appetites and hatreds.

But though Mill, writing between 1848 and 1871, could not foresee the implications of national self-determination for liberty and peace, his own considerations could lead to the conclusion that a state comprising several nationalities offered from the point of view of liberty a healthier diversity and less danger of an oppressive uniformity of public opinion. The identification of state and nationality is the desire of a historical period, nothing inherent in the eternal nature of man or society. State and nationality belong to two different orders of things. The progressive state is not a tribal community, but a society based on reason and law, an association of spiritual loyalty; nationality is a fact of nature which subjects the state to its own needs and tries to bind men in a close collective will to which every other influence must defer. It is true that Mill defined nationality not as based primarily upon "natural factors" like race or descent, limits of geography or language, but as constituted through the feeling of common sympathies, the will of forming a nationality and being under a government of its own. Yet natural factors and influences of the past played in most cases a decisive role in the determination of the sympathy which lay at the bottom of nationality.

Mill's contemporary, Lord Acton, clearly foresaw the danger,[16] that a state which identifies itself with one definite single object, be it one nationality or one class, tends to become absolute. On the other hand, in a multi-national state, nationality can become not only a limit to the excessive power of the state but also a bulwark of self-government. A nationality which is the state inclines towards the absolutization of the sovereign will; a nationality within a multinational state based on freedom efficiently counteracts the tendencies of absolutism. "Liberty provokes diversity, and diversity preserves liberty by supplying the means of organization. It is a firm barrier against the intrusion of the government beyond the political sphere which is common to all into those departments which escape legislation. Intolerance is sure to find a corrective in the national diversities. The coexistence of several nations under the same state is a test, as well as the best security of its freedom.

It is also one of the chief instruments of civilization, and indicates a state of greater advancement than national unity. The combination of different nations in one state is as necessary a condition of civilized life as the combination of men in society. It is in the caldron of the state that the fusion takes place by which the vigor, the knowledge, and the capacity of one portion of mankind may be communicated to another."

The state in the era of liberty must be able not only to tolerate but to welcome differences and to do justice to the peculiar character of various races. In a multinational state which believes in liberty, an attempted excessive centralization would be destructive of the state itself, while liberty could achieve its most glorious results. For the cohabitation of several nationalities within one state supplies the greatest variety of intellectual resources, the most abundant elements of self-government, and the fullest security for the preservation of local customs. "If we take the establishment of liberty for the realization of moral duties to be the end of civil society, we must conclude that those states are substantially the most perfect which include various distinct nationalities without oppressing them. Those in which no mixture of races has been made are imperfect; and those in which its effects have disappeared are decrepit. A state which is incompetent to satisfy different races condemns itself; a state which labors to neutralize, to absorb, or to expel them, destroys its own vitality; a state which does not include them is destitute of the chief bases of self-government." Nationalities, like families or communes, should be the foundation of self-government and of all the guarantees of liberty which it implies against the possible tyranny of the state. But they cannot form the basis of the state because they tend to sacrifice the true aims of the state, liberty and prosperity, to the necessity of making the nation the mold and measure of the state.

Nor, in an age which demands ever higher forms of integration, does the multiplication of sovereignties by national independence seem advisable. Mill himself rightly pointed out that "whatever really tends to the admixture of nationalities, and the blending of their attributes and peculiarities in a common union, is a benefit to the human race. . . . Nobody can suppose that it is not more beneficial to a Breton to be brought into the current of the ideas of a highly civilized people—to be a member of the French nationality, sharing the advantages of French protection, and the dignity and prestige of French power—than to sulk on his own rocks." Mill could have added that the French nationality of Bretons like Lamennais, Renan or Clemenceau was of benefit not only to them but to France and mankind. Mill hoped that with the disgrace of atrocious misgovernment removed, the Irish would not be insensible to the benefits of connection with England.[17] He underestimated the power of "the memory of the past" over rational considerations. As the will-to-power is an inherent element in human history, so the will to national independence is a potent moving factor in modern history. There is no gain in disregarding wishfully the immense driving power of these wills over many minds and hearts, but there is the question whether these tendencies should be consciously encouraged by praise and propaganda or rather controlled and checked in the interests of human liberty and peaceful progress. In a liberal multiracial state or empire citizens may be free and their human dignity safeguarded by law without national independence; in an independent nation citizens may be subject to a despotism which entirely disregards the rights of the individual and the elementary human freedoms. Nothing seems more important at present than the clarification of the current misunderstandings of independence and freedom.[18]

To the liberal mind progress seemed to be based not on national independence and sovereignty but on a growing combination of the principles of individual liberty and federal self-government. In both these fields the institutions of Britain and of the United States appeared to point the way. Mill followed the English tradition in his wish to apply both principles to the consolidation of the British Empire, for the maintenance of which he believed there were strong reasons. "It is a step, as far as it goes, towards universal peace, and general friendly cooperation among nations," he wrote. It protects its members "from being absorbed into a foreign state, and becoming a source of additional aggressive strength to some rival power, even more despotic or closer at hand, than Britain." The empire "has the advantage, specially valuable at the present time, of adding to the moral influence, and weight in the councils of the world, of the power" which, whatever its grievous errors in the past, has stood for liberty. The transformation of the empire toward a loose federation based on self-government, broad tolerance of diversities, respect for individual liberty, and equality of justice and consideration— a process which began in Mill's time and since has progressed far toward its realization—was welcomed by Mill. With his experience in the administration of dependencies he knew all the difficulties of the task assumed, which he regarded as the highest moral trust which can devolve upon a nation. "There are in this age of the world few more important problems than how to organize this rule so as to make it a good instead of an evil to the subject people." [19]

What Mill and the liberals of his day proposed has since become the common policy of all British parties. The ferment of liberal policy worked faster than many expected. The idea of liberty and law which England brought to the less advanced parts of her empire contrasted sharply with the habits and customs prevailing there and became a model in influencing and invigorating the dependent communities. They began to judge themselves by this new ideal, they absorbed it and were transformed under its guidance; it was the most potent ferment

of regeneration. Millenary traditions of abject human degradation, of hideous superstition, of cruelest oppression began to
give way. When Macaulay in 1835 presented his memorandum
on the introduction of English education in India, he foresaw
that beneficial influence of liberty: "It may be that the public
mind of India may so expand under our system that it may outgrow that system, and our subjects having been brought up
under good government may develop a capacity for better
government, that having been instructed in European learning, they may crave for European institutions. I know not
whether such a day will ever come, but if it does come it will
be the proudest day in the annals of England." England, by
the inherent and inevitable expansion of her own principles,
spread the ideas of freedom and self-government everywhere
in her empire. The task of the empire became, to use the
words of the Montagu-Chelmsford Report on Constitutional
Reforms in India in 1918, "a common realization of the ends for
which it exists, the maintenance of peace and order over wide
spaces of territory, the maintenance of freedom and the development of the culture of each national unity of which the empire is composed. The existence of national feeling, of the love
of and a pride in a national culture, need not conflict, and may
indeed strengthen, the sense of membership in a wider commonwealth." The growing realization of the principle of individual liberty and federative self-government over vast areas
sets an example to the world; it may help to promote wider
unions and to overcome everywhere the growing tension between national and wider interests, a tension dangerous alike
to the causes of peace and of human liberty. For these reasons
Mill wrote in 1870: "For my own part I think a severance of
the empire would be no advantage, but the contrary, to the
world in general, and to England in particular; and though I
would have the colonies understand that England would not

oppose a deliberate wish on their part to separate, I would do nothing to encourage that wish." [20]

True prophets foresee developments; not only are their words valid for the hour in which they are spoken, but they offer a guide amid the growing complexities and changes which have developed since their time and of which they forewarned. The burning questions of Mill's day—individual liberty and national independence, the justification of war and of intervention, the ever growing need for peace and social reform—are still with us. Whether all the answers he attempted will stand the test of time only the future can show. At present there is less certainty than to Mill's prophetic mind whether the achievements of the English peoples of the seventeenth and eighteenth centuries, the dignity of the individual and the free state, will prove the lasting foundation of universal civilization as the nineteenth century believed. Perhaps in this state of uncertainty, the words which Mill addressed eighty years ago to a correspondent in Southport, Connecticut, who had written him indulging in abuse of the British people, seem worth recalling: [21] "No one disapproves more than I do of the narrow patriotism of former ages, which made the good of the whole human race a subordinate consideration to the good of the country of one's birth. I believe that the good of no country can be obtained by any means but such as tend to that of all countries, nor ought to be sought otherwise, even if obtainable. If my country were peopled, as you seem to think, by the scum of the earth, and if its existence were a standing nuisance to all other nations, I for one would shake the dust from my feet, and seek a better country elsewhere. But, speaking as one who has never kept any terms with national vanity, nor ever hesitated to tell his countrymen of their faults, I do not admit the charges brought against them in your letter. England is to the populations of Europe the representative, by no means perfect but still the representative, of the same principles of social and political freedom which Americans so justly cherish. Any weakening of her influence would be simply so much additional discouragement to popular institutions and to liberty of thought, speech, and action throughout the old continent, and strengthening of the hands of despotism all over the world. A war between Great Britain and the United States, were such a calamity possible, would give a new lease to tyranny and bigotry wherever they exist, and would throw back the progress of mankind for generations. Let me remind you that what you say about the grasping disposition and aggressive spirit of the English, is exactly and literally what the ignorant and prejudiced part of the higher and middle classes of Great Britain sincerely think and say concerning America. In neither of the two cases is the accusation true; but the profound ignorance of each other which it exhibits in both countries, is a most serious danger to the world, which all who wish well to mankind must earnestly desire to cure, and which can only be aggravated by the indulgence of such feelings as you express."

Chapter Two

FRANCE: MICHELET

Je regarde, ainsi que je l'ai toujours fait, la liberté comme le premier des biens; je vois toujours en elle l'une des sources les plus fécondes des vertus mâles et des actions grandes. Il n'y a pas ni tranquillité ni de bien-être, qui puisse me tenir lieu d'elle.
—TOCQUEVILLE, *January* 7, *1856.*

Le libéralisme, ayant la prétention de se fonder uniquement sur les principes de la raison, croit d'ordinaire n'avoir pas besoin de tradition. Là est son erreur. L'erreur de l'école libérale est d'avoir trop cru qu'il est facile de créer la liberté par la réflexion, et de n'avoir pas su qu'un établissement n'est solide que quand il a des racines historiques.
—RENAN (1858), *Nouvelle Revue, vol. LXXIX, p. 596.*

2

THE French Revolution grew out of the ideas of the eighteenth century and carried on the administrative and military traditions of the monarchy, but such was its consuming fire that it appeared to the generation who lived through it and to the generations who have since lived by it as an unprecedented new beginning. Like all revolutions it followed a complex and contradictory course. It began in the clear light of the eighteenth century and of English influences as a movement to abolish the arbitrariness of absolute power, to secure constitutional liberties and to bring peace in the spirit of humanitarian cosmopolitanism. Soon, however, resolute minorities seized power as the representatives of the people, the new sovereign, in whose names wars were started, liberty suppressed and violent passions aroused. Stirred into great hopes and expectations, filling the earth with the spectacle of its arms and the air with the clarion call of its messages, the French people proclaimed the start of a new period of history. The relations of man and society changed; his liberties triumphed over the traditional fatalities. Man had discovered his power to shake and change the foundations of society; he claimed that power as his right. The heavenly city was brought down to earth, France became the promised land, Paris the new Jerusalem, the Revolution a turning point of the ages.

In 1848 when the new revolutionary wave rose to its climax, Renan—who was then twenty-five years old and had broken three years before with the Church—wrote a long book of democratic fervor; it was not published until forty-two years later. In it he praised the Revolution as marking the transition of mankind from childhood to maturity, from an age of guidance by instinct, caprice and the will of others, to a period of responsible liberty. "One can call all preceding periods of history the irrational epoch of human existence which one day will count as little in the history of mankind, and in that of our nation, as at present the chapter on the history of Gaul counts in the history of France. The true history of France begins in 1789. All that precedes is but a slow preparation and of interest only as such." [1]

Since 1789 France has lived in the lights and shadows of that gigantic period. The French Revolution never became for France an accepted settlement. The debate on its meaning and merits has never ended. Its hopes and hatreds have lived on, and almost every half century—in 1848, in 1898, in 1938— they have been rekindled into the flames of open or latent civil war. The message of the French Revolution has been interpreted in the last one hundred and fifty years by many poets and prophets, historians and moralists. None among them has shown a more fervent faith in its messianic nationalism or a deeper devotion to its democratic mysticism than Jules Michelet. The trinity whose prophet he became was People, Revolution and France. With all of them he was intimately connected by his origin. Born in 1798 under the First French Republic, he prepared the Second and he died under the Third Republic. His birthplace was the heart of France, Paris, the city of the Revolution where all the three republics originated and whence they radiated over France and even over Europe. He was a child of the people, the revolutionary people of the city, and he was prouder of his roots and ancestors than any old nobleman on his inherited estates could ever be. Throughout his life he felt himself the man of the People, of the Revolution, of Paris and France. To them he dedicated his life, he wrote their history, he wished to arouse their moral sentiments. When he composed at the age of 71 a preface to the many volumes of his History of France, he addressed the hero of his life with the tender words of a lover. "Dear France with whom I have lived and whom I leave now with so great regret. How many passionate, noble, austere hours have we spent together. I have worked for you, I have gone and come, I searched and wrote. I have given day after day all and everything I had, perhaps even more. Now then, my great France, if it has been necessary in order to recall you to life that a man give himself, that he cross and recross so many times the river of the dead, he has found his comfort in it and he is grateful to you. His greatest sorrow is that he must leave you now." [2]

Michelet's father had a small printing shop which was ruined by Napoleon's suppression of the press. The family was living under conditions of great poverty, and the boy had to work hard helping his father. As he himself said, he grew up like a blade of grass between the cobblestones of Paris. Parental ambition and his brilliancy secured his admission to schools of great distinction, where he kept apart from his wealthier companions. It took him a long time of hard work to establish himself; poverty and people stayed with him for years. He was twenty-six years old when three events became decisive in his life. In 1824 he married his first wife, with whom he remained united until her death fifteen years later; he met Edgar Quinet, the son of a wealthy middle-class family, five years his junior, and between them a lifelong friendship founded on a wide community of thoughts and actions grew up; they shared the discovery of two authors, little known in France then, Vico and Herder, and the affinity they felt filled them with enthusiasm and gave a new direction to their minds.

Michelet translated into French Vico's *Principi di una scienza nuova*, and Quinet translated Herder's *Ideen zur Philosophie der Geschichte der Menschheit*. Through these works history gained for the young men a new importance and a new dignity. It became a source of poetry and inspiration, a subject which opened vast horizons on the march of mankind through the centuries. From Vico Michelet learned the importance of great turning points and crises in the growth of civilization, the meaning of myths and symbols as motive forces in history. From Herder he accepted the optimism of the Enlightenment and the idea of a Volksgeist, of national souls and of nations as living manifestations of the spirit, as the origin of all intellectual life, and learned to love France as a person, a self which the historian-poet re-creates in his own self, and to regard her history as a record of her moral growth. He and Quinet shared from now on the dream of a new France and a better mankind, dreams of young enthusiastic minds which when grown old they were not to repudiate.

Quinet, under the influence of his Protestant mother, was of a deeply religious nature. The moral seriousness of his mind found itself attracted and engrossed by German ways of thinking. He read Herder first in an English translation, but he wished to read the original and to study Herder's background. He went to Heidelberg, where the intellectual and social life of the quiet and lovely university town charmed him. He acquired a better knowledge of German cultural and social trends of the period than perhaps any other Frenchman of his generation. He spent many years in southwestern Germany, especially in Baden, a land long open to French influences and separated from France only by the Rhine. In his introductory essay on Herder he paid a deeply felt tribute to Germany as "the land of the soul and of hope where under the oaks of Arminius the pure spring of moral beauty gushes forth and where sooner or later the neighboring peoples will come to quench their thirst." His attachment to Germany grew when he fell in love with a young German woman whom he met in Heidelberg, and whom he married after a long betrothal. No wonder that he wrote "je dois tout à Heidelberg." His enthusiasm was contagious; through him Michelet learned to love and admire Germany though he never knew her well. He remained faithful to his love for Germany his whole life.[3] His attitude to history shows deep traces of his acquaintance with German romantic thought and scholarship, especially with Jacob Grimm, whose interpretation of the traditions and symbols of law influenced his own work.

Quinet and Michelet were in no way alone in France in their love and admiration for German letters and thought. Things had completely changed since the eighteenth century. Then, in the great era of liberty and cosmopolitan ideas, France had been in the closest cultural contact with England. The bitter wars which filled the century did not influence the French or English intellectuals; their minds were above emotions and passions of national rivalries and united in the serene atmosphere of freedom and progress. Only as a result of the French Revolution rational cosmopolitanism gave way to national passion. Many intellectuals now shared and fanned national jealousies. France, for so many centuries the leading power on the European continent, found herself surpassed by Britain in power and wealth, in the art of government and in industrial advance. When the Revolution tried to reassert France's primacy in the world, it found itself thwarted by England, the triumphal march of her army was broken, the light of her revolution extinguished. The French forgot Leipzig and Blücher; they remembered Waterloo and Wellington.

Britain, whose conquests of liberty had stimulated the rise of the French Revolution, appeared overpowering and insolent; Germany, whose thinkers were to reject the ideas of French liberty, seemed peaceful and idyllic. She was hardly known except through the eyes of her discoverer, Mme. de Staël, who in her *De l'Allemagne* drew a heart-warming picture of a serious people of poets and thinkers who led a peaceful, modest and virtuous existence in small picturesque towns without any practical interests or any ambitions for power. Thus was created the legend of a Germany which had ceased to exist even before the book was written. Mme. de Staël, who knew little German, was entirely unaware of the forward-driving forces which were creating a new Germany in her day; she was more interested to present to France, from which she was exiled, the example of an imaginary virtuous country, and to counter the coldness of Empire classicism with the inspiration of German poetical enthusiasm, with which her own heart overflowed. German Romanticism aroused her ardent sympathies, which she communicated to the young generations in France. A Germanomania swept intellectual France. Her scholars went to school in Germany. Young Victor Cousin, through whom Michelet met Quinet and to whom Quinet dedicated his French translation of Herder, lectured at the Sorbonne to enthusiastic students on German philosophy. He confirmed the eager intellectual youth of France in their admiration of Germany. Victor Hugo wrote: "La France et l'Allemagne sont l'Europe. L'Allemagne le cœur, la France la tête."

II

Waterloo had left France in a state of physical exhaustion and spiritual humiliation. Napoleon's rule had been Janus-faced. His armies had aroused the peoples of Europe from lethargy; Germany and Italy, Spain and Russia, owed him their awakening. To them the new principles of law and administration which he brought meant light and progress, the first breaking of ancient fetters, the emancipation of man. To France, on the other hand, Napoleon meant only disaster. His rule consummated what the Convention and the Terror began: the exaltation of democratic dictatorship based upon the mystical will of the nation instead of a free interplay of forces based upon the liberties of the individual; administrative centralization instead of self-government; a tyrannical suppression of freedom instead of which conquests and triumphs were offered, and the appeal to arms and to patriotic passions. Since 1793 democracy had become identified, for France, with the defense of the fatherland and very soon with its military greatness. To use Quinet's words, "La liberté s'était perdue dans la gloire." In 1815 the glory went, but the liberty was not regained. The promise of both was rekindled by the legend of Napoleon [4] which came from the lonely isle where the Eagle languished in cruel British captivity; a legend of Napoleon as a hero of democracy, of the people's sovereignty, of its true human and social interests, and at the same time as a friend and liberator of all nations, the creator of a united Europe. Waterloo appeared now to fervent nationalists and democrats as a decisive defeat of the human spirit, a cruel destruction of the greatest hopes of universal liberation, the crucifixion of a redeemer, a new Caucasus or Calvary.

The July days of 1830 seemed to realize many of the expectations of the Napoleonic legend. The people of Paris rose, and their rising was a signal for Europe. The order imposed by the victors of Waterloo was threatened; Poland rose against Russia, Italy against Austria, the French-speaking Belgians against the English-supported Dutch, Paris against the Bourbons. France's primacy in the cause of human liberty, of the friendship of all progressive peoples, seemed re-established. In the white heat of those enthusiastic days Michelet began to write history "conceived as an eternal July." *L'Introduction à l'Histoire Universelle* which appeared in the following year was the fruit of his studies of Vico and Herder, an interpretation of the advance of humanity culminating with France as "the glorious pilot of mankind's ship." Universal history became an introduction to France's history, which was its climax and fulfillment.

History appeared to Michelet as a growing struggle of man's freedom against the fatality of nature and tradition. To him the least fatalistic, the most human and the freest continent in the world was Europe; the most European country was France. For had she not alone, by her spirit of ceaseless activity, fused out of a welter of various provinces, races and classes a national union overcoming all the natural and traditional obstacles. France's origin was free fusion, her life was action. Thus, Michelet declared, by her character she will be able to group for the first time all peoples in a true union of intelligence and will. France's social genius aspired to liberty in equality, an ideal which can be best reached by a nation which has neutralized within itself the opposed fatalities of races and climates, by a nation created for action but not for conquest, by a people which desires equality for itself and for mankind. Rome had begun the liberation of the world through Christianity and universal rational law, France has carried on that work throughout the Middle Ages and modern times and has consummated it when she alone understood in the Revolution that liberty without equality was incomplete. Napoleon, himself a Frenchman and an Italian, had continued Rome's and France's mission of liberation and unification. In the seventeenth and eighteenth centuries France had given to Europe her language and literature and had unified Europe spiritually in a republic of letters; now the spirit of France, rekindled by the fires of July, will bring to Europe unity through liberty and democracy. France, the people of law and action, cannot but legislate and agitate the world. She is the mediator and interpreter among the nations, the great world auditorium through which ideas and arts gain world importance and radiate everywhere. In such pictures in the enthusiasm of July, Michelet saw the past, its culmination in the present, its projection into the future.

In the fulfillment of her historical mission Michelet wished France to collaborate with Italy and Spain, her Latin sister nations. He felt deep sympathy with Germany. He conceded to England the quality of a heroic nation which opened up the path to modern political liberty. But he found England a country of individualistic pride, subject to the fatalities of the traditionalism of caste and the materialism of industry and commerce. She had never been able, he thought, to overcome the fatality through the spirit. His passionate hatred of Britain made him blind to the fact that from his own philosophy of history he should have praised England above all as a nation offering a brilliant example of the victory of human liberty over fatality. Within a few centuries a poor agricultural people had overcome the fatalities of nature and grown into a maritime commercial and industrial power of the first rank, had created through human activity wealth on an unprecedented scale, and with a very small population had founded a mighty empire.[5] But Michelet saw in England only the hereditary enemy of France: for eight hundred years the two nations had been locked in contest; and only recently France had been compelled to cede the leadership to Britain. Michelet could not forget nor forgive.

III

The high hopes of a glorious France, roused in July, were soon dampened by the peaceful mediocrity of Louis Philippe's reign; the England of the settlement of 1689, not the enthusiasm of the Revolution, seemed the belated guide of the new monarchy. France refused the appeal of Michelet and his friends to assume the leadership of Europe in the struggle for liberty. The Poles, for all European liberals the ever-present symbol of this struggle, were abandoned to Russian tyranny. But Michelet had found his vocation: to arouse and to educate France and her people to a truer understanding of their mission. He did it in the lectures of his classrooms, and in innumerable books. In 1831 he began the writing of his lifework, *The History of France*, of which the first two volumes appeared in 1833, the last one in 1874, the year of his death. In the Preface of 1869, looking back on many years and volumes, he wrote: "I conceived this laborious work of forty years in one moment, in the lightning of July. In these memorable days a great light suddenly burst forth and I saw France." What Michelet saw was France's people, its agitation through centuries of darkness, its slow climb, its sudden eruption to light in the Revolution. He did not try to analyze the past in historical perspective, he tried to resurrect it as if it were to be lived again. He participated in it as fully as if it were his own life. He could do it best where he found in history trends and forces with which he felt a deep affinity. Much remained disjointed, arid and even bizarre in the work, especially in its later volumes. But where his heart vibrated, history grew under his evocative pen into a great national epopee, perhaps the greatest monument of national historiography.[6]

Albert Thibaudet called Michelet a republican Bossuet; like the great bishop of Meaux, Michelet wrote the book of a faith and of a propaganda. While Bossuet educated the heir to the monarchy, Michelet educated the people, the new heir; while Bossuet interpreted the whole of history for the glorification of the church and the French monarchy, Michelet undertook the same task for the glorification of the people and the French Republic.[7] For both France was the center of a universal faith; to Michelet the destiny of France was closely linked with the progress of mankind. And as France was the mediator of Europe, so Paris was the mediator of France: "Who says Paris says the whole monarchy. How could this great and complete symbol of the country form itself into one city? One would have to tell the whole history of the country to explain it. The genius of Paris is a most complex and at the same time the highest form of France. It might seem that something which resulted from the destruction of all local spirit, of all regionalism, must be something that is purely negative. It is not so: of all the negations of material, local, particular ideas results a living generality, a positive thing, a life force. We have seen it in July." The history of France confounded itself for Michelet with the history of the people of Paris, with the history of democracy and revolution; in short, with Michelet himself.

In 1838 he was called to the Collège de France, the famous institution of learning founded by Francis I, where he occupied the chair of Histoire et Morale, a name which meant research in the history of ideas but which he interpreted to imply a two-fold task: to teach history and to arouse the moral sense of French youth. Instead of continuing the quiet research which had characterized the Collège, Michelet soon turned his chair into a pulpit. He was joined in his educational crusade in 1842 by Quinet, who received a chair for the literatures of Southern Europe, and by the Polish poet Adam Mickiewicz, who became professor of Slav languages and civilization. The three professors did not confine themselves to their fields. Their lectures dealt with the moral problems of the day, they proclaimed the faith of a new lay church which would liberate mankind from its subjection to the traditions of the past and would usher in a period of liberty and progress. A fever of messianic expectation filled the air; the new messiah was on the march—France, Poland, the People, all the oppressed peoples, mankind itself. Visions of the absolute emancipation of man, of the reign of justice and virtue here on earth, of a jubilant and unending progress toward the City of God which would be the City of Man filled the hearts.

One of the earliest and most powerful expressions had been given to these expectations in the *Paroles d'un Croyant* of Félicité-Robert de Lamennais, a Catholic priest who had developed from a firm upholder of ultra-conservative church authority after 1830 to his hope of a church which would rule men's minds not by fear or outward power but by spiritual forces exercised in perfect freedom. His *Paroles* were written in the exalted poetry of the Apocalyptic prophecies of the Bible. They were influenced in their style by Lamennais' Polish disciple Mickiewicz, whose *Books of the Polish Pilgrims* appeared in Paris in 1832 and were condemned by Pope Gregory XVI, in a breve directed against Lamennais, as "a pamphlet full of malice and temerity." They were translated into French by Count Montalembert, at that time Lamennais' most prominent disciple.

The *Paroles* are hardly readable today but when they were printed, the printers were moved to tears in setting them up. They were dedicated to the People in a spirit which Lamennais himself defined in *De l'esclavage moderne* (1839): "What the people wills, God himself wills; for what the people wills is justice, the essential and eternal order, the fulfillment in mankind of that sublime work of Christ, That they be One, my Father, as You and I are One. The cause of the people is therefore the sacred cause, the cause of God; it will triumph. But in order to triumph faster with the least possible of useless perturbations and vain sufferings, the People must first draw tighter the moral tie from which unity springs by the devotion of each one to all, by the complete sacrifice of himself." Lamennais believed that the people, once politically free, would regain without hindrance their other liberties, and bring about all possible economic and civic improvements. In 1848 he adhered to a democratic and socialist republic. The rise to power of Louis Napoleon's dictatorship condemned him to silence. But as his faith in the People had profoundly molded the generation of 1830, his attempt to reconcile Christianity and Republic, the Church and the People, set an example followed by later generations. Péguy owes him as much as he owes Michelet.

Lamennais believed that the true church was the People, a free community of love united in God and Liberty. He shared this faith with Dostoevsky. But the people of Lamennais was the progressive people of democracy, creating in a joyful spirit of Western activism; the people of Dostoevsky was the primitive mass of peasants submitting to authority and finding their redemption in suffering. Both expected the impossible from the

concrete historical representatives of their mystical faith: Lamennais from the Pope, Dostoevsky from the Czar, both from
their People. The Pope disillusioned Lamennais and in his en-
cyclical *Singulari vos* condemned the *Paroles* as a book "small in
size but huge in depravity." The People, being an abstraction,
could disillusion neither Lamennais nor Dostoevsky. The Russian prophet, who made his peace in the service of nationalism
with Tsar and Church and People, died respected and venerated by all of them; Lamennais, faithful to his invisible church
of democratic liberty and human brotherhood, died rejected
and forgotten and was buried without religious rites in the
potter's field.

Lamennais hailed the People as the true interpreter of Christianity; soon however, the revolutionary fervor detached the
messianic expectations from their Christian origin. The People
no longer were regarded as fulfilling the promise of Christianity, but as rising against it; no longer were they to create a new
earth under a new heaven, the earth alone seemed a sufficiently
vast empire to occupy men's energies. "It's here on earth, not in
a fantastic heaven, that the life of the spirit will be realized,"
Renan wrote in 1848. "Let's attach ourselves courageously to
the earth," Jean Reynaud proclaimed. And Daniel Stern
(Countess d' Agoult) in her *History of the Revolution of 1848*
analyzed the trend of the time: "If it is true to say that socialism
seems at first glance an extension of the principle of fraternity
which Jesus Christ brought to the world, it is at the same time
and above all a reaction against the essential dogma of Christianity, original sin and expiation. One could, I believe, with
greater justification regard socialism in its general principle as
an attempt to materialize and to bring about without delay the
spiritual paradise and the future life of the Christians. Perhaps
that is the fulfillment of the law, but it is its fulfillment by its
suppression." The earth and the worker: that was the new gospel of the people. "O travail, sainte loi du monde," Lamartine

exclaimed. And Victor Hugo hailed the new Age of the People as the approaching kingdom of God:

> Tout sera dit. Le mal expirera; les larmes
> Tariront; plus de fers, plus de deuils, plus d'alarmes;
>   L'affreux gouffre inclément
> Cessera d'être sourd, et bégaiera: Qu'entends-je?
> Les douleurs finiront dans toute l'ombre; un ange
>   Criera: Commencement!

In these feverish years [8] leading up to 1848 Michelet's attitude toward Christianity also changed. In his history of medieval France he had treated the faith and the Church with respect and piety. They had formed part of the greatness of France. The French Revolution itself appeared to him then as a fulfillment of the Christian promise, as the return to the true spirit of Christianity. In 1843 he finished the last volume of his history of the Middle Ages, carrying it to the death of Louis XI. When he resumed the writing of the *History* with the volume on the Renaissance, in 1855, he had completely changed his outlook. In the intervening twelve years he had dedicated himself to a struggle for the People and against the Church. This task was discharged in his courses at the Collège de France. Out of them grew the books with which his fame will forever be connected: *The History of the French Revolution* which he began to write in 1846 and the three volumes, *The Jesuits* (1843), *The Priest, the Family and the Woman* (1844), and above all *The People* (1846), which in itself sums up Michelet's philosophy.

In these years Michelet, Quinet and Mickiewicz appeared as prophets before the youth of the Collège, calling up its desire for enthusiasm and action.[9] In 1843 Michelet and Quinet lectured in their courses on the Jesuits and published their lectures as a book. In it they did not yet attack the Church itself nor the Catholic faith; they claimed to protect the Church from the

Order which undermined the morality and thereby the faith. Soon, however, Michelet was to go further. His book *The Priest, the Family and the Woman* became a direct attack on the Church. Abandoning the Catholic faith Michelet turned not only against the Church but against Christianity itself. The French Revolution appeared to him no longer the fulfillment of pure Christianity against the corruption of the Church, but a rejection of Christianity and all that it implied.

Quinet did not follow Michelet: his religious faith was more deeply anchored, he never turned against Christianity itself. For him the religious problem always occupied the center of his thought and democratic and social regeneration was indissolubly connected with religious reformation. Christ remained for him the supreme embodiment of the moral forces of mankind. For Michelet mankind itself became the creator and bearer of the Divine message; for Quinet all spiritual life sprang from religion, the perpetual revelation of God. Later Quinet, in an interesting study of the French Revolution, reproached it for its lack of religion and considered that lack its fundamental weakness.[10] He praised the Revolution for having liberated France from the domination of the Church; he found the rejection of the Church justified, for it had proved in 1793 its antinational character by remaining unmoved by France's mortal danger. But the Revolution had not replaced Catholicism by any new religion and had thus left a void. There had been the opportunity for a Reformation, but France had missed it. The Revolution did not only destroy; its terror remained sterile and therefore unbearable. For Quinet religious forces were needed to regenerate mankind.

While Quinet continued to regard the democratic revolution as an event in the line of true Christianity of which Catholicism was only an aberration, Michelet saw in the Revolution and the modern mind which was its outcome a rejection of the Christian faith in salvation by Divine forces. The Revolution was for

Michelet a new epoch, but no isolated fact; it was synonymous with modern civilization and enlightenment, with rational thought and the forces of democracy, with the whole development of the last three centuries in which the French Revolution was the decisive turning point. Through it man became the artisan of his own destiny. The Revolution had destroyed the Divine authority of religion by the grace of God and the traditional secular authority of government by the grace of God. It had put in their place a new authority, the sovereignty of the people, Rousseau's general will, which now became the voice of God, the interpreter of law and reason. The people had become God.[11]

IV

Michelet dedicated *Le Peuple* to Edgar Quinet.[12] In the famous introduction he summed up his personal experiences and his political ideals and presented the book as a *summa* of his life and thought. "This book is more than a book; it is myself," the dedication began, "therefore it belongs to you. We live by the same heartbeat, a beautiful harmony which can astonish; but is it not natural? All the variety of our labors has germinated from the same living root: our feeling for France and the idea of the fatherland. I have made this book out of myself, out of my life, out of my heart. It came from my experience rather than from my study. To know the life of the people, their labors and their sufferings, I had only to question my own memories. For I, too, my friend, have worked with my hands. I merit in more than one sense the true name of modern man, the name of 'worker.' From my childhood I have preserved the impress of work, of a hard and laborious life, I have remained one of the people."

The heartbeat of the age of the rising masses vibrated in Michelet's message. New multitudes were knocking at the gates of the city, demanding entrance. "Often today one compares the rise of the people, its progress, to the invasion of the bar-

barians. I like the word, I accept it. Barbarians! That means full
of a new life-giving and rejuvenating sap. Barbarians, that
means travelers toward the Rome of the future, marching
slowly, each generation advancing a little, to be halted by
death, but others are marching on. If the superior classes possess
culture, we barbarians have more vitality and warmth." Michelet felt himself one of the people; his learning added responsibilities, for he had gained the knowledge of France's grave situation and the power of reflection about its causes. He wrote the
book to save France, which he felt endangered in the very hour
of an approaching crisis when mankind needed her most. He
knew that a unified France was necessary, conscious of her
mission. But instead of mutual love he found division and
estrangement.

"I suffer more than others from the deplorable rift between
the men and the classes, I who have them all in me. France's
situation is so serious that I could not hesitate. I do not exag-
gerate the power of a book; but its writing is a question of *must,*
not of *can.* I see France going down hourly; while we quarrel
the country sinks. This ruin is absurd and ridiculous; we alone
cause it. Who has a literature which still dominates European
thought? We do, in spite of our weakness. Who has an army?
We alone do. England and Russia, two weak and bloated giants,
deceive Europe. Great empires, but weak peoples! Let France
be One, for one moment; she will be strong like the world." For
the critical times ahead he exhorted France to trust only in her
own strength. Was not France surrounded by enemies? "Perpetual peace which some promise you (while the arsenals
smoke . . . see that black smoke over Kronstadt and Ports-
mouth!), let's try this peace by beginning it among ourselves.
One people! one fatherland! one France! . . . Let us never
become two nations, I implore you. Without unity we perish.
Frenchmen of every class and party, you have on this earth only
one sure friend, that is France." Did not all other nations fight

France fifty years ago because France had wished to redeem the world? The nations did not forget that France was the Revolution. "In the face of Europe, France will always have only one name, an inexpiable name which is her true eternal name: the Revolution!"

The whole book was a call to France to unite, to find her strength in the people and her mission in the Revolution. He began with a moving analysis of the social and moral state of France under Louis Philippe. He found modern society holding all classes in bondage; the poet and the patriot in him taught that from the hatreds which this thraldom engenders only love can free men—love liberating through the forces of nature and of the fatherland. He accused French society of remaining divided into classes in spite of the Revolution; and the machine age, which he disliked, of mechanizing life. He wished to overcome these dangers to the substance of France by an uplifting of the hearts, by the association of all men of good will. Michelet saw the source of real strength in the common people, he found the root of weakness in the bourgeois who had fallen victim to class egoism, mechanization and foreign influences. Writing under the Orleanist monarchy with its consistently peaceful policy—which Michelet regarded as a policy of servitude to British and capitalistic interests [13]—he began his chapter on "The Bondage of the Rich and of the Bourgeois" with an accusation of the pacifism of the industrial and financial classes.

He found the France of his day lacking in greatness, fearful of her heroic vocation. Was not the pusillanimous policy responsible for France's abandonment of her leadership? "The only nation that has a genuine army is the one which counts for nothing. That can not be explained by the weakness of a cabinet or of a government; unfortunately it is caused by a more general condition, the decline of the ruling class, a very young and very worn class. I speak of the bourgeoisie." Only in the people he found still surviving "the sentiment of military honor always renewed by our heroic legend, the invisible spirit of the heroes of our wars, the wind of the old flag. . . . Oh, I have no hope but in it. May it save France, that flag, and the France of the army. On the day of the supreme battle between civilization and barbarism (who knows whether it will not be tomorrow?) the Judge must find the young soldiers irreproachable, their swords clean, their bayonets shining. Whenever I see them pass, my heart is moved; here alone force and idea, valour and right, which elsewhere are separated, go hand in hand. If the world can be saved by war you alone will save it. Sacred bayonets of France, take care that nothing will darken that light which shines over you and which no eye can bear."

Michelet judged men and classes according to the strength of their patriotic sentiment and their devotion to the fatherland. He found that in national feelings as in geology the warmth is always deep down. The poor people loved France more than the rich ones did. The common people were men of sound instinct and ready action, the source where the educated classes will find rejuvenation and strength. Michelet's love turned to all those whom he knew to be beginning the upward march of life; his tenderness bowed deep down full of kindness and mercy to all those whom he believed growing up from the roots, the poor, the simple, the children, all those yet outside the City, the backward peoples and the savages in Africa and even the animals. He called all of them into the great and all-inclusive City of Man from which he wished to exclude no one. He knew that cities fell and empires crumbled because their narrow and exclusive foundations had not been strong enough. "I have lent words in this book to those who are unable to know if they have a right to this world. All those who moan or suffer in silence, everything that aspires and rises to life, that's my people. That is the People. Let them all come with me. O that I could enlarge the City to make it secure. As long as it is incomplete, exclusive, unjust, its foundations shake and totter. Its justice is its strength.

It will be divine when instead of jealousy shutting its gates it will rally all the children of God, the least ones, the most humble ones. Let all without distinction, feeble or strong, simple or wise, bring here their wisdom or their instincts. Those who are infirm and incapable, who can do nothing for themselves, can do much for us. They have within themselves a mystery of unknown power, a hidden fecundity, sources of life at the bottom of their nature. In calling them, the City calls the life which alone can renew it." In the true fatherland all men and all nature will celebrate, after so many separations, a happy reconciliation. Nobody, from wherever he comes, will be excluded from this great association, this great friendship.

For Michelet the nation was, since the French Revolution, the fatherland of man, the fountainhead of love, the source of those great moments in which men feel different from ordinary life because they are touched by the eternal, the transcendent. In these moments their little lives and their inconclusive existences gain purpose and meaning; their irrelevant occupations, their daily routine are lifted into the realm of ends; they themselves are united out of isolation and loneliness into something vaster and greater which yet is themselves. Michelet felt that in the crisis of the century France and the world could be saved only by that spirit of association and by that willingness to devotion and sacrifice which presupposes a sense of the Divine, a God in Whom men recognize and love each other.[14]

This God, Michelet believed, was revealed to the world in 1789. Has any epoch in history, he asked, shown greater examples of the spirit of sacrifice than the new era starting in 1789? "In which century has one seen such great armies, so many millions of men suffer and die, without revolt, gently and silently? The God of 1789 has given to association its vastest and truest form, that which alone can unite us and through us save the world. France, glorious mother, you who not only are our mother but who must bring forth every nation to liberty, make us love each other in you." Thus Michelet prayed to the divinity of the new age, the Patrie. In her supreme moment, when the message went forth, she had been united as never before: in the great national festivals of July 14, 1790. This unity had to be regained so that France might fulfill her mission.

In strong words Michelet attacked a cosmopolitanism of uniformity; every modern nation represented to him an important idea which cannot be suppressed. What had been formerly countries and populations had become through the French Revolution personalities, in whom the life of humanity was now pulsating, through whom it was advancing. The fatherland was the necessary initiation to mankind. That was even more true in the case of France. "Suppose for one moment that France be eclipsed and finished, then the bond of attraction of mankind loosens, disintegrates and probably will be destroyed. Love which makes the life of this globe would be affected by it in its core." France, through the Revolution, has brought to all nations the gospel of equality. She may be inferior to others in wealth or strength, in systems of philosophy or in works of art, but she has given what she has, her soul, and the world lives on it. Rome was the pontiff of the dark ages, France has been the pontiff of enlightenment. France has lived through the ages as no other nation: Italy has been great in past centuries; Germany and Britain in modern times; but France alone has had a history complete through both periods. She has continued the work of Rome and of Christianity, but what they only promised, fraternal equality, she has given as the law of this world. She is more than a nation, she is a haven for the world, her history is that of mankind. When France becomes conscious that upon her depends the salvation of mankind she will teach her children France as a faith and religion, she will find herself alive and strong like the earth.

Michelet closed his paean to France—like Apollon, the healer of mankind—with an appeal for education in the religion

of the fatherland. That was the true task of government; but in
Michelet's opinion only the government of the Revolution had
really given itself to that task. It was France's tragedy that even
the Revolution did not keep its own faith to the end. It found
the people unprepared, and was unable to transmit its spirit
through education. It did not understand itself as the manifestation of the genius of France, and lost faith in itself. An all-
pervasive education must re-create faith in France and the Revolution, a patriotic education resurrecting the whole past of
France and animating the whole life of the citizen, from childhood to manhood. Here Michelet saw the need for a unified
common-school system bringing up children of all classes and
conditions together; for national festivals; for an adult education in which the sons of the bourgeoisie as mediators of the
classes would bridge the gulf between them, bring instruction
and beauty to the masses, and make the cultural heritage of
France and mankind a common national possession.[15] Thus the
unfinished work of the French Revolution would be resumed.

V

Michelet's *Le Peuple* has remained one of the chief documents of the prophetic nationalism of 1848. Its weakness lies
less in the obvious patriotic exaggerations of the second part
than in its idealization of the people, the exaltation of their instincts, their truth, their rights—in the sentimental faith that
the true wisdom of the world, the guiding light for the future,
may be found in the weak and the simple, in children and
women. In Michelet's passionate appeals the individual is in
danger of drowning in the embrace of the community, reason
in the torrent of emotion. There is much of Rousseau in Michelet and little of Montaigne, Descartes or Voltaire. Michelet
deeply believed that spontaneity was the source of life, imitation the source of death; and he thought of France's spontaneity

in instinct and vitality rather than in reflection, in the mystical national will rather than in the thinking individual, in the heart rather than in the head. He was convinced that nationality was the indestructible fountainhead of spontaneity and that the Revolution alone could create true national unity.

This faith found its expression in his course on nationality [16] which he opened in the Collège de France the very day on which *Le Peuple* was published and which served as an introduction to his work on the Revolution. He taught that neither Church nor monarchy could really incarnate nationality, only the People could. He regarded the Catholic Church as an enemy of nationality. Fortunately, so he thought, the emerging national spirit broke in the time of the Renaissance and the Reformation the false unity imposed by the Church. As a result of this triumph of national sentiment, the three centuries between the Reformation and the Revolution have been much more fertile for human progress than the preceding ten centuries. The nationalities have begun to build a better unity than the Church did, a unity respecting the diversities and spontaneous forces of life: first they created the unity of international law, established by Grotius and the treaty of Westphalia; then the spread of French literature under Louis XIV brought the unity of civilization; the next stage of unity was achieved through Voltaire's rational criticism of religion; finally the French Revolution produced a growing unity in liberty through political and civil rights. After the efforts of the Church and of the monarchy to organize French nationality had failed, the Revolution incarnated France in the People and thus created the indestructible personality of France and through its example of all other modern nations. They had gained their souls.

Michelet's great history of the French Revolution thus represents the summit and the center of all his creations. In writing it he was at the zenith of his powers. The hero of the Revolution was to him the People, and the people alone. He showed the Revolution as the work of collective forces in which the so-called leaders, the heroes of so many other historians, were more led than leading. His sympathy induced him to justify, at the beginning of the Revolution, all the actions of the masses and to regard their passions and prejudices as a judgment of history. But while he refused to judge the people, he never denied the responsibility of individuals, of the leaders, of strong and assertive minorities. He did not believe the crimes of history —terror and tyranny—could be excused as products of historical necessity. To him the tragedy of the Revolution consisted in the fact that the people had not been strong enough to carry through their sublime vision. They fell victim to tribunes and ambitious agitators, to sectarian parties and to generals who led the Revolution to the atrocities of the Terror and the tyranny of the Empire.

Michelet never condoned the invocation of the *salut public*, of the *raison d'état* as a valid justification for injustice or inhumanity. Their application, in his opinion, weakened the sense of right and the moral fiber of the people, and in the long run no nation could ever gain by it. When the French monarchy for reasons of interests of state arranged the St. Bartholomew massacre or revoked the Edict of Nantes, it undermined the morale and sapped the strength of France; the expulsion of the Huguenots profited only Britain, Holland and Prussia. Nor was the Terror of the Revolution any better; neither public safety nor success could excuse or legitimize it. It did not save France, it destroyed the Revolution. Michelet knew that France would continue to pay dearly for the Terror, and for its sequence, the Empire. Territory might be won, but the souls of men were lost. From that history full of blood they kept the adoration of force and of victory; of force which was not true strength, of a victory which ultimately brought only defeat.

"La Révolution hier était une religion; elle devient une police. La police de ce Salut Public, qui a tout perdu. En la jetant dans un crescendo de meurtres, qu'on ne pouvait arrêter, elle rendit la France exécrable dans l'Europe, lui créa des haines immortelles. Perdu, en ce que les âmes brisées, après la Terreur, de dégout et de remords, se jetèrent à l'aveugle sous la tyrannie militaire."

The wars and the Terror changed the character of the French Revolution. At the beginning it had been the common work of all, not only of the middle class, of politicians and professional revolutionaries. But then the war had sent the more valorous elements of the people to the frontiers to fight. Those who remained easily became a prey of forceful minorities who did not shrink from any excesses in carrying through their ideas. They violated all the divine and human laws, they terrorized the Convention, turning it away from its fertile work of legislation, and they terrorized the people, destroying its union. For the Revolution had begun as a great commune of brotherhood. Its real climax was the fête of Federation on July 14, 1790, with its spontaneity of the popular masses, its upsurge of enthusiasm and loyalty, its joy and union from which none was excluded; where there were no parties and no classes, but only the French people, the new nation. Men and women in Paris and in all the cities and towns of France dedicated themselves to the fatherland. "At no other time, I believe, has man's heart been wiser or more spacious, at no other time have distinctions of class, of fortune and of party been more completely forgotten." In those happy days the Revolution appeared to bear out Michelet's faith in the nobility of the people and his humanitarian interpretation of nationality.

VI

The early spring of 1848 reawakened the old hope and joy of the Revolution. Did not the people in their enthusiasm accept that mission of devotion and sacrifice to which Michelet had called them two years before in *Le Peuple?* His dreams seemed approaching realization: this time the Revolution would not degenerate into war and a police-state, it would bring human freedom and social progress to all peoples. Soon however the disillusionment came. There was neither unity nor harmony. The bloody June days of the civil war revived all the fears of the first Revolution: classes and parties interlocked in deadly combat, envies and hatreds, the irreconcilable clash of hostile ideologies. Again the road led from the Terror to the Empire; the election of Louis Napoleon as president by an overwhelming vote of the people, the rise of a new clerical regime, the abolition of civic and political liberties, the centralized police-state—all these came in the name of democracy and of social progress with the acclamation of the masses. Michelet and Quinet witnessed the rapid ruin of all their hopes for France and mankind. Their shattered dreams brought them a new and deeper understanding.

The Revolution of 1848 failed in France as it failed in Germany. The pseudo-democratic dictatorship and the paternal socialism of Napoleon III were in many respects paralleled by similar attitudes of Bismarck. Yet what a difference between the two men and their innermost dreams and fundamental loyalties! But even greater and more significant was the difference in the attitudes of the leading intellectuals and representative citizens of the two nations. In Germany the great 1848'ers soon bowed to Bismarck's success and welcomed his promises of national power and of the people's prosperity. Masses and intellectuals found themselves in harmony in their common adoration of the great hero and his work. In France the 1848'ers went into opposition against Napoleon III, which for many of them meant long years of silence or exile. They could not be bribed by apparent success, by dreams of national glory or by promises of welfare for the masses. They insisted on individual liberty, on

their humanitarian ideals, and turned away from the acclaim of
the masses, from the popular will to which the dictator catered.
The German attitude led to the well known consequences of
Bismarckism; in France Napoleon III was followed by the
third Republic. It came to be accepted, with its individual liberties, its distrust of militarism and clericalism, its civilian character, by the great majority of the French people. In the crises
through which it had to pass it was shaken, but never destroyed.
Like Paris it could claim of itself: Fluctuat nec mergitur. It
showed its vitality in men like Jaurès, Péguy and Clemenceau
who each one in his own inimitable way guarded the common
heritage of France. Through its politics the republic might
again and again drift to the brink of ruin, but the deeply rooted
mystique républicaine, to use Péguy's words, would in every
crisis restore faith and vigor and save the liberties of France.
This mystic republicanism in France owes much of its ethos and
its vitality to Michelet.

In his last years at the Collège de France, Michelet worked
for the growth of a spirit of reconciliation and respect for liberty in France.[17] Perhaps his own experience also guided him
in that direction. In the catastrophe of his hopes for the nation
he found personal happiness in meeting at the end of 1848
Atanais Mialaret, a girl thirty years his junior, whom he married a few months later. Their marriage, in spite of their extreme differences of age, character and background, became,
after storms, sufferings and difficult adjustments, an unusually
happy and harmonious relationship based on mutual respect and
affection. He now could understand that the great achievements in public and private life which endured were settle-
ments through adjustments and tolerance, "a union with a slow
fusion of differences, assimilation by tactful consideration, a
careful respect of mutual liberty. Un tendre respect pour la
liberté, telle sera la vertu moderne." To heal and to conciliate in
a profound respect of individual liberty now appeared to him

as the task. He reproached the masses for being subject to superstitious idolatry which led to the reign of men like Robespierre or Napoleon. Only an education based on science and law as the seventeenth and eighteenth centuries established it—the principle of truth in science, the principle of justice in law—could help human progress. In his course in 1851 he addressed a fervent appeal to the youth to fight against the rapid growth of reaction. The government dismissed teachers in increasing numbers, others were carefully watched. Soon fate overtook Michelet and Quinet. In April of 1852 both were deprived of their positions in the Collège de France. As Michelet refused to take the oath required from all officials he also lost his position in the National Archives, which had been so dear to him. The hard life of his early years returned. But he kept his faith in the mission of France and of liberty. Quinet, who went into exile, also carried on their struggle for human emancipation. The experiences of 1848, of Louis Napoleon's rise, matured his philosophy of history. He taught that "idolatry is no longer permissible. Away with prejudices; away with sanguinary systems, away with historical fetishes—Caesar or Robespierre; away with the deification of people."

VII

Michelet and Quinet did not cease to grow and develop. They learned from experience as the history of the century unfolded. True to their innermost faith, they adapted their concrete attitudes to the emerging realities. In December of 1847 Michelet and Quinet sent a petition to the king of Prussia asking for an amnesty for Polish insurrectionists condemned to death by Prussian tribunals. In that petition Michelet wrote: "France and Germany, suffocated between two giants of whom one rules the sea and the other the land, have no better security for the future than their union. It would be a misfortune for the

world if there were to be blood between France and Germany."
Michelet until his very last years regarded Britain as the enemy.
"The war of all wars, the struggle of all struggles, is that between Britain and France; the rest are episodes." England appeared to him as the anti-France.[18] Like others in the thirties
and forties of the nineteenth century, he thought that social
unrest would rent her unity and free trade ruin her commerce
and he hoped that France would inherit social peace and prosperity.[19] He characterized the English genius as purely negative, Hobbes as a teacher of hatred, Locke as the theoretician
of a utilitarianism without greatness. The Revolution of 1688
seemed so insignificant compared with the French Revolution,
it had brought only the victory of the aristocracy not of the
people. Montesquieu and Voltaire had glorified England, because they interpreted her through French ideas. France could
never find an example in Britain. Britain was rich but without
soul or idea. Her greatness was sterile.

But in his last years, in his *Histoire du XIXe siècle* which carried the history of France through the Napoleonic Wars to
Waterloo, Michelet wrote: "The Channel seems already
bridged by common ideas and even by common interests. I am
happy to learn of the project of a tunnel from Calais to Dover
which would restore the two countries to their real neighbor-
liness, their kinship, their geological identity." [20] The nineteenth century now appeared to him as the struggle between
British industrialism and Napoleonic militarism. He still hated
industrialism and the machine; like Péguy he loved his people
of peasants and craftsmen. But the factory the rigors of which
had been attenuated by the moral values of Methodism was now
in his eyes the lesser evil, compared with the regimentation of
the barracks which mankind owed to Napoleon. Napoleon and
his heritage, not England, had become to Michelet the enemy
of Europe. Napoleon I was the ancestor of Napoleon III and the
godfather of Bismarck. Michelet had learned much; the events

of 1848 and of 1851 convinced him of the immense value of England's constitutional liberty and her tradition of law for the cause of human dignity and freedom. He declared himself for Britain against Philippe II, against Louis XIV, against Napoleon, against all the tyrants of Europe.[21]

Michelet was as slow to understand Germany as he was to appreciate Britain. In his old age he loved liberty more than the interests of France, hated despotism more than her enemies. In the very last minute he tried to stop Napoleon's war against Germany. He ended a letter of July 10, 1870, with the words: "Let us plant the flag of peace. War alone to those who could wish war in this world." He signed an appeal which Marx, Louis Blanc and other revolutionaries of the two nations who lived in exile in London addressed to the German and French peoples. The manifesto terminated with the words of the *Marseillaise:* "The peoples are for us brethren and the tyrants enemies." [22] The war and the peace imposed upon France came to him as a terrible shock, the revelation of the new Germany as a bitter disappointment.

Quinet with his deep knowledge of Germany had been much more farsighted. With a rare perspicacity he had divined trends unnoticed by most observers. When he returned for the third time in 1831 to his beloved Heidelberg, where many friends and his fiancée waited for him, he found them full of hostility and contempt for France. He became conscious of the dreams and desires which agitated Germany and of which his fellow countrymen did not know anything.[23] He saw the Germans, even in southwestern Germany, more and more looking toward Prussia for guidance. In 1832 he published his first warning, an article "De l'Allemagne et de la Révolution," in which he pointed out that the renowned German ideas which seemed so ethereal were striving to gain body, to pass from the minds into the wills, from the wills into actions, and to transform themselves into social power and political might. "Now all these ideas which we believed would remain unfathomable and without body operate like all other ideas, and rise before us with all the destiny of a nation; and this nation puts itself under the dictatorship of a people who are not more enlightened than it is, but more greedy, more ardent, more exacting, more efficient. The Germans have loaded that people with their ambitions, their rancors, their rapines, their trickeries, their diplomacy, their violence, their glory, their outward force, and have reserved to themselves only the honest and obscure discipline of inner freedom. You know who that people is. Since the end of the Middle Ages the strength and initiative of the German states have passed from south to north. So Germany intends at present to make Prussia her leader instead of Austria? Yes; and if we let Prussia go ahead she will slowly push Germany from the rear to the assassination of the old kingdom of the Franks." Germany turned to Prussia, which she thought capable of realizing her innermost aspirations; she was ready to accept the hard yoke of Prussian leadership because Prussia alone could offer it. When Quinet sent the manuscript to Michelet the latter advised against publication; Quinet's prediction of the rise of an aggressive German power under Prussia seemed incredible. But Quinet insisted: "I think that I fulfill the duty of a citizen in revealing what could become a menace to our country. My friend, I respect you, I love you more than a brother; believe me, there must be pressing reasons to decide me to resist your suggestions." [24]

Quinet, who throughout had shown a profound sympathy for, and a keen appreciation of, German thought and literature, regarded the relations between the two peoples as primarily a conflict between two civilizations. "L'esprit allemand et l'esprit français sont de nature si opposée que presque toujours l'un exclut l'autre." Quinet knew that the same words have a very different meaning in different languages and civilizations, and that nothing is as dangerous as to confound these meanings by

the same words. He saw France, under the governments of
Louis Philippe and Louis Napoleon, abdicating her mission of
spreading freedom; Germany was ready to step into the void
with her own ideas, to begin, in the realm of power but even
more in that of ideas, a new era, the German century. He
warned in 1840 and again in 1867. He saw clearly the end of
the great period of German idealism and spiritualism; in 1836
he predicted the rise of a philosophy of materialism, the fall of
the German mind from one extreme into the very opposite extreme. "Quand l'esprit allemand n'est pas dans la nue, il rampe;
il lui reste à apprendre à marcher."

Even after Prussia had crushed Austria at Königgrätz,
Quinet's Cassandra calls went unheeded. France, eager to continue the complacent happiness of the preparations for her
World's Fair of 1867, did not listen when told that she was
facing not a political or military crisis, but "un état nouveau du
monde," a completely new world situation. Quinet was the
first to foresee all the consequences of 1866. He could not prove
them from documents, he wrote, because decisive changes in
the mind are not revealed in diplomatic notes or the diaries of
statesmen; they can be caught only in scattered words, in songs
or dreams. Quinet warned that it was useless or insufficient to
imitate Prussian armaments: a new Germany could only be
countered by a new France, a France more alive to her own
traditions of liberty. Nothing was more dangerous than a despotism assuming the mask of liberty and of democracy and calling them by new names; for then all notions of true and false,
of just and unjust, get hopelessly confounded and harm is done
to the very soul of the people. To a France governed by Napoleon III in the name of a new democracy, Quinet called out:
"There is nothing older in the world than people who acclaim
success, who greet in the evening what they cursed in the morning. It is useless to create for that a new word: authoritarian
democracy, as if any authority placed in the stead of law were

not the very negation of democracy. Is that the way to form great nations? I have so often seen democracy and liberty taken in by cheap promises of establishing freedom sometime in the future after strength and union have done their work. But meanwhile the masses have become impenetrable to the ideas of justice and liberty."

The terrible defeat of 1870, the importance of which few could clearly foresee at the time,[25] filled the hearts of Frenchmen with despair. It was then that Renan expressed the fear that "France and even Britain—which suffers at bottom with the same malady (the weakening of the military spirit, the predominance of commercial considerations)—will soon be reduced to a secondary role; the stage of the European world will be exclusively occupied by two colossal powers, the Germans and the Slavs, who have preserved the vigor of the military and leadership principle, and whose struggle will fill the future." [26] In spite of this pessimism, France recovered with surprising speed. Michelet and Quinet were no longer there to witness it —the former had died in 1874, the latter in 1875—but the light of the liberal and humanitarian tradition which they had so faithfully tended burned on, sometimes in wise or kind men like Renan or Jaurès, above all in the people. True, the mood of 1846 when Michelet wrote Le Peuple with its messianic fervor and its heroic patriotism—which had much of nationalistic idolatry in it—was gone. One hundred years later the mood was infinitely more sober, modest, and humanized.[27] But in this chastened form the spirit has survived, or rather has been rekindled again and again, as in his Le Peuple Michelet had predicted: "I have acquired the conviction that this country is one of invincible hope. With France, nothing is finished. Always everything begins anew."

Chapter Three

ITALY: MAZZINI

E perocchè più dolce natura in signoreggiando e più forte in sostenendo e più sottile in acquistando nè fu nè fia, che quella della gente latina, siccome per isperienza si può vedere, e massimamente quella del popolo santo nel quale l'alto sangue troiano era mischiato, Iddio quello elesse a quello ufficio. Perocchè, conciossiacosachè a quello ottenere non sanza grandissima virtù venire si potesse, e a quello usare grandissima e umanissima benignità si richiedesse, questo era quello popolo che a ciò più era disposto. Onde non da forza fu principalmente preso per la romana gente, ma da divina provvidenzia ch'è sopra ogni ragione. E in ciò s'accorda Virgilio nell' primo dell' Eneida, quando dice, in persona di Dio parlando: A costoro (cioè alli Romani) nè termine di cose nè di tempo pongo: a loro ho dato imperio sanza fine.

—DANTE, *"Il Convivio," Trattato IV, Capitolo IV.*

3

THE words and wars of the French Revolution brought the first awakening of political life to Italy. The slumber of centuries was broken. For the first time the word "Italy" was used as a political reality; created by the French for their own purposes, it evoked a memory and a longing which were not to die when, after 1815, Italy and the rest of Europe returned to the apparent quiet of the Restoration period. Under the surface the stir and fermentation went on. The French Revolution had sown the seeds: the words "liberty," "people," "republic," spelled a sacred destiny. The memories of the great days made life on the continent of Europe seem shallow to youth suffering from the *maladie du siècle*. In a century which had started as an heroic epopee but which degenerated into a pseudo-idyll of hypocrisy and mediocrity, Napoleon and Byron, the deed and the song, stood out as a promise and inspiration. In the stillness of the air, which was heavy, the old seemed irretrievably dead, the new not yet born. In the twilight between two epochs the youth, waiting for the dawn, longed for a new word, a new song which would bind men together in a new hope and call them to new deeds. Regeneration demanded a new faith which could come to life only through sacrifice and action. Its sacred dogmas were received from the French Revolution—liberty and equality, people and humanity—but the fire of 1789 had burned out and failed to regenerate mankind in their service. Only a stronger faith could build more secure and lasting foundations. Giuseppe Mazzini devoted his life to becoming the prophet of the new faith; he wished to found it on the rock of eternal Rome and on the mission of the Italian people.

Mazzini was neither an original thinker nor a profound one. He had neither the analytical power nor the patience of a student of history or society. He was not eager to describe or to understand; he was driven to transform man and mankind. As a believer, he was satisfied with a few dogmas which he borrowed from the French Revolution and the French Romanticists, from Condorcet and Saint-Simon, and to which he added a fervent Italian nationalism; as an agitator, he repeated these few dogmas again and again in innumerable articles and letters; as a poet he endowed these dogmas with a beauty and passion which sent other men out as apostles of the new faith. He himself was the indefatigable messenger of the new word. He never achieved a social position or popular recognition, he never founded a family or a home. Life for him was not the quest of happiness, but the pursuit of duty; not pleasant and joyful, but earnest and resigned.[1] Like the prophets of old he consumed himself under the burden which the message imposed upon him. Like them, he called his people to a stern ethical life far above their readiness. Like them, he found few willing listeners, was maligned in his lifetime and honored only after his death. Like them, he suffered and yet went on to the very end without flinching or failing. As a young man he made up his mind, and in the remaining forty years he never changed; in his writings of the early 1830's are expressed all his fundamental ideas, even the forms of locution, which reappear in a monotonous repetition to the very last articles he wrote in the early 'seventies. While the world changed around him he did not veer. When he left this world he found his message unheeded, the new faith unkindled.

Like Michelet and Quinet, Mazzini underwent the influence of Vico and Herder. From Vico he learned to view the history of mankind as a unity following its providential course, subject to the same universal laws; from Herder and Condorcet he accepted the idea of the irresistible progress toward ever greater harmony, and like Herder he regarded the peoples as the collective individualities through which the process of history is carried on. But the French Revolution had politicized Herder's concept of peoples into nations. Mazzini, in a temper entirely different from Herder's, demanded a nation. Michelet and Quinet lived in a nation; Mazzini had to create one. When he was a young man, the Italian nation was not more than a vague hope for a few men—it was neither an actual force moving the hearts of a people nor a political aspiration guiding its actions. None of the Italian states offered the slightest encouragement to national ambitions. Almost no one believed a united Italian nation possible, very few believed it desirable. Politically and economically life in Italy was more stagnant than in any other European country; even after unification, Italy was to remain in every respect by far the weakest of the European powers. Yet it was upon the Italian people and upon the creation of an Italian nation that Mazzini founded his faith and based his plans for the regeneration of mankind. Mazzini became the prophet of Italy's mission. As the present seemed nowhere to vouchsafe any future greatness for the Italians, he had to look to the past to inspire and legitimize his hopes. Like Vincento Gioberti, his fellow subject of the King of Sardinia and fellow exile as a revolutionary, Mazzini proclaimed the moral and civic primacy of the Italians.[2] But while Gioberti based it upon the Papacy and the Catholic Church, the Rome of the Middle Ages and of his own day, Mazzini looked to the Italian people and a new faith, a third Rome which would harmonize and outshine the Rome of antiquity and the Rome of the Middle Ages.

Until then the Italian patriots and liberals had always looked to France for initiative and inspiration. The awakening of the European continent began with the great example of 1789; from that time Paris was the beacon of hope, France the second fatherland for all European lovers of liberty. In the hot July of 1830, in the early spring of 1848, whenever a new great hope stirred Europe, the initiative came from France and spread to Italy and over the continent. For a whole century, from Rousseau to the Commune, revolutionary thought and example first germinated in France. French leadership, however, was not confined to progressive movements; as a result of the deep division produced in France by the Revolution, all counter-revolutionary doctrine, from Bonald and De Maistre to Maurras and Sorel, was first thought in France though it came to fruit in other nations which rejected the ideas of 1789. Italy accepted them, but Mazzini and Gioberti rejected the leadership of France and denied her right to initiative. Was not Italy the older sister, the rightful heir of the Rome of the Caesars and of the Rome of the Popes which for fifteen hundred years had brought their civilization and law to an ever widening circle of peoples? Italy, Gioberti proclaimed, contained within herself, above all through her religion, all the conditions necessary for her national and political resurrection and had no need, therefore, to imitate foreign examples. "In the Italian nationality are founded the interests of religion and the civil and universal hopes of mankind. Italy is the chosen people, the typical people, the creative people, the Israel of the modern age." [3] With greater force than Gioberti, Mazzini claimed for Italy the initiative and the moral leadership in the regeneration of humanity, and he called upon the Italians to live up to their mission. From this faith he drew the inspiration to sustain him in his struggle; his burning flame was able to kindle responsive sparks in the hearts of his people. But his apostolate, based on a claim not supported by reality, aroused dangerous illusions and gnawing disappointments, the bitter harvest of which later generations were to reap. He burdened the young and weak Italian nation with a legacy of the past which like a will-o'-the-wisp drew it from the patient mastering of reality to the world-embracing dreams of Roman ghosts.

The great passion of Mazzini's life, however, in which his deep religious mysticism found its expression, was not Italy but unity. Unfolding itself on three ascending levels, this unity in every stage answered one of the fundamental needs of the age. Unity of man was to overcome the dispersion of modern man in an industrialized mass civilization through an identity of thought and action, fused into wholeness by a faith which would give a new heart and center, meaning and end, to man's manifold activities and self-contrarieties. Unity of nation was to bind all the free individuals of democracy into a community of liberty and equality and by the unity of feeling and thought counteract the atomization, the egoism, and the competitive struggle which threatened to undermine modern society. Unity of mankind was to assure the peace and collaboration of all nations working in harmony under a common law of progress toward the common goal of a better world. Rome was, to Mazzini, the symbol of this threefold unity, the eternal source of inspiration to bind all men for the realization of God's ends. History and geography had selected Rome for her mission; did not her name itself, *Roma*, spell to his mystical faith in its palindrome *amor*, a message of Love? He never became aware that by this identification of man's destiny with Rome he narrowed his ideal of unity and lowered his faith in universal regeneration. The vision blinded his perception of reality; later on, void of its ethos and disfigured beyond recognition, it was to lead his people repeatedly to catastrophe. Yet Mazzini found it an anchor in his quest for guidance. He felt that an epoch of mankind was drawing rapidly to its end, that a critical time was approaching, that a new gospel was needed, as in the time of the disintegration of antiquity and the birth of Christianity. The nationalistic spell of the past made Mazzini believe and proclaim that the new word and the new law would sound forth from a third Rome.

II

Mazzini was born in 1805 in Genoa, a city where traditions of its republican past and memories of recent French rule survived even after it became in 1815 part of the possessions of the King of Sardinia.[4] He grew up in a cultured middle-class family and joined the revolutionary patriotic movement of the Carbonari. He never felt any loyalty to the royal house, nor any roots in its lands. Thus his thought early centered on Italy and on liberty. He participated in the uprisings of 1831. The failure of the movements of 1830 left a lasting impression. He became deeply disappointed with the Carbonari, whose weakness he explained as due to the lack of any comprehensive program based upon principles, and with France where the revolutionary fire died down in the *juste milieu* policy of the Orleanist monarchy. From that time on his course was set; he never swerved from it: Italy and mankind were to be freed by a policy based upon principles, not under French leadership, but through the moral strength of an awakened Italian people. Untiringly he called them to the struggle. The Italian governments regarded him as their foremost enemy. He lived his remaining life in exile, first in France and Switzerland, then after 1837 in London which became his second home. He returned to Italy only to plan or lead armed insurrections. For a brief while in the spring of 1849 he was one of the triumvirs responsible for the fate of the short-lived Roman republic, where in the modesty of his personal conduct and in the moderation of his counsels he set a noble democratic example. But the dream collapsed; the hated papal old order returned. Again he found the revolution betrayed by France, where the Catholic party and Louis Napoleon's dictatorship buried the hopes of 1848. Italian unity and liberty seemed farther away than ever. Young Italy had failed as did the Carbonari two decades before.

Young Italy was the instrument which Mazzini forged for the transformation of Italy and of Europe, when the uprisings of 1831 failed through the hostility of the princes, the pusillanimity of the middle classes, the inertia of the masses. Salvation could come only from a youth educated in the right spirit. To that task Young Italy, founded by Mazzini in Marseilles in 1831, dedicated itself. The *Carbonari* had been sectarians under the influence of the eighteenth century and of France; Young Italians, apostles of a national religion, precursors of the new age, had to free Italy from the influence of foreigners and the spirit of the past age. But their task was more than education, it called for action. Mazzini thought much about insurrection and revolution and he developed the theory of the leadership of dictatorial elite which a century later was applied so successfully. He stressed the need for a small and homogeneous minority, determined to armed action, highly disciplined and ranged in the hour of need as a compact phalanx, which in a combative spirit of "energetic initiative" would foment insurrection which "forms the military education of the people, and consecrates every foot of the native soil by the memory of some warlike deed." The movement would become a crusade teaching the people "that war is inevitable—desperate and determined war that knows no truce save in victory or the grave. The secret of raising the masses lies in the hands of those who show themselves ready to fight and conquer at their head." The struggle may be long and the goal distant, therefore until it is fully attained Italy must be governed by "a provisional dictatorial power, concentrated in the hands of a small number of men." Only, when total victory has been achieved and the foundations securely laid, will the dictatorship give way to the perfect democracy of a nation united in liberty and equality by a common faith.[5]

Faith alone, faith in God and the people, could give a movement and a nation strength for great deeds. Everything had to serve this faith, otherwise it would lose its meaning. Art had to be a national manifestation,[6] not "the caprice of this or that individual, but a solemn page of history or a prophecy." The Italian poet or artist could not hark back to history, he had to be a prophet. "To do this it was necessary to interrogate the latent, slumbering, unconscious life of the people, to lay the hand upon the half-frozen heart of the nation, to count its rare pulsations and reverently learn from them the purpose and duty of Italian genius." But true art would be possible only in a united and independent nation. "Without a country and without liberty we might perhaps have some prophets of art, but no art. Therefore it is better to consecrate our lives to the question—are we to have a country? and turn directly to the political problem." Mazzini forgot that art did bloom in exemplary greatness in Italy in the late Middle Ages and in the Renaissance, when there was no Italian country, and had inspired mankind when it did not seek to arouse a nation. The Italian fatherland since its creation certainly has produced nothing approaching anywhere the cultural and spiritual manifestations of an Italy which had been no nation. Like so many nationalists Mazzini in the fire of his apostolate misread history.[7]

It is true that for Mazzini the liberation of Italy was never the ultimate goal. His vision aimed much higher: a regenerated Italy had to serve the regeneration of mankind at a turning point in its history. For the age which had begun with the Christian Middle Ages and the Reformation had run, Mazzini taught, its full course in the French Revolution with its emphasis on individuality and rights. The French Revolution was to him not a beginning, it was an end, the consummation of the skeptic and materialistic eighteenth century. A new epoch was to dawn, no longer of materialism and self-interest but of faith and devotion; not of rights but of duties, not of individuals but of association. The French Revolution had broken old and obsolete forms which had to be swept away; it had emancipated man from fetters and set him free. But it had been a negative performance. It had established liberty; but it did not tell how to use the liberty. It had pointed out no new goals. On the ruins of the old world a new faith had to rise, a positive message inspiring men to great actions and answering their quest for the meaning of life. There was a deadening void in Europe. France could not fill it; the initiative could come only from Italy. Behind Mazzini's calls for Italian nationhood was "a presentiment that regenerated Italy was destined to arise the *initiatrix* of a new life, and of a new and powerful unity to all the nations of Europe." Italy would surpass herself in the future, Italy which Mazzini without any historical justification identified with Rome. Twice Rome had guided mankind in the past; would not Italy rise to even greater heights in the future?

"The worship of Rome was a part of my being. The great Unity, the One Life of the world, had twice been elaborated within her walls. Other peoples—their brief mission fulfilled—disappeared for ever. To none save to her had it been given twice to guide and direct the world. There, life was eternal, death unknown. There, upon the vestiges of an epoch of civilization anterior to the Grecian, which had had its seat in Italy, and which the historical science of the future will show to have had a far wider external influence than the learned of our own day imagine—the Rome of the Republic, concluded by the Caesars, had arisen to consign the former world to oblivion, and thence she had borne her eagles over the known world, carrying with them the idea of right, the source of liberty. In later days Rome rose again, greater than before, and at once constituted herself, through her Popes—as venerable once as abject now—the accepted center of a new Unity, elevating the law from earth to heaven, and substituting for the idea of right an idea of duty—a duty common to all men, and therefore source of their equality. Why should not a new Rome, the Rome of the Italian people—portents of whose coming I deemed I saw —arise to create a third and still vaster unity; to link together and harmonize earth and heaven, right and duty, and to utter, not to individuals but to peoples, the great word Association— to make known to free men and equals their mission here below?" [8]

Rome had united mankind in a universal monarchy. It had secured peace and justice and had produced a unity of civilized life. Mankind had never ceased to cherish the dream of such a union. Napoleon had attempted its realization. After his downfall the Holy Alliance tried to resurrect a dead past based on throne and altar and the association of princes. Young Italy took the initiative for future unity, based upon God and the people and an association of free nations. Mazzini called up against the Holy Alliance an alliance of the youth of Europe, the "vanguard of nation and liberty in a fraternity of peoples." In Switzerland on April 15, 1834, seven Italians, five Germans, and five Poles drew up the Pact of Fraternity, establishing Young Europe, "an association of men believing in a future of liberty, equality and fraternity for all mankind, and desirous of consecrating their thoughts and actions to the realization of this future." Its general principles proclaimed that there was one sole God, His law the one sole ruler, humanity the one sole interpreter of that law. "To constitute humanity so as to enable it through a continuous progress as quickly as possible to discover and apply the law of God: that is the mission of Young Europe. Every people has its special mission, which will cooperate toward the fulfillment of the general mission of humanity. That mission constitutes its nationality. Nationality is sacred." [9]

Young Europe was a secret revolutionary organization. National committees were set up, insurrections planned. The Swiss authorities dissolved it on August 11, 1836, and expelled its members. The leaders and the national committees soon quarrelled among themselves. The venture failed as Young Italy had failed. But the idea lived on; new organizations sprang up, a Young Switzerland, a Young Spain, and others. Though they

were only ephemeral, a new word had been coined which reverberated as far as Young Turkey and Young China; an idea
had been set upon the course which it still pursues: humanity is
one, obeying one law, marching toward one goal, and it has to
be organized by the association of free nations. The gospel of
liberal nationalism was on its march; Europe was the cradle,
Young Europe the nucleus of a development which ultimately
would embrace the world.[10] But first the map of Europe had to
be redrawn according to nationalities.[11] "The question of the
nationalities was destined," Mazzini declared, "to give its name
to the century and to restore to Europe the power of initiation
for good."

III

The years of Young Italy and Young Europe were a period
of stirring hope and feverish action, of youth and comradeship.
Looking back thirty years later Mazzini remembered these
"years of young life" as a time "of such a pure and glad devoted-
ness as I would wish the coming generation to know." In the
dreary years of exile the exhilarating happiness soon vanished;
his faith remained unshaken. In all his writings he celebrated
the new "religion whose center is the fatherland, and whose
circumference embraces the whole earth." [12] Mazzini was a
deeply religious man; he was not a seeker after God, he possessed the certainty of faith. His religion sustained him against
the blows of fate and the doubts of reason. His God, like the
God of the Bible, was the God of history who realizes Himself
in the development of mankind. World history becomes the
way to salvation, a moral struggle in which the forces of good
fight for the progressive realization of the Divine truth. Man's
task on earth is to serve faithfully in God's cause. History has
an end, life is a mission toward its realization; virtuous is the
man who sacrifices to duty his heart and passion, his hopes and
interests. His efforts will not be in vain: the coming age will see

the glory of the reign of the moral law; man will find his true liberty by assuming his share in the divine mission of mankind. In the present period of history men are fighting the good fight in associations called nations. The nation which most devotedly lives up to the duties of man will lead mankind into the coming age.[13] Mazzini hoped that that nation would be Italy.

Mazzini regarded religion as the greatest need in the crisis through which he saw Europe passing. In 1871 he addressed the Italians in the "Program" of his new organ, *Rome of the People*. "Without a common faith, without conception of an ideal that shall bind the nations together, and show to each its special function for the common good, without unity of standard for its whole moral, political, economic life, the world today is at the mercy of caprice, of dynastic and popular ambition and egotism. The initiative, which France has lost since 1815, lives no longer, visible and accepted, in any people. England deliberately abdicated it when she introduced, under the name of non-intervention, a policy of local interests.[14] Germany threatens to sterilize all her vast power of thought, by surrendering the action that should be collective, and the formation of her unity, to a military monarchy hostile to liberty.[15] The Slav populations, who have so great a part in the future reserved for them, dismembered and without center of national life, still hesitate between the rule of a Czar fatal to them all, and the old difficulty of local antagonisms. And, faced by such a void, we— who are ready to hail and applaud the initiative wherever it may arise—we cherish as the ideal of our heart the sacred hope that it may arise on the ruins of the Papacy and of every similar lie, from the third Rome, from the ROME OF THE PEOPLE. Reborn at the cradle of an Age, Italy and Rome are called to inaugurate it, if only they know their destinies, and the moral force they have behind them." [16]

Mazzini never wavered in his conviction that public like private life is an ethical duty, a religious mission. He believed that "to make politics an art and sever it from morality is a sin before God and destruction to the peoples. The end of politics is the application of the moral law to the civil constitution of a nation, in its double activity, domestic and foreign." [17] The great war cries of the age, Fatherland, Liberty, Nationality, Equality, Progress, Fraternal Association, were to him "holy and prophetic sounds of a new order of things, a complete translation of the words of Jesus, 'That all may be one.'" He regarded the struggle of the peoples of Europe as "a sacred struggle," the logical consequence of the doctrine of the unity of God and therefore of the human race. He never tired of repeating that every man, made in the image of God—irrespective of color, birth, or fortune—ought to be a temple of the living God; the earth, the altar upon which he sacrifices to God; the task accomplished by him, the incense of his sacrifice; love, his prayer; love realized or association, his power.

For a man like Mazzini the true liberation of Italy could come only through ethical principles and religious enthusiasm. Like the prophets of old, Mazzini summoned the Italians to rely on the power of the spirit and not on the crooked ways of diplomacy. He had no use for Machiavelli, whose theory reflected to him "a period of corruption and degradation which it was necessary to bury with the past." He hated the little Machiavellians of his own day, the worshippers of facts who did not understand that ideas precede and generate facts. He believed that great revolutions were the work of principles not of bayonets, and were achieved first in the moral, and only afterward in the material sphere. Machiavelli could not be a guide to a new life, which can be founded only "in the stern worship of morality, in the energetic affirmation of the right and true, in the scorn of all expedience, in the consciousness of the unity of the religious, social and political movement." A nation addicted to Machiavellianism, to immoral opportunism, would in spite of all outward successes and all its power, fall prey to inner decay and finally to foreign invasion.

Yet it was intelligent diplomacy and a daring use of opportunities, not the spirit of the prophet, that brought about the unification of Italy. As Mazzini bitterly complained, Machiavelli prevailed over Dante, Mazzini's great hero in Italian history. He had imbibed much of his own doctrine of the primacy of Italy and the identity of her interests with those of the human race from Dante's *De Monarchia*. On Dante he bestowed a praise which fitted the nineteenth-century nationalist much more than the medieval poet. "The idea of his nation's greatness illumines every page of Dante; it is the ruling thought of his genius. Never man loved his country with more exalted and fervent love; never man had more sublime and glorious visions of the destinies in store for her." [18] Though Dante and Mazzini had in common a faith in the oneness of mankind, only Mazzini regarded nations as the indispensable link between the individual and humanity, a thought which would have been incomprehensible to Dante. But for Mazzini, too, mankind was above all nations. He never failed to stress that man has duties to himself, to his family, to the nation, to mankind; and of them all, those to mankind were the highest. For him as for Dante the general and universal took precedence over the limited and concrete. "Your first duties," Mazzini told the Italian working people, "first not in point of time but of importance, because without understanding these you can only imperfectly fulfill the rest, are to humanity. You are citizens in order that in a limited sphere, with a concord of people linked to you by speech, by tendencies and by habits, you may labor for the benefit of all men, a task which each could ill do by himself, weak and lost amid the immense multitudes of his fellow men. Those who teach morality, limiting its obligations to duties toward family or country, teach you a more or less narrow egotism and lead you to what is evil for others and for yourself. Country and family are like two steps of a ladder without which you could not climb any higher but upon which it is forbidden you to stay your feet."

Mazzini never regarded nationality as an end; it was for him only a means to a higher purpose. No nation could therefore be sovereign. While all sovereignty rested for Mazzini on a much higher level than that of nations—in the moral law, in humanity, in God—nations were the individuals of humanity, providentially constituted to represent, within humanity, the division of labor for the common good. Sovereignty had its place in the goal, the ideal. *Il solo fine è sovrano*. But the knowledge of the ideal needed an interpreter. This interpreter, according to Mazzini, could only be the nation. A true cosmopolitan had to be a nationalist. *Chi vuole Umanità, vuole Patria*. Nationality is thus the consciousness of a mission to be fulfilled for the sake of mankind. It does not depend upon race or descent, but upon a common thought and a common goal. These were, for Mazzini, the essential elements in determining a nationality; without them none could exist. Certain objective factors might help the formation of a nationality: language, geography, historical traditions. In that respect Italy seemed more highly favored than other nations: few had so clear-cut a geographic contour; few, a history and language comparable in nobility to that of Rome and Dante. Yet the determining factor was to Mazzini the unity of the mind, the national idea—*un pensiero comune, un fine comune*—though sometimes he sounded like the Pan-Germans, demanding the union of all the populations speaking Italian dialects.

Mazzini stressed the difference between the spirit of nationality understood by him as a starting point for the common work of mankind, and the narrow spirit of nationalism with "the stupid presumption on the part of each people that they are capable of solving the political, social and economic problems alone, forgetful of the great truth that the cause of all peoples is one." He demanded of the Italians that they ask themselves whenever they set out to do something for their family or their fatherland whether, if such an action were taken by all other people, it would help or harm humanity. "And if your conscience answers that it would harm, then desist; desist even if it seems that from that action some immediate advantage for your fatherland or your family might come." But on the other hand, the individual seemed not a sufficient basis for the fulfillment of humanity's goals. Men can work for the common good only in association. Mazzini was convinced that "the idea of nationality arose at the opportune moment, to multiply the forces of the individual and make known the means by which the labor and sacrifice of each man may be rendered efficacious and beneficial to humanity." Sometimes, however, he realized that nationality was a passing phenomenon, a stage in the flow of history, and should not be put at the same level as the individual and the family, more eternal and essential elements of the life of mankind than is nationality. "The fatherland, sacred today, will perhaps some day disappear when every man shall reflect in his own conscience the moral laws of humanity; but the family will endure as long as man endures. It is the cradle of humanity."

IV

Throughout Mazzini's life Young Italy and Young Europe remained closely connected in his mind. The age of nationality which he predicted was to usher in a new organization of Europe, a league of democratic peoples, each one free in its internal organization, but all gradually uniting in their international life. "The Europe of the peoples will be one," he wrote in 1849, "avoiding alike the anarchy of absolute independence and the centralization of conquest." In 1871 he predicted the basic principles of the modern League of Nations. Deploring the absence of any rule to govern the international relations of the peoples, he demanded open diplomacy and collective security. "Like the members of one family, the peoples are jointly bound, in proportion to their power, to combat evil wheresoever encamped, and to promote good wheresoever it may be accomplished. The nations who stand by, inert spectators of unjust wars inspired by national egotism, will, when attacked in their turn, find in the surrounding nations mere spectators." [19]

Mazzini's hope lay in the brotherhood of the peoples of Europe—and through Europe, of all humanity; in a Europe kept at peace through the unity of ideal and civilization and through a real balance of power of almost equally large states. As one of the essential elements of this balance Mazzini favored a federation of the smaller nations, mostly Slavonic, living in the belt between the Baltic Sea and the Aegean. He hoped to see Italy become not the least of the great powers but the center and soul of a league composed of the minor European states protecting themselves against the possible usurpations of any of the great powers. "The true object of the international life of Italy lies in our alliance with the Slav family." Mazzini wished Italy to help the northern and southern Slavs achieve their independence and federation. He feared that otherwise they would seek the aid of Russia and submit to the leadership of the Russian autocrat. "In that case the result would be a gigantic attempt to make Europe Cossack; a long and fierce battle waged by despotism against all the liberties we have already won; a new era of militarism; Constantinople, the key of the Mediterranean and all the paths to Asia, in the hands of Russia instead of a confederation of the Slavonic groups, friendly to us and liberty; the creation of a hostile Pan-Slav unity, governed by one despotic will, instead of a barrier erected against tyranny by the organization of free men from the Baltic to the Adriatic." [20]

But Mazzini's vision reached farther than that of a united and democratic Europe. He saw all the great lines of modern European development converge upon Asia, whence the first germs of civilization had once fertilized Europe. Now Europe was "providentially tending to carry back to Asia the civilization developed from those germs in her own privileged lands." In an article written after the unification of Italy and Germany, a few months before his death in 1872, Mazzini's picture of the future broadened into the one world with its growing unity of civilization and common tasks in which, inspired again by the tradition of Rome, he wished to secure for Italy her rightful place. "Europe is pressing upon Asia, and invading her various regions on every side: through the English conquests in India, through the slow advance of Russia on the north, through the concessions periodically wrung from China, through the advance of America across the Rocky Mountains, through colonization, and through contraband. Shall Italy, the earliest and most potent colonizing power in the world, remain the last in this splendid movement?"

For united Italy Mazzini set out an international policy of imperial destiny. He hoped she would follow it with the same tenacity with which for the last two hundred years Russia has followed her colonizing plans. Writing in his *Roma del Popolo* in 1871 he demanded "to lay open to Italy every pathway leading to the Asiatic world, and to fulfill at the same time the mission of civilization pointed out by the times, through the systematic augmentation of Italian influence at Suez and Alexandria, and by seizing the earliest opportunities of sending a colonizing expedition to Tunis. In the inevitable movement of European civilization upon Africa, as Morocco belongs to Spain and Algeria to France, so does Tunis, key of the central Mediterranean, belong to Italy. Tunis, Tripoli, and Cyrenaica form a part—extremely important from its contiguity with Egypt, and through Egypt and Syria, with Asia—of that zone of Africa which truly belongs to the European system. And the Roman standard did float upon those heights in the days when, after the fall of Carthage, the Mediterranean was named our sea. We were masters of the whole of that region up to the fifth century. France has her eye upon it at the present, and will have it if we do not." [21]

Thus Mazzini saw the future: the liberation movements of the Slav peoples which were to lead to the disintegration of the Turkish and Habsburg empires on behalf of the principle of nationality; the League of Nations and the political structure of Europe as it emerged from World War I through the triumph of national self-determination; the new imperialism with its expansion of the American empire into the Pacific, the Westernization of Asia and the Europeanization of North Africa; and finally the colonial ambitions of his own country. Fifteen years after his death one of his prominent disciples, for many years a fervent republican and a leader of the extreme Left in the Italian parliament, Francesco Crispi, started the conquering march toward the gateways of Asia, after he had seen France plant her standard over Tunis and Carthage. The year in which the fiftieth anniversary of the creation of the kingdom of Italy was celebrated witnessed the advance of Italy into Tripoli and Cyrenaica. And the claim for the Mediterranean as "our sea"— a claim based upon the unfortunate identification of the modern Italian nation with ancient Rome—was to haunt many Italians in the two great European wars of the twentieth century, wars fought primarily, as Mazzini again had foretold, for the control of the smaller nations inhabiting the belt between the Baltic Sea and the Aegean Sea.

V

Unlike the German patriots, Mazzini never separated national independence and unity from individual liberty. Fatherland and liberty were equally dear to him, they were intimately and indissolubly connected in his mind. "The religion of the fatherland is most sacred; but where it is not governed by the sentiment of individual dignity and the consciousness of the rights

inherent in the nature of man—where the citizen is not convinced that he must bestow renown on the fatherland rather
than receive it—it is a religion which can make the fatherland
powerful, but not happy, famous before the foreigner but not
free." [22] He never wavered in his devotion to all the political
and individual rights gained by the Anglo-Saxon and French
Revolutions in the seventeenth and eighteenth centuries; he
praised England as the home and guardian of these liberties; and
he became after 1860 even more insistent in his emphasis on
liberal democracy and the expansion of individual rights in the
new Italian kingdom. He did not reject the Declaration of
Rights of the French Revolution. He accepted it whole-
heartedly. He saw the French Revolution not only denying the
dead past, feudalism, aristocracy, monarchy: "Amid all those
negations, a mighty Yea arose—the creature of God ready to
act, radiant with power and will—the *ecce homo*, repeated after
eighteen centuries of suffering and strife, not by the voice of
the martyr but on the altar raised by the Revolution to victory
—Right, individual faith, rooted in the world forever." Mazzini
understood the great affirmation of the French Revolution, the
fruit of the spreading influence of the English ideas of liberty.
He was a Western radical democrat.[23]

In all his writings Mazzini never denied the value or rejected
the validity of the French Revolution.[24] But he felt the need of
going beyond it. For it seemed to him that in freeing man it had
not pointed out any positive and social goals except those of
individual happiness, which were not strong enough as a foundation of society nor noble enough as an inspiration of the heart.
Human evolution had to go on beyond the French Revolution,
but the march of progress did in no way destroy or weaken the
achievements of the past; it preserved them in a higher synthesis.
The French Revolution secured forever the individual rights of
man. The sacred principle of liberty had been gained, but the
equally sacred principle of union and association, of man's duties

toward society and humanity, was missing. The new age had its task set: the harmonization of the liberty and rights of the individual with the needs and duties of society.

In the quest for this harmony Mazzini, following therein the Rousseau of *The Social Contract*, often went too far in his emphasis on unity, on the need of a communion of faith for all citizens. His democracy had a religious and almost totalitarian character. It harbored the danger involved in the romantic longing for the ideal state based upon community, *Gemeinschaft*, with its possible disregard for the legal and rational relations of society. Thus Mazzini could complain that "liberty of belief destroyed all community of faith, liberty of education produced moral anarchy." He demanded a system of compulsory democratic national education which would bring up all children in the same spirit. In spite of his long residence in England he never fully understood the working of parliamentary representation and the necessity of parties. His religious democracy did not help toward education of a politically immature and economically backward people in the art of modern self-government.[25]

In fusing the provinces and the social traditions of the new Italian nation into a common nationality, nothing could have been more helpful than the spirit of representative institutions and the growth of party life and political discussion. It mattered little whether that fusion was effected in a constitutional monarchy or a republic. Not only for practical reasons inherent in the historical situation of Italy and her dynasties, but out of his unitarian mysticism, Mazzini rejected for Italy a constitutional monarchy or a federation after the model of Switzerland or the United States, and demanded a unitarian republic. It became one of the central dogmas of his creed. He overstressed the importance and wholeness of the form and neglected the realities of the content and of the parts. Here, too, the stress upon the presumed originality and mission of Italy could usefully have given way to a closer study of the politically more advanced Western nations.[26]

With all his insistence on unity and his identification of religion and politics, Mazzini remained in the tradition of individual liberty and political rights. He opposed socialism not only because its class struggle threatened national unity, but also because its realization would violate liberty. "Working men, my brothers, are you disposed to accept a hierarchy of masters of the common property—masters of the mind through an exclusive education, masters of the body through the power of determining your work, your capacity and your needs? Is this not a return to slavery?" He opposed the excessive centralization and bureaucratization of the state and demanded a wide program of self-government for townships and cities. Like John Stuart Mill he was a fervent champion of complete political and social equality for women. But to him "unity remains intellect's first law. The reformation of a people rests upon no sure foundation unless based upon agreement on religious faith." He wished to found the Italian republic on a National Pact, elaborated by a constituent assembly, elected by universal suffrage. But the pact should not be a simple constitution clearly limiting and balancing the powers of government and a Bill of Rights guaranteeing the freedom of the individual, as in the United States. It would be a declaration of principles and not of rights, a manifesto of a religious character, the cornerstone of a new faith which would "become the expression of an epoch." Mazzini wished the young and inexperienced nation to fly to heaven before it even learned how to walk firmly on earth.

VI

From the bitter exile which he bore with great integrity and dignity, Mazzini misjudged more and more Italian reality and the men working for Italy's unity. He never understood that

Louis Napoleon, though working with very different means, cherished the same dream of regenerated nationalities and European unity as he himself did. He was unjust to the patient efforts of the Italian moderates. He idealized the Italian people, with whom he had no close contact. He had no part in the actual unification of Italy. When it was achieved, largely through the aid of France which he distrusted, through the Sardinian monarchy which he abhorred, and through unscrupulous diplomacy which he detested, he returned to Italy as an exile in his own land. He lived there his last years a lonely life under an assumed name, unhappy and broken by the way in which his dream had been realized.

Rome was Italian, but it was the seat of a wretched and despised monarchy—while the republic had been proclaimed in that Paris which he judged unworthy of the honor. He saw "a mockery of Italy" ruled by "a medley of opportunists and cowards and little Machiavellis that let themselves be dragged behind the suggestion of the foreigner." His vision of unique greatness and universal leadership had turned into the reality of a poor and discontented nation. Without principles or real unity it was painfully struggling through parliamentary combinations, veiled dictatorships and favoritism, to find the road to orderly progress and democratic traditions. Would Mazzini have recognized the sincere and serious efforts which slowly prevailed and brought Italy a high and promising cultural life, vitalizing reforms and growing prosperity? Would he have rejected the grandiose ambitions which led to the humiliations of Dogali and Adua, of Libya and Greece? There was a great call but also a great temptation in Mazzini's prophetic words and political teachings. Mazzini had thought of calling up the soul of Italy, and now he saw only her corpse.[27] His lifework seemed a failure, his years of toil and sacrifice in vain.

But history proved that his feeling of defeat was not justified. Mazzini was the father of Italian democracy. Italy, for whose nationhood he had labored more than anyone else, was no ideal nation—but it was a nation. The seeds Mazzini had sown fell on fertile ground, though it would take patient efforts through many years for them to shoot out roots and leaves. Under his inspiration the Fascist rejection of the principle of 1789 never took deep root in the consciousness of the Italian people. In his spirit an Italian freedom movement—to which no parallel could be found among the masses of Germany or Russia—carried on the struggle against an autocracy which denied individual liberty and the rule of law. When Fascism claimed to express a new epoch of higher national integration, when it appealed to ancient Roman grandeur, to the enthusiasm of youth, to the sacrificial spirit of faith, it took up some of the great—too great —words of Mazzini. But it divested them of their ethical and libertarian content and turned them often into their opposite.

Many Italians perceived this. For before Fascism "interpreted" Mazzini to its own ends, the Italian liberals—men like Count Cavour, Carlo Cattaneo and Giuseppe Ferrari, hated by Mazzini as unitarian monarchists or republican federalists—had directed Italian democracy from the religious romanticism and the Italocentrism of Mazzini toward the common road of Western liberal development. When Cavour built railroads he thought not only of the unification of Italy but above all of her closer connection with Europe. He hailed the Alpine tunnel as shortening the distance which separated Italy "from the countries that march ahead of civilization, from London and Paris, the centers of enlightenment." The independence of Italy was to him a step toward raising her to the level of the more advanced Western nations. His ideal was the closest possible collaboration with France and Britain. He was the most jealous guardian of parliamentary prerogatives and civic liberties. He was proud that Italy had achieved nationhood "without sacrificing liberty to independence, without having passed through the dictatorial hands of a Cromwell, without having unshackled herself from monarchical absolutism by falling into revolutionary despotism." [28]

The Italian liberals fought the nationalist belief in the primacy of Italy and in the need of originality in her political and social development. Even Cesare Balbo, who in his younger years was Gioberti's friend, rejected all pride and trust in Italy's past glories: "Of all the dreams which distract from reality, the dreams of the past are the worst because they are impossible to realize; even the most improbable future may succeed, but the past will never succeed again." He saw the great advantage for Italy of being a young nation unburdened with a past, for Rome was not Italy and the Italian nation was a creation of the nineteenth century. "One of the great advantages of new nations," he wrote, "is to be unable to fall insanely in love with one's own past; to belong entirely to the present and to the future. That was precisely the case of ancient Rome, that is the case of the present Anglo-American nation." [29] In like manner Ferrari considered Italy happy in that she had no national past but that nineteenth-century liberalism had to create everything, the political customs, the laws, the fatherland itself. "What good fortune," he exclaimed, "that liberty could give us all."

The Italian nation had to look to the leaders of modern liberty for her inspiration. The rational cosmopolitanism of Cattaneo emphasized that "every true and good idea, from whatever land or whatever tongue it will come to us, should be immediately ours as if it had germinated on our own soil." Ferrari and Giuseppe Montanelli looked to France for leadership; Cattaneo proposed the harmonization of union and liberty in an Italian federation after the model of the United States or Switzerland, and he suggested that Europe should follow that example and become the United States of Europe. Above the hatreds and conflicts separating nations he saw the unity of European civilization, of the human mind. "We must devote what little strength we have to the common enterprise of humanity. We must participate in the struggle between progress and inertia, between thought and ignorance, between gentleness and barbarism." Progressive intelligence and individual liberty were the only true sources of the wealth and welfare of nations. The Anglo-Saxons ruled the sea, Cattaneo thought, precisely because they were the most faithful to the cult of liberty. He taught the Italians that individuality and liberty characterize modern European civilization, of which the young nation was an integral part.[30]

The rational thought of the liberals, the progressive action of Cavour, and the moral enthusiasm of Mazzini, created Italy. When Mazzini died he set an example and left an inspiration for Italy and Europe at a time when material satiety and apparent security began to silence the call of liberty and the turmoil of the market place to mute the voice of conscience. One month after Mazzini's death Carducci summed up his place in Italian history: "I have always venerated and adored the great character, the great soul, the more than heroic life of Giuseppe Mazzini. Italy has probably had no one since Roman times resembling him in integrity, steadfastness, and unity of life."[31] Perhaps Mazzini proposed the truest judgment on himself in a letter to Malwida von Meysenburg, a judgment sincere in its insight and moving in its modesty: "Je crois que mon cœur est supérieur à mon intelligence, tandis que chez la plupart des gens c'est l'intelligence qui est supérieure au cœur. Voilà pourquoi les autres n'agissent pas." Action dominated his life. But it was always activity guided by the highest purpose. "There is only one goal," he wrote to Daniel Stern, "that is the moral progress of man and of humanity. From this point of view I judge everything that is done."[32] For almost half a century his heart had consumed itself in action; the great heart and the untiring action came to rest in 1872. His noble words, reiterated with rhetorical pathos, perhaps sound trite today. But his ethos, divested from the heavy tribute which he paid to the exigencies of the period and the pride of nationalism, will survive to guide those who seek the peace and progress of the European peoples in liberty and unity.

Chapter Four

GERMANY: TREITSCHKE

Man denke sich den Wiener Stephansturm, den Strassburger und den Freiburger Münster, den Kölner Dom, die Hamburger Petrikirche und so viele andere architektonische Trophäen des deutschen Geistes in den Ringmauern einer einzigen Stadt vereinigt, und man frage sich, ob sich in dieser Stadt dann nicht notwendig auch eine granitne Kaiser-Burg erheben müsste, und ob der darin thronende Kaiser nicht mit der Rechten den Scepter der römischen Imperatoren und mit der Linken den ehemals karthageniensischen, jetzt grossbritannischen Dreizack schwingen würde.—FRIEDRICH HEBBEL, *dreaming in 1849 of the future capital of the German Reich, in "Erinnerungen an Paris" (Sämtliche Werke, ed. R. M. Werner, Berlin, 1903, vol. X, p. 20).*

4

MACHIAVELLI was a man of the Italian Renaissance; yet Mazzini shows no trace of Machiavellian thought, and Mussolini's attempt to revive Machiavelli in his homeland failed lamentably and ignominiously. Italy lacked the power and the hardness of character which Machiavellianism presupposes. Piedmont was an imitation Prussia, but only imitation. Machiavelli's ideas bore real fruit in nineteenth-century Germany. The German inclination to force ideas in the "free realm of the mind" to their logical and absurd conclusions without regard for the limitations of reality and common sense combined with Prussia's power and hardness of character to implant Machiavellianism firmly in Germany.[1] While German statesmen like Frederick II and Bismarck were Machiavelli's ablest disciples, his noblest teacher and prophet was Heinrich von Treitschke.

Like Michelet, Treitschke was a patriotic historian; like Mazzini, he was the apostle of national unity. But while Michelet and Mazzini died disappointed, the one overlooking the ruins of a prostrate nation, the other an exile in his fatherland united by forces and methods which he utterly rejected, Treitschke saw his dream and idea of a Prussian monarchy over Germany fulfilled. He was indisputably one of the master-builders of the triumphant national edifice which seemed to stand in rocklike strength, able to weather all storms of the future. By his pen and his word he had prepared his generation for Bismarck's deed, he had anchored it in the course of preceding history and charted its road into a glorious future, he had aroused the enthusiasm and deepened the faith of countless young Germans who in their turn became educators of youth and administrators of the empire. He had himself longed to be a man of the deed; deafness kept him from the career of officer or statesman. He had no need to regret it. His influence as a teacher from the classroom, as a publicist from his study, was mightier than any "practical action" could have been. His editorship of important reviews like the *Preussische Jahrbücher* and his long membership in the German Reichstag broadened his influence; they added little to its force and depth. He was above all an enrapturing teacher who filled the largest halls with overflowing audiences, and an inspired historian who made the past live again and serve the present and the future as he wished to mold them.

He was as little an objective historian as Michelet. He was a poet who appealed to the heart, a prophet who wished to arouse his people. In the last years of his life he protested against the misuse by his critics of Ranke's famous saying that history must be written with complete detachment, *"sine ira et studio."* [2] He not only pointed out that Ranke himself little followed his own rule, but he emphasized that man understands only what he loves and that only a strong heart which feels the fate of the fatherland like one's own woe and joy can reveal the inner truth of history. The greatness of the ancient historians lies, according to Treitschke, as much in their emotional power as in the perfection of form. He himself possessed both in abundance. But neither the passion and power of the heart nor the beauty of presentation decides ultimately the value of the prophetic mission; from Hebrew time on the true prophets were judged by the moral and universal content of their message. The triumphant edifice which Treitschke erected on what seemed to him the impregnable rock of might, collapsed half a century after his death like a house of cards. He, like most Germans of this time, did not understand that modern nations draw their strength from individual liberty and universal ideas. From them, and not from the state, flow the vital forces and inspirations which give to the society of Western civilization a cohesion and a resilience unknown to the more primitive communities based upon the might of the state with the hero as its law.

Bismarck and Treitschke firmly and finally established in nineteenth-century Germany the cult of might and of the hero. This cult was unknown to the German intellectuals of the eighteenth century, who thought only of individual liberty and universal ideas. Their heritage survived, gradually dwindling to a pale memory and ineffectual lip service, for more than a century, but long before the decisive turning point of the 1860's German liberalism had sacrificed the Western ideals on the altar of the fatherland. No sudden transition allows us to distinguish a "good" pre-Bismarckian and a "bad" post-Bismarckian Germany. In reality the German liberals of 1815 and of 1848 had in their large majority been more German than liberal. Bismarck embodied their innermost dreams, and they rallied as enthusiastically around him after his success as, for the very same reason, their descendants rallied around Hitler. The liberals of 1815 and 1848 were in their great majority the true ancestors of Pan-Germanism, of the policy of might and the cult of the hero.[3]

Treitschke followed and even led the march from liberalism to nationalism. He was born in Dresden, the capital of Saxony, in 1834. His life span linked the idyll of the cosmopolitan idealism and the peaceful *Kleinstaaterei* of the German *Biedermeier* with the "blood and iron" epic of Bismarck which he helped to write. His father, a Saxon general and commandant of the fortress Königstein, throughout his life remained deeply loyal to his king and country. The old man suffered grievously when his beloved and gifted son turned violently against his native land and extolled its most relentless enemy, Prussia. In his struggle against pretty princely courts and stagnant police regimes young Treitschke called himself a liberal. Even as a boy in the stormy year of 1849 he distrusted and hated the popular forces of democracy, but he resented deeply the fetters with which an obsolete order frustrated the creative ambitions of the rising educated middle classes. Soon his concern with liberty was over-shadowed by his burning desire for national unity and inde-pendence. Whatever remained of liberalism with him, as with most other German liberals, became a mere means to national ends.

As a student at the University of Bonn in 1851 he received his decisive inspiration from two of his teachers who were typical German liberals. Ernst Moritz Arndt, then eighty-two years old, lectured to a jammed classroom on the "Origins and Princi-pal Parts of the European Nations" and filled his audience with his pride in the German race and his confidence in German greatness. Treitschke's feelings for Austria, the friend of his native Saxony, did not grow friendlier when he heard Arndt say: "The Habsburgs wish to mix their dirty Slav pap with our clean German waters. But that is due only to their egoism, they don't care at all for Germany." [4] Of even greater influence upon the young student was Friedrich Christoph Dahlmann, who gave a course on German history since Charles V. In it he glorified Luther as the first voice of the rising German nation, Protestantism as its lasting foundation and Prussia as its present leader. Dahlmann, who in a speech in the Frankfort National Assembly on January 26, 1849, had declared: "The road of power is the only one which can satisfy and satiate our growing urge for freedom—for it is not only freedom which the German desires; he strives to an even greater extent for power which has been withheld from him so far," was deeply grieved in 1851 by Austria's diplomatic victory over Prussia at Olmütz. In his notes for a book which he then planned, he reaffirmed his deep faith in Prussia and in the early dawn of a new strong Germany. On the realization of this hope would depend, he believed, the outcome of the coming great struggle, "whether our European continent will be able in the future to defend its position against America which is developing so differently." [5]

These student years put a final seal on Treitschke's determination to devote his life to the unification of Germany under Prussia. To this one ideal he remained faithful all his life. He judged all events and all his readings from the point of view only. When he reread Machiavelli in 1856, he wrote his father in defense of the Florentine: "He sacrifices right and virtue to a great idea, the might and unity of his nation. This fundamental idea of the book—the fiery patriotism and the conviction that even the most oppressive despotism must be welcomed if it warrants the might and unity of the fatherland—these are the ideas which reconcile me with the many objectionable and terrible opinions of the great Florentine." [6] Treitschke's mind, guided by his one central aspiration, found food for his visions of future German greatness in his research deep into the German past and in his glances far across the oceans. When Prussia acquired from Oldenburg in 1853 the mouth of the small Jade river to build there a naval base, the future Wilhelmshaven, Treitschke recalled the glorious days of the Hansa and greeted the bold venture as a "resolute step to wipe out the old shame that the first seafaring nation of the world has been alienated from the sea." [7]

II

At the beginning of his career as a university teacher in Leipzig, Treitschke tried to solve the dilemma common to his generation in Germany between the liberalism of the eighteenth century and the West and a nationalism based upon the might and precedence of the state. In his essay "Die Freiheit" (1861) he attempted to define his concept of liberty against that of the Western nations. He took issue with John Stuart Mill's essay "On Liberty" and Edouard Laboulaye's article "*L'état et ses limites.*" He objected to their conclusions which led the Englishman to proclaim the political development of the United States as a desirable end, and the Frenchman to regard the nineteenth century as an epoch in which the Christian ideal of the dignity of the individual would be realized. Against them, Treitschke wished to subject all liberty to political limits, limits set by the state in the realization of its own aims. Not liberty from the state or against the state but only liberty within the state could be the goal for Treitschke, who concludes his essay with a stirring appeal: "If there is one thought able to spur today a true German to ethical courage more effectively than the commandment of universal human duty, then it is the thought: Whatever you do to become better, more mature and freer, you are doing it for your people." In this essay,[8] young Treitschke still strove for a synthesis of the free individual and the powerful state; although he subordinated the individual to the state, he stressed his freedom as the best foundation for a strong state. This was the high-water mark of Treitschke's liberalism. Its tide was to recede more and more until like all German liberalism it lost itself in the flood of Bismarckism.

In the following year, in a lecture on "Fichte and the National Idea" delivered at the centenary of Fichte's birth, Treitschke traced the road which in his interpretation led the idealistic philosopher from the local loyalty of a Saxon subject to a newly found German patriotism, from cosmopolitanism to nationalism. But this time the concluding sentence was an unmistakable clarion call: "Our living generation will preserve Fichte's spirit most faithfully when all nobler minds among us will work to the end that in our fellow citizens there may grow and mature the character of the warrior who knows how to sacrifice himself for the state." [9] But more congenial to Treitschke than Fichte's idealist liberalism was the fierce patriotism and hatred of the French of the unfortunate German dramatist, Heinrich von Kleist. In his essay on Kleist the young historian with his genuine love for poetry and his creative gift for letters is perhaps at his best. The essay which rediscovered for the German public the almost forgotten dramatist vibrates with the same passion, the same poetic depth, the same pride which filled and broke Kleist himself. Like Kleist's greatest drama, which he wrote in glorification of the victorious banners of the Prussian army, the essay ends with the battle cry of the Prussian officers storming forward to victory: "Into the dust with all enemies of Brandenburg," [10] a battle cry which reverberated infinitely more strongly in Treitschke's passionate heart than in the hearts of Kleist's contemporaries.

When Bismarck became Prussian prime minister in 1862 and provoked the famous constitutional conflict with the Prussian Lower Chamber, Treitschke, like most German liberals, sided with the Landtag against Bismarck, who was violently attacked for his ruthless despotism. In spite of this opposition, Treitschke clung passionately to his faith in Prussia and in the Hohenzollerns and their German mission. Bismarck's success in 1866 converted him, as it did almost all German liberals, into an enthusiastic Bismarckian. National unity and might triumphed definitely in him and his generation over liberty and constitutionalism. Bismarck's *Realpolitik* had conquered not only in the field of diplomacy and battle, but even more disastrously in the field of the German mind.[11] But this triumph was made possible only by the fact that for the last fifty years the German mind had been preparing for it.

Hegel's faith in history and the state as vehicles for the Divine, and the romanticists' distrust of the potentialities of the free individual, diverted the German mind farther and farther from the liberalism of Western civilization. Bismarck's success in wars which the Germans regarded as ideological or ethical conflicts seemed to confirm the superiority of the German way. His victories over Austria and France were interpreted as victories over the Western world, the world of Roman universalism and of Western liberalism. They seemed to justify Treitschke's burning faith in the Protestant Prussian military monarchy and its unshakable superiority. The prophet had seen his visions come true, his labors rewarded. It was easy for him to communicate his faith to the German youth. From the chair at the University of Berlin to which he was called from Heidelberg in 1874, he interpreted in his courses on politics and on history the essence of the state as primarily an instrument of might. Though, like many of the most active German sponsors of Prussianism in the nineteenth century, by birth and family not a Prussian, he loved Prussia with all his heart because he saw in it the embodiment of might. Whatever Germany had gained in the last centuries it owed to Prussia's sword.[12] Not in the German lands of the west and south which had undergone the influence of Roman civilization, but in the new colonial territories east of the Elbe River which the German sword had conquered from the Slavs in the thirteenth century, the new state-forming forces of German history had risen in Prussia, the weapon-proud eagle land of the north.[13] To its origins and its spirit under the Teutonic knights Treitschke devoted one of his most famous studies, which he chose to head his collection of "Historical and Political Essays." The origins of Prussia seemed to guarantee its leading role in the unification of Germany.

The unification of Italy had preceded and inspired that of Germany. Treitschke watched it with great sympathy and stressed the affinities of the military monarchies of Piedmont and Prussia. "Both states cherish the ambition of conquerors; the diplomacy of both shows often that combination of duplicity and indecision which is characteristic of weak states hemmed in by strong ones. Both are the sword of their nations and both win the only glorious victories of which their nations can boast in their recent history. Both earn for the deeds of their arms the irreconcilable hatred of radicalism. In both countries for a long time the ideal of the Piedmontese aristocracy seemed realized: a king who rules, a nobility which surrounds him, a people which obeys." [14] For the unified monarchies of Germany and Italy Treitschke set the task of collaborating in breaking French preponderance on the European continent. He desired a lasting alliance of the two powers which according to him would assure the peace of Europe.[15] In 1866 he supported Bismarck's collaboration with the Italians against the Habsburgs. German political unity under Prussia was to him the absolute goal which even justified a war of Germans against Germans. He agreed with his friend, Gustav Freytag, who had written in 1848: "If, in order to bring about this unity, we must even march against Germans (which God forbid), Prussia will march, and perhaps that is what fundamentally distinguishes us Prussians from other Germans, for we are ready to shed our last drop of blood to have our way. We have an object in view, a great ideal for which we live; our opponents have no such ideal. What should we fear? Are we not a nation of warriors?" [16] Treitschke himself wrote, twelve years later: "I wish Prussia to take an intelligent and honest step and to start now the war which will in any case break out within a few years. Prussia should—at the risk of a terrible struggle—finally, finally, demand that Denmark pay its debt of honor to Germany. Should then follow the war with Napoleon; let it come: our hands are clean and the struggle would be a popular war which must bring Prussia immeasurable moral gains, if not the German crown. . . . It is unworthy of Prussia, in a period of such rapid change, when all other powers vie in ambitious plans, to do nothing herself to give the world a new shape." [17]

III

The decisive year of 1870 found Treitschke wholly on Bismarck's side. The spokesman of the educated middle classes still feared that the Junker, despite the audacity and mobility of his mind, had little understanding for the moral forces in the life of nations.[18] In a letter to Franz Overbeck in May of 1871 he blamed Bismarck for undermining the prestige of the Reichstag by leaving it to long, sterile talk without provoking any initiative. But in spite of some residual misgivings Treitschke had taken irrevocably his stand on the side of unity against liberty, of national power against constitutional progress. In a letter to Bismarck himself in 1865, Treitschke mentioned his liberalism but at the same time emphasized that he was free of the "prejudices of his party" and that he put the Prussian state and its right higher than any party interests.[19] In January 1870 he wrote in a letter that: "We must become more radical in questions of unity and more conservative in questions of liberty." [20] The liberal party, he declared, has always been ready to sacrifice every other political goal and ideal to German unity.

When the war of 1870 broke out, Treitschke published in the August issue of the *Preussische Jahrbücher* an article in which his later development was clearly forecast: "It does not become the German to repeat the commonplaces of the apostles of peace and of the priests of Mammon, nor to shut his eye to the cruel truth that we live in an age of wars." That the strong prevails over the weak was to him an indisputable law of life. He accepted and praised this "inevitable" fact as ethically good. He warned his readers of the "equally disgusting examples" of the Western nations: France with her readiness to war and her inability to see who is the stronger; the formerly great England with her ignominious cowardice. The complete victory of the Prussian military monarchy convinced Treitschke, as he wrote in February 1871 in his review, that all the former admiration for republican or democratic forms of state will now be ended. He saw clearly—and he accepted the fact—that the very essence of the new Prussian German state which ran counter to all nineteenth-century thought with its desire for peace, prosperity and individual liberty, will arouse universal fear and distrust among other nations.

Indeed the new Prussian Germany presented the unexpected resurgence of a type of state which in the nineteenth century was believed to be obsolete. It formed, as Moltke had foreseen in 1841, a nation "regarding itself even in the midst of peace as a great army in its encampment and facing a mighty enemy." Democracy seemed to have finished its part for the moment—to paraphrase Moltke's wishful prophecy of September 1848— but there would no doubt be other severe struggles coming; what was needed, and what seemed to have arrived, was an age of heroes after a period of "brawlers and scribblers." German intellectual and economic life—professors and writers, industrialists and agrarians—fell eagerly into line with, and served, the new state. Few were the men who thoughtfully doubted the wisdom or desirability of the new development, small was the number of them who had the courage or the ability to speak out. Their lonely voices were fast drowned in the general chorus of approval. Yet it might be fitting to mention the little known protest of a German historian and patriot, Georg Gottfried Gervinus. He, too, had dreamt of German unity, but as a liberal and a European. Like Mazzini he died almost immediately after his nation's unification, irreconciled to its methods. After his death a memorandum on peace was published, written in 1871 to the Prussian royal house. Its words, unheeded then, might serve as a guide even for the present; their sober warning has been revealed as a true prophecy:

"Europe has watched for one thousand years over German power developments, because this country and people have by their strong central position an immeasurable advantage for every warlike policy. The expansionism of the great German imperial dynasties of the Middle Ages with their lust for conquest has produced in domestic and foreign policy nothing but hatred and discord, uprisings and wars, defeat and decline. Since the seventeenth century it has been a principle of European policy that the organization of the Germanies must be federal; the German Confederation has been created for the very purpose of forming in the center of Europe a neutral state which would by its federal organization guarantee peace. By the disruption of the Confederation in 1866, two-thirds of the German territory have been transformed into a warrior-state ever ready for aggression, in which one can see, without being an enemy of Prussia and Germany, a permanent threat to the peace of the continent and to the security of the neighboring states.

"Prussia has been reproached with having by its war and its methods transformed the whole of Europe into one armed camp; it would be impossible to regard as a malevolent phrase in the mouth of an enemy what can be simply proved by facts. It is not wise to disregard out of patriotism that the events of 1866 have revived for the whole continent and for the whole epoch the dangers of a system which was generally held to be vanishing, and to have immeasurably magnified them. After the hopes and strivings of half a century to outgrow the military systems of former times, there has been here created a permanent military power of such tremendous superiority as the world has not known even in the iron age of the Napoleonic wars.

"This interpretation of the situation could have been regarded as exaggerated before the events of 1870. These events have strengthened the military power even more and have by necessity increased its self-confidence. Whatever be the momentary impressions and sentiments evoked by these miraculous deeds and events, they will arouse distrust against us." To avoid that outcome, Gervinus suggested the decentralization of Germany, the cult of pacifism, the initiative for disarmament, and the transfer of the center of the German confederation from the capital of its most powerful member to a city which would symbolize a policy of peaceful civilization. In vain he warned against the national intoxication with a success which might have been due as much to the chances of the situation as to permanent national virtues. Bismarck's policy hardly aroused any protest; the whole press and the entire educated nation applauded wildly, at the risk of abandoning the cause of their domestic liberty.[21]

IV

In Bismarck's Reich Treitschke found the fulfillment of his prophecies. It seemed established for ages to come, anchored in the leadership of the Hohenzollerns, whom history had destined for it, and in the virtues of the Germans who willingly followed their leaders. The new Germany was an expanded Prussia of which Treitschke himself called the new Germany an "extension of Prussia"; the constitution of the Reich in 1871 had indirectly "extended the might of Prussia over the whole Reich." [22] Ranke had already declared that Prussia's "true destiny is to be and to remain a military monarchy. It is impossible not to submit to what is historically due." The triumph of Prussian arms vindicated the ideal of the Prussian state and the traditionalism of German historicism against the Western ideals of the rights of man and the peace of peoples.

This historicism undermined the optimistic faith in reason and progress and the respect for universal law. It stressed the forces of the past and their inescapable hold on national life, determined entirely by its own growth and separated from all fellow nations. Hegel expressed the ideal of the Prussian state as opposed to the "civil society" of the West: "Were the state to be confused with civil society, and were its fundamental end to be regarded as the security and the protection of property and personal freedom, then the interest of individuals as such would be the ultimate purpose of their association. Membership of the state would then be optional for the individual. But the state's relation to the individual is totally different from such a relation. The state is the true embodiment of mind and spirit, and only as its member the individual shares in truth, real existence and ethical status." [23] The social system did not, as in English thought and politics, exist for the growth and happiness of the individual and therefore limited by his rights; it was an ethical totality, all-embracing, self-determined, the "Divine Will as it exists on earth"; only as an integral part of it could the individual lead a true life and fulfill his duty.

Thus in Germany the state became the main concern and the highest regulator of all life; its self-preservation, the supreme end; its might, the foundation of right. True, the state never did realize itself in might alone: [24] it was the fountainhead of law, culture and ethics; its might protected and nurtured them, they depended on it, they existed only within the state and through the state. The German state was the fountainhead of specific German culture and ethics; it had to nurture them and protect them against alien influences. German culture differed from Western civilization and Eastern barbarism as much as German ethics differed from the morality of others; in their profundity, which no other people could completely follow, they revealed their superiority. This conviction gained an ever firmer hold on the German mind. Their successes in war, in science and economics could be due only to the preëminence of the German character. Were not the Germans the creative and masculine element in modern history, the source of all renovation? [25] Had they not to live up to a mission which could be fulfilled only through the might of the state?

Treitschke taught the Germans the "devout and earnest attachment to the state" (*fromme Hingabe an den Staat*) necessary for the realization of German ideals. He demanded a high and serious morality based not on freedom but on stern duty. He formed with Sybel and Droysen a phalanx of scholars whom Lord Acton characterized in 1886 as "the first classics of imperialism, a garrison of distinguished historians that prepared the Prussian supremacy together with their own, and now hold Berlin like a fortress." [26] It was an almost impregnable fortress, but like all fortresses it limited the view of the outside world and distorted the perspective. More and more Treitschke extolled the Prussian garrison state and abandoned the liberal principles of his youth. He lost faith in the educated middle class and their creative forces. The will of the king and the Prussian nobility, not the people or public opinion, was to him determining history.[27] He denounced the middle classes as selfishly pursuing only their own economic interests; parliament, as a docile instrument of these narrow and conflicting interests; while he hailed the king as the disinterested guardian of the national soul and mission, a knight in shining armor high above the sordid market place, surrounded by the paladins of the Prussian nobility. Treitschke reminded his readers that Brandenburg and Prussia did not owe their superiority to cultural achievements or the arts. In the sands of these northeastern German marshes no saint ever grew up; no minnesingers were heard at the courts and manors there; the townspeople preferred their rough existence and hard work to the laurels of the scholar or the artist. Only by their military force and their powerful pride did they rise over the other Germans and create the new Germany.[28]

Yet this reliance upon the state, its might and its hero, proved in the long run a weakness; the forces of individual liberty, of political initiative and responsibility, so little developed throughout Germany, withered away in the uncongenial climate of Prussian Germany and could not endow the state with that vital spontaneity without which modern progressive nations cannot exist. These serious dangers to the national structure were revealed when the genius of Bismarck, Treitschke's hero, was replaced at the helm of the ship of state by Wilhelm II, Hindenburg, and Hitler, who led a docile and adoring people from catastrophe to catastrophe. Nor were the Junkers the disinterested paladins of the Prussian legend; they were politically and socially an anachronism, caring above all for their own interests without any understanding for the needs of a new epoch. No salvation could come from the middle classes and the people, who were kept from maturity and responsibility and were educated to dependence upon authority and to dangerous illusions about the outside world.

Shortly before Treitschke's death, a young scholar who was to become Germany's most brilliant social scientist, Max Weber, delivered his inaugural address on "The National State and Economic Policy." He shared Treitschke's fundamental position and Bismarck's faith in the power state, in Machiavellianism and in the importance of great leaders. Throughout his life he taught the Germans that "It is not our task to pass on to our descendants for their journey through life peace and human happiness, but rather the eternal struggle for the maintenance and enhancement of our national way. The power and interests of the nation are the last and decisive interests which economic policy has to serve. The *raison d'état* of the nation-state is for us the ultimate yardstick for economic considerations." Like other Germans, Weber never understood that "tolerance, fairness, love of freedom, not the *raison d'état* of the power state form the traditional character of the English people and the true liberal state." He was unable "to see the moral element inherent in any political power, provided human beings rose above the level of animals." But though for him German interests and power remained the supreme law, he was farsighted enough to see the inner weaknesses of the German state: "The dynasty of the Hohenzollerns knows only the corporal's form of power: to command, to obey, to stand to attention, to boast." Even worse was the people's willing acceptance of the situation. Bismarck "left behind as his legacy a nation without any political education, a nation without any political will, accustomed to have the great statesman look after its policy for it. He left a nation submitting fatalistically to anything which was decided for it, without criticizing the political qualifications of those who now sat in Bismarck's empty seat and assumed leadership with incredible ingenuousness." Weber considered the German middle classes and the German workers equally immature and incapable of political leadership, and their spokesmen, harmless and timid small men, without any spark of revolutionary energy or national passion. But Weber could not find any remedy because he too did not grasp the underlying values of Western political life; all his thought centered on power—Germany's might remained for him the highest value and norm.[29]

V

Weber, however, had a keener understanding of modern economic life, of the importance of the industrial proletariat, of the need of the masses, than Treitschke who followed Bismarck in his struggle against the working class and social democracy. When the German professors, known as "socialists of the chair," founded the *Verein für Sozialpolitik* to plead for social reform and for the attenuation of the most crying economic and social inequalities, Treitschke opposed them violently. He praised the value of slavery and he insisted that all society must be organized hierarchically. "Class domination," he wrote, "by necessity follows from the nature of society. Social democracy desires, as the name implies, something nonsensical. It is in no way the task of society to educate all men to the enjoyment of the goods of civilization. The participation of all men in all the blessings of civilization is not only a perhaps unobtainable ideal, but no ideal at all." [30] The "socialists of the chair" desired a benevolent paternal socialism to strengthen Germany's national unity. Their leaders, Adolf Wagner and Gustav von Schmoller, Treitschke's colleagues at the University of Berlin and equally influential in molding public opinion, shared Treitschke's faith in the German power state and its foundations. They regarded the struggle against English and French political and economic liberalism as the German mission, and wished to substitute the superior and more ethical German way for the individualistic economics of the West. They opposed the "social monarchy" of the Hohenzollern—a concept differing only in degree from the "Prussian socialism" of Oswald Spengler and the "national socialism" of Adolf Hitler—to the social democracy of Western and therefore alien origin. Though they rejected Treitschke's economic policy, they saw eye to eye with him in his pan-Germanism, his hatred of Britain, and his anti-Semitism.[31]

In 1879 Treitschke published in the *Preussische Jahrbücher* the first of his anti-Semitic articles. In its opposition to Western ideas of individual liberty and human equality, German nationalism was by necessity anti-Semitic. "The fatherland of modern anti-Semitism is Germany, where the systems were thought out and the slogans coined. The German literature is the richest in anti-Jewish writing." [32] Treitschke, influenced in his anti-Semitism by Ernst Moritz Arndt and other early German liberals, never went so far as other German writers of the nineteenth century. As early as 1815 a professor of history at the University of Berlin, Friedrich Rühs, demanded the exclusion of the Jews from all civil rights, especially public offices and the army, and asked that the "Hebrew enemy" should wear a special sign on his garment to make him easily recognizable. In the first half of the nineteenth century Jewish pogroms swept many German cities amidst shouts of "Hep, Hep, Jude verrecke!" (Hep, Hep, let the Jew die like a beast!) and in these pogroms students took the lead and organized the mob.

In Treitschke's day, Moritz Busch, a German liberal publicist and Bismarck's press agent, conducted a violent campaign against the Jews; a prolific philosopher, Eugen Dühring, wrote in 1881 a book "The Jewish Question as a Racial, Ethical and Cultural Problem. With a World Historic Reply" in which he suggested those "remedies" which Adolf Hitler later was to apply; and Adolf Wagner joined Adolf Stöcker in the leadership of the "Christian Socialist Workmen's Party," which the influential cathedral and court preacher founded in 1878, to organize the proletariat on a strictly monarchist and paternalistic basis against Marxism and bourgeois liberalism, which were regarded both as inspired and as dominated by Jews. In 1881 a mass petition by Bernhard Förster, Nietzsche's unwelcome brother-in-law, signed by 250,000 citizens, demanded the social segregation, the economic boycott, and the removal from public life of all Jews. Treitschke never participated in these excesses. He called anti-Semitism "a brutal and hateful but natural reaction of the German folk-sentiment against an alien element which has occupied too large a space in our life." He saw in the Jews a danger which threatened the innermost nature of Germanism. He demanded the complete assimilation of the German Jews and a stoppage of Jewish immigration from the eastern borderlands of Germany. But his prominent position as national scholar and popular prophet gave to anti-Semitism in Germany a recognized standing, perhaps even more than Richard Wagner's racial Jew-baiting. Treitschke's words, "The Jews are our misfortune," served as a rallying banner for the German anti-Semitic movements of the next sixty years.[33]

VI

Though the Jews were the immediate target of the agitation, it ultimately aimed at the liberalism which had brought about Jewish emancipation. The ideas of 1789 were felt as a threat to the very substance of German ideals. Treitschke hated the liberal middle-class society of the West and despised its concern with trade, prosperity and peace. He saw England as the home of liberalism, and the French Revolution as the main vehicle for its spread. His later writings expressed contempt for "degenerate" France and the "sub-Germanic" peoples of the Slavic East, but reserved their main venom for the English character, intentions and history.[34] "This new Carthage," as Treitschke called England, was the chief obstacle to the world-encompassing march of German ideas and German power alike. Yet, in view of the apparent decay of the Western world through liberalism and individualism, only the German mind with its deeper insight and its higher morality could regenerate the world. Against all "historical justice," the British Empire stood as a firm structure of the ideals of liberty, peace and law; it hindered German expansion across the seas, which would facilitate Germany's mission. Treitschke and many Germans thought that this worldwide influence of England and English liberal ideals had become possible only through the opportunity afforded by Germany's disunity and the lack of leadership and unity in Europe. This situation had to change now. "The world position of Germany," Treitschke wrote in defense of his claim for colonies, "depends upon the number of German-speaking millions in the future. Therefore, we must see to it that the outcome of our next successful war shall be the acquisition of colonies by any possible means." [35] Otherwise, Treitschke foresaw "the appalling prospect" of a division of the world between the English-speaking nations and Russia. "In such a case it is hard to say whether the Russian knout or the English moneybags would be the worse alternative."

Only one English thinker of the nineteenth century found grace in Treitschke's eyes. He called Carlyle "the only Briton who had completely understood the Germans," Germany's "warmest and most faithful friend," the only one among many millions who "lovingly understood the nobility of the German national soul." Carlyle and Treitschke met in their admiration for Frederick II of Prussia. Carlyle saw in him "his own ideal, the strong man," and wrote the first great biography of the prince whom Treitschke called "one of Machiavelli's greatest practical disciples" and "the greatest king that ever reigned on earth." [36] Frederick's concept of state and monarchy set an example for Prussia and Germany. In Frederick's spirit Treitschke saw the Reich based upon the army as "the real and effective bond of national union." To Treitschke, trade, art and science, and parliamentary institutions appeared dangerous; the former because they are cosmopolitan and lead beyond the limits of the nation, the latter because they rather disunite the nation. "An army organized on a really national foundation" seemed the sole means of binding citizens in a real union. "Such an army is suitable only to a true monarchy, like the German one, for the Germans are the most completely monarchial people of Europe." The absence of military universal service in England explained to Treitschke "the want of chivalry in the English character, which so strikingly differs from the simple loyalty of the Germans." [37]

As power, within and without, was the very essence of the state, war naturally embodied the beauty and sublimity of history. "We have learned to perceive the moral majesty of war through the very processes which to the superficial observer seem brutal and inhuman," Treitschke wrote. "War must be taken as part of the divinely appointed order. It is both justifiable and moral, and the idea of a perpetual peace is not only impossible but immoral as well." Therefore, a state which would neglect its strength in order to promote the idealistic aspirations of the welfare of man would commit the sin against the Holy Ghost.[38] Treitschke despised small states. He thought them ignoble and ethically undesirable because they demanded little from their citizens, tended toward complacent prosperity, and opposed the heroic ideal. Like many present-day worshippers of big power, Treitschke denied that small states could exist except as satellites of great powers. A state without might seemed to him incomplete by its very nature. Such states, like the Netherlands, Belgium or Switzerland, could never develop a "healthy" international law. By living in constant fear of aggression they, by necessity, viewed international relations

sentimentally and were inclined to make, "in the name of humanity, demands upon the victor which were unnatural and
unreasonable and irreconcilable with the power of the state."
Treitschke proceeded from the assumption, which he treated
as self-evident, that great powers will always endanger small
countries. He never doubted that the United States would impose its dictatorial hegemony on the Western Hemisphere.
"Nothing," he wrote, "obliges the Union to place any restraint
upon its actions, and the small South American republics have
been spared a direct interference with their affairs only because
the connection between them and their greater neighbor is still
slight." Treitschke hardly understood moral restraint in international relations.[39] That Belgium or the Netherlands, Portugal
or Denmark, lived safely, and felt secure in the Pax Britannica
of the nineteenth century, that the United States did not annex
Canada, Mexico or the Antilles, seemed unnatural to him. The
world was a battlefield, history the relentless struggle of nations, power the only guarantee of survival, national morale and
military virtue its foundations. In the heart of nineteenth-century Europe, amidst the hopes of growing peace, prosperity
and trade, the stern ideal of Sparta was defiantly revived.

VII

In an obituary speech for his friend and fellow historian,
Max Duncker, Treitschke praised in 1886 the kindness of the
fate which had privileged them to live as Germans in this German century. One year before his death, the twenty-fifth anniversary of the war against France gave Treitschke the opportunity to revive in memorable words, before the students of the
University, the exhilaration and elation of the generation which
had lived through "that happiest of all wars." He complained
bitterly that in the new Reich materialism, democracy and
mechanization threatened to undermine the heroic idealism

which had created the Reich. Under its inspiration "the German sword had dealt blows as unerringly and as forcefully as Thor's hammer, and had forced, against all experience, the fickle fortunes of war to faithfulness." Now Germany appeared to the old man disunited and dispirited. He appealed to the youth to remember the miraculous time when the whole nation had been united in one great common enthusiasm and therefore invincible. He painted the war of 1870 in colors which forecast the great events of 1914 and 1939. "King William was a hero of our age," Treitschke declared, "the commanding monarchial führer of an immense democratic mass movement which stirred all the heights and depths of our people and, confident of its goal, inexorably swept on." German victory, Treitschke claimed, had been a blessing for Europe; the strong power in the heart of the continent kept its peace not by the panacea of pacifists, disarmament, but by its very opposite, the general rearmament. "Germany's example forced everywhere the transformation of armies into nations, of nations into armies, so that wars became a tremendous risk." On that, Treitschke based his hope for peace. But should that hope fail, he appealed to the German youth to follow the example of their fathers of 1870. No doubts seemed to trouble the aging prophet that Thor's hammer might be blunted and that the fortunes of war might turn against war's most faithful worshippers.[40]

Treitschke died at the climax of what he could call the German century, his century. Overlooking his land and the world, he could feel gratefully and happily that his prophecies had come true. He could not conclude his scholarly lifework, "The German History of the Nineteenth Century," which he had intended to carry on to 1871, the founding of Bismarck's Reich, the consummation for Treitschke of all the hopes and promises of German history. He finished only five volumes, which brought the narrative to March, 1848. His famous lectures on politics which he first delivered at the University in Freiburg in

1863 and which became his favorite course during the twenty-two years in Berlin, were only compiled and published after his death from the notebooks of his students.[41] But his lifework was no torso; it was the representative revelation of a man, an age, and a nation.

It is a great work, beautiful in its form, noble in its content. Nobody can read it without being grateful for a memorable experience, enriched by much knowledge, stirred by a stern call. Yet this prophet with the ringing voice held forth no generous promise to mankind, no deeper insight into the troubled mysteries of the human heart. Unlike Mill, Michelet or Mazzini, he had no universal message. He had no faith in the unity of law on earth nor in the triumph of justice over force. In spite of his Christian piety which grew on him with advancing age, he never, like the Hebrew prophets or Kipling's "Recessional," called his people to repentance and to the realization of the futility of might. His obsession with state, might and hero oversimplified human motives and relations as much as a naïve faith in man's goodness or in exclusively economic incentives could do. By obscuring reality it became a dangerous guide. Treitschke traced the will-to-power in history and in man's heart, and glorified it. Will-to-power with all its tragic consequences is an integral part of human nature and one of the compelling motives in history. But it does not need glorification; it needs restraint. The state with its apparatus of power is a necessary element of human society. But its glorification leads to the danger of its growth into a monster which enslaves man instead of being an instrument to safeguard his freedom.

Treitschke, like so many nationalists of modern times, confounded national independence and individual liberty under the one magic word "freedom." He thus made the essential— liberty in the human and universal sense—contingent upon something external and accidental—independence in the age of nationalism. The individual and the human suffered; the nation gained, but at the danger of becoming more and more self-contained, setting itself apart from the outside world, cultivating its own native culture, expecting the dawn of its day in history. Such a closed nation-state grew up in the eighteenth century in Russia and Prussia. It found itself in opposition to the open society of Western nations with their emphasis upon individual liberty, universal intercourse, and common progress. This opposition developed in the nineteenth and twentieth centuries into a challenge to Western civilization.[42] A conflict involving fundamental principles seemed inevitable. Treitschke was its prophet in nineteenth-century Germany; Dostoevsky, in nineteenth-century Russia.

Chapter Five

RUSSIA: DOSTOEVSKY

One cannot understand Russia by reason
And measure her by a common yardstick,
She has a peculiar nature,
One has just to believe in Russia.
　　　　　　—FYODOR IVANOVICH TYUTCHEV, *1860.*

Amid this chaos . . . the eye spontaneously turns toward the East. There like a dark mountain looming in the mist appears a hostile threatening state; at times it seems that it approaches Europe like an avalanche, like an impatient heir ready to accelerate its slow death.
　　　　　　—ALEXANDER HERZEN *to Michelet, 1851.*

Il y a aujourd'hui sur la terre deux grands peuples qui, partis de points différents, semblent s'avancer vers le même but: ce sont les Russes et les Anglo-Américains. Tous deux ont grandi dans l'obscurité; et tandis que les regards des hommes étaient occupés ailleurs, ils se sont placés tout à coup au premier rang des nations, et le monde a appris presque en même temps leur naissance et leur grandeur. Tous les autres peuples paraissent avoir atteint à peu près les limites qu'a tracées la nature, et n'avoir plus qu'à conserver; mais eux sont en croissance; tous les autres sont arrêtés ou n'avancent qu'avec mille efforts; eux seuls marchent d'un pas aisé et rapide dans une carrière dont l'œil ne saurait encore apercevoir le terme. L'Américain lutte contre les obstacles que lui oppose la nature. Le Russe est aux prises avec les hommes; l'un combat le désert et la barbarie; l'autre la civilisation revêtue de toutes ses armes. Aussi les conquêtes de l'Américain se font-elles avec le soc du laboureur, celles du Russe avec l'épée du soldat. Pour atteindre son but, le premier s'en repose sur l'intérêt personnel et laisse agir, sans les diriger, la force et la raison des individus. Le second concentre en quelque sorte dans un homme toute la puissance de la société. . . . Leur point de départ est différent, leurs voies sont diverses; néanmoins, chacun d'eux semble appelé, par un dessein secret de la Providence, à tenir un jour dans ses mains les destinées de la moitié du monde.

—Tocqueville.

5

THE modern Prussian and Russian states originated at about the same time in an effort to gain strength by introducing Western methods and techniques. Both were motivated by the wish to resist the West successfully and, eventually, to triumph over it. Prussia's effort was, like Japan's a century later, a miracle of will-power and national discipline: a small country without any important national resources procured for itself the armor of a great power. Russia had the advantage of vastness of space and abundance of resources. Yet there was another and more important difference. Prussia rose in the borderlands of a Germany that had been an integral part of Europe; Prussia did not become a free state like the Western nations, but she was a law-state, a *Rechtsstaat*. Russia lived on Europe's far border, virtually separated from it for many centuries. The vitalizing intellectual and social revolutions which have shaped modern Europe, the reception of Aristotelian philosophy and of Roman law, Renaissance and Reformation, did not reach and fertilize Russia. While their fruit grew in seventeenth-century England in the mighty tree of modern liberty, the seeds of which spread from there to America and western Europe, in Russia the fragile roots of lawful life and traditional freedom which had existed before the Mongol invasion withered away. Thus the gulf between Russia and Europe created by the Mongol rule remained. Liberty under law was unknown in that semi-Asiatic region. People and their property, nobles and serfs alike, were humble material for the autocrat's arbitrary will, without any legal protection or rights of their own. Peter I, who though attracted by the West distrusted it and wished by the adoption of Western methods of production and organization to prepare his country to withstand it, tried to overcome the inertia and backwardness of the people by a ruthless despotism and regimentation. His reign was a period of almost unceasing preparation of war and actual warfare. Through him, Russia laid the foundation of great power and of an unbroken march of conquest in all directions toward an ever-expanding empire. Her subjects, however, enjoyed neither liberty nor law. They were reared, to quote the words of a great Russian historian, in "an atmosphere of arbitrary rule, general contempt for legality and the person, and to a blunted sense of morality."

The Europeanization of Russia on a large scale began in the eighteenth century through the court of St. Petersburg. In the nineteenth century the task was carried on, with infinitely more understanding, by the new class of Europeanized intellectuals. They presented a brilliant succession of reformers and liberals, beginning with Alexander Radishchev as a rivulet and broadening into a mighty stream with men who fought devotedly against a stubborn autocracy for constitutional liberties after the English model in the Dumas of the beginning twentieth century. The leading Russian historians—among whom Vasily Klyuchevsky was a great master of his art—far from idealizing the national past, as so many Prussian historians did, exposed the backwardness, ruthlessness and brutality of the Russian state and society. They promoted the struggle for liberty under law, the true Europeanization of Russia.

With an astonishing eagerness the best thought of free Europe was assimilated, foreign literatures were translated, science and knowledge popularized. The example of Europe and the slowly growing individual liberty produced in the highly gifted Russian people with their untapped intellectual resources a flowering of the mind unprecedented in its sudden glorious eclosion. The works of Pushkin and Lermontov, Gogol and Turgenev, Dostoevsky and Tolstoy rose like stars of the first magnitude over the sky of Europe. The brightest among them was *The Brothers Karamazov*. In that unmistakably and specifically Russian novel, a novel of nineteenth-century Russia, Dostoevsky reached those sublime heights beyond any limitations of space or time where Hamlet, Don Quixote and Faust dwell. He was one of the greatest artists of all ages, a poet who with a rarely equalled, never surpassed intuitive power lit up the darkest corners of the human heart and its eternal strife and riddle, anguish and hope. But he saw himself above all a national prophet, and was hailed as such by his contemporaries. He cherished his journalism, which appears to us undistinguished, as part of his mission of national educator and spokesman; in it as in his novels he voiced the Russian national idea. No less a student of Russia than Thomas G. Masaryk has regarded Dostoevsky as the representative Russian and his ideas as the key to an understanding of the Russian revolution and of the Russian problem in general.[1]

Dostoevsky had neither the clarity of thought and integrity of intelligence of a Mill or Renan, nor the historical insight and broad knowledge of a Treitschke or Quinet; he fully shared with Mazzini the fiery heart and the burning passion for national mission and greatness. Both devoted their whole life to the vision of a third Rome as the world's center and leader. Both were imbued with a deep mystical faith: with Mazzini the faith of a Western liberal who accepted the English constitutional development and the French Revolution as his starting point; with Dostoevsky the faith in a semi-Asiatic autocracy which scornfully rejected the examples of the West. The problems facing them differed even more than their faith. Mazzini found Italy disunited, no state at all, only a venerable civilization flowering since Dante, in many ways heir and mother of Europe's proudest cultural traditions. Russia, on the other hand, was a mighty state, united and rapaciously expanding since Ivan the Terrible, secure in its imperial mission, but entirely

uncertain of its civilization, geographically half in Europe, culturally hardly yet of Europe.

Nowhere were Russians subject to foreign domination; as
masters they ruled many peoples in west and east. The Russian
empire, in spite of its vastness and its undeveloped resources,
was always expanding further and further. It had only recently
stood its test: it had defeated Napoleon who had subjected the
whole of Europe and threatened Britain; the Russian army had
marched victoriously into Berlin and Paris. The empire's fast-
growing population, its bigness, guaranteed its future. Russians
were certain of its grandeur and foresaw its leadership over
Europe and Asia. When in 1831 all liberal Europe sympathized
with the Poles in their struggle for independence from Russia,
Pushkin turned violently against Poland's friends with a fierce
warning to the Europeans, who had nothing to seek in a strife
among Slavs. He saw in Europe's sympathy not the desire to
help an oppressed nationality to liberty but ungrateful hatred
of Russia, of that very Russia which had not bowed to the insolent will of Napoleon and had with its blood redeemed Europe's freedom, honor and peace. Let the Western liberals heed
the warning; any enemy of Russia would be destroyed, like Napoleon, by her innumerable warriors who, from the cold cliffs
of Finland to the flaming Colchis, were ever ready to meet
again Russia's foes, not with words but with deeds.[2]

This mighty Russia, proudly asserting her powerful position,
suffered by the contrast of her backward and primitive civilization; she suspected Europe of looking down upon her with contempt or condescension. The anomalous situation was resented
even more because many Russians were filled with sincere
admiration for the rich and progressive civilization of the West.
They were torn between a desire for imitation, envy and self-
assertion. The question of the relations of Russia and Europe
was ever present before their minds: was Russia to become a
part of Europe, was she to follow the lead of Europe and accept

its values and standards, or was Russia to remain conscious of and to cultivate her deep difference from Europe? And in that latter case, was Russia to use her superiority to destroy Europe or to save it? Since many Russians liked to think of themselves as the only true Christians and full of brotherly love, they naturally decided to save Europe. The all-consuming quest for the meaning of Russian history and of the peculiar Russian way received an added impetus from the fact that Russia entered Europe during the age of revolutions, the rational revolution of the eighteenth century and the political and social revolutions of the nineteenth century. Should Russia reject the revolution and lead the counter-revolution, as an unshakable rock upon which the revolutionary wave would break and recede, thus saving Europe from chaos and destruction? Or should Russia accept and head the revolution and thus lead Europe and mankind, as she alone could, out of suffering and darkness to justice and light?

Russia's feelings for Europe were ambivalent in their strange amalgam of attraction and hatred, of inferiority and superiority. While the Russians felt humiliated by Europe's free society and civilization, and looked to her greatness with admiration and envy, many of them could not forget that Moscow was in the Russian tradition the third Rome; the rightful heir, since the fall of Constantinople to the infidels, of the imperial mission and of the true faith.[3] Were the princes of Moscow not the legitimate successors of the Roman emperors, like them the protectors of the Church? Had they not established their claim by great wars and conquests? Did not the imperial greatness of Russia dwarf that of Rome? Karamzin, the Russian historian of the beginning nineteenth century, expressed a widespread feeling when he wrote that "looking on the immensity of the Russian monarchy, which is unique in the world, our mind feels overwhelmed. Never did Rome equal it in greatness." Out of the very consciousness of her backwardness and lack of liberty grew extravagant dreams of Russia as the founder of a new civilization, as the bearer of universal salvation.[4]

This inner struggle of attraction and pride, this ambivalent relation to Europe, made many Russians look at Europe with a critical insight to which the weaknesses in Europe's armor revealed themselves more easily than its intrinsic but more hidden strength. As a result, some Russian observers—alike in that respect to Spengler and other Germans—never understood the West and underestimated it so much that their descriptions and judgments often resembled caricatures. Yet, did not European critics themselves confirm this interpretation? De Maistre in France, Carlyle in England, and many German thinkers abused modern Europe and castigated its decadence and shallowness. They looked longingly to a past which they idealized romantically. Should Russia eagerly accept this modern civilization which was so far from perfection? Was Russia not better off for the very reason of her backwardness? Had her seclusion from Europe not been a blessing? Rousseau had contended that the "noble savage," the primitive man with his unspoiled feelings, was nearer to God and nature; he condemned the civilization of modern cities as empty and superficial, separating man through reason from the truly life-giving sources of existence. His disciple Herder had hailed the Slav rural people of his day as the embodiment of primitive man and had prophesied their glorious future.[5] What wonder that the Russian nationalists regarded rapturously the Russian peasant, the common folk, as a superior type compared with the bourgeois of the West? Their enthusiasm was the greater, the less they knew of the real life and mind of the masses. The peasants appeared to them living in an organic and natural community based on mutual love and harmony, while Western society was held together, in competition and conflict, by the coldness of law and the brutality of force. The longings of European reactionaries and European utopians seemed reality in Russia. Russian nationalists used concepts borrowed from Europe to idealize and mobilize everything Russian against Europe.

In modern Russia the influence of Descartes and Locke, of Hume and Kant, on Russian thought remained slight. An infinitely more profound impression was produced by German romanticists and historians, who emphasized German peculiarity and uniqueness against the West and the differences in the past of Germany and Western Europe rather than their common development. They rejected liberalism, individual rights and modern industrial society as products of the West, unsuited to Germany, which had to find in her own past and in her own character her own solutions for her problems. They flaunted their alleged superiority and depth defiantly and triumphantly before the West. The West seemed old, Germany young, and a struggle between them was often visualized in almost apocalyptic imagery.

The German romantic rejection of the West was adopted and surpassed by the Russian Slavophiles. They borrowed the guns from the Germans—but they turned them not only against what the Germans considered the West but also against Germany herself. Even for the fight against the West, these anti-Westerners were dependent on the West, in spite of all their insistence on the uniqueness and originality, the *Eigenart* or *samobytnost*, of their respective *Urvolk* or folkish archetype. With a far greater remoteness from the common traditions of Europe, and with an even greater readiness to go to extremes and to reject and despise the common sense of the middle road and of moderation—what Dostoevsky and the Russians call their "broad nature"—the Russians went farther than the Germans ever did in their rejection of the West and in their apocalyptic expectations. There were many shades among the Russian opponents of the West: Slavophiles, Pan-Slavs, conservative bureaucrats, and lovers of the Russian common man. All were united in their hostility to the West, in their idealization of Russia, and in their extreme nationalism often expressed in assertions of all-embracing love and disinterested service. Their foremost spokesman, in Russia and before Europe, was Fyodor Mikhailovich Dostoevsky.

II

Dostoevsky was born in Moscow in 1821, the son of a middle class family. He spent his childhood in poverty and loneliness. His literary gifts revealed themselves early. He was already a well known minor author when he was arrested in 1849 with some fellow conspirators for a rather innocuous and mild participation in the troubled agitation of 1848. He was condemned to death, but was pardoned at the last minute to years of hard labor and military service in the wilds of Siberia. There the contact with criminals and the masses changed him. He returned from Siberia ten years later as a repentant revolutionary. He had left Russia in the stifling atmosphere of Nikolai I; he now found Russia animated by the high hopes of liberty and progress aroused by Alexander II. In the liberal atmosphere of St. Petersburg Dostoevsky started at the beginning of 1861 to publish with his brother and some friends a periodical, *Vremya* (Time). There his later attitude was already clearly forecast. The group called itself *pochvenniki*, men rooted in the soil, the native soil of Russia. They taught that only from the Russian soil, and from the Russian peasant masses attached to the soil, could the Russian intellectual draw life-giving forces. If he uproots himself, he loses his substance and becomes a mere parody of himself. Twenty years later, in his famous speech on Pushkin, Dostoevsky was to return to his attack upon the uprooted intellectual who strays away from soil and people and as a *skitalets*, a homeless wanderer, seeks for alien traditions and sources.[6]

The journal was closed by the authorities as a result of a misunderstanding early in 1863; a second journalistic venture

was even more short-lived. These failures did not brighten
Dostoevsky's life; the 'sixties were years of difficulty for him,
though two events in 1866 were full of promise: he published
Crime and Punishment, which overnight made him one of the
most popular authors in Russia, and he met his second wife, a
woman many years younger than he, with whom he was to live
in a most happy marriage. But most of the time he was haunted
by poverty and disease. His debts forced him to spend many
years abroad in order to escape his creditors. There, in Switzerland, Italy and Germany, his hatred of Europe grew into an
obsession. Everything seemed to him vile and mean, and in contrast everything Russian seemed infinitely noble.[7] His letters
were full of bitter complaints about the rotten and still rotting
West; as a result of his experiences his works glorified Russia
even more eagerly and restated the problem of Russia and Europe even more insistently.[8]

The political events which he witnessed, the wars of Italian
and German unification, drew his attention to the international
situation. He changed from a Russian nationalist to a Pan-Slav
imperialist. He expected a war between Russia and Europe, a
war which for him was not simply a military or political event
but the inescapable clash of two irreconcilable worlds, of two
opposite principles of life and society. To strengthen Russia
for that struggle, the help of all Slavs was to be enlisted. This
racial nationalism, based like Pan-German nationalism upon
affinity of language and supposedly common descent, hardly
corresponded to cultural realities. The Poles and the Czechs are
peoples of the West; the humanism of the Renaissance and the
yeast of the Reformation produced these high civilizations; the
Universities of Prague and Krakow date from the fourteenth
century and are among the oldest in Central Europe; the first
university in Russia was founded in Moscow in 1755. The
Dutch, the German-speaking Swiss and the Alsatians have a
closer racial and linguistic relationship with the Germans than

have the Czechs or Poles with the Russians; culturally they are
as far apart from the Germans as the Western Slavs are from the
Russians. Yet the Russian nationalists appealed to Pan-Slavism
for political and military reasons, as the German nationalists
had appealed to Pan-Germanism. Dostoevsky was among their
leading spokesmen.

He was in Germany at the time of the Franco-Prussian war.
His sympathies were on the French side, but all his thoughts
were turned to Russia and to his deep conviction of the approaching inevitable struggle between Russia and Europe. He
was convinced that all of Europe was united against Russia. He
worried whether Russia would use the time well for preparation, build enough railroads and fortresses, improve the army,
strengthen the border territories. "These things are the things
that are needed, and the rest, that is, the Russian spirit, unity—
all this exists and will endure, and it will be so strong, it will
have such wholeness and sacredness that even we are impotent
to fathom the whole depth of that force, to say nothing of
foreigners; and my idea is that nine-tenths of our strength consist just in the fact that foreigners do not understand and never
will understand the depth and power of our unity." [9]

Pan-Slav imperialism and its hostility to Europe found at the
same time a famous expression in the widely read and discussed
writings of Nikolai Danilevsky. Impressed by Prussia's expansion of 1866, Danilevsky published a series of articles which
were collected in 1871 in book form under the title, *Russia and
Europe*. In these articles he anticipated two of Spengler's basic
interpretations of history: the cyclic theory, according to which
history knows no progress of development but only a succession
of sharply separated civilizations, each one in turn maturing and
decaying; and the wishful interpretation of the present, according to which Western civilization, which he identified with the
Roman-Germanic world, was in a state of utter disintegration.
That civilization, the ninth of the ten types which Danilevsky

recognized, was, according to him, based upon individualism and violence. Catholicism, "a product of lie and arrogance," and Protestantism, "the denial of all religion," were not able to provide a spiritual basis for the decaying civilization which vainly claimed to be destined to serve for all mankind and to spread over the earth. This role (Danilevsky held) will be fulfilled by the tenth type of civilization, to which the future belongs and which is completely opposed in its ideas to Western civilization. This will be the Pan-Slav civilization, with Russia as its center, based on peace and collaboration. It will bring about a harmonious synthesis of all aspects of civilization, and will solve above all the social question. Russia, a compact giant, not having any colonies but spreading and extending on all its borders, is "too great and powerful to be just one of the great European powers." It is in a better position to build a new cooperative society, for private interests have never been the driving motive of Russian life. As soon as the Russian people decide to build the new order, the transformation will take place with unusual speed and without opposition, because the Russian masses, once the Europeanized intelligentsia is eliminated, will show a spirit of limitless sacrifice and obedience as no other people. The Orthodox Church as the only true faith will be the cornerstone of the new civilization. But fundamentally it will be a racial Slav civilization (though the Poles as Romanized Europeans were excluded from participation). For every Slav, Slavism must be the highest ideal, high above all ideals of culture or liberty.

From these premises, Danilevsky went on to prophesy a great war between Europe and Slavism which would last and characterize a whole period of history. Without any considerations for other values, Russia must destroy "the rotting West" and create a Slav federation under her leadership, which would include Hungarians, Rumanians and Greeks, "whose historical destinies have attached them by indestructible bonds to the Slav world." Constantinople and the Straits (he said) will be annexed to the federation, which will promote the spiritual unity of all Slavs and the recognition of the Russian language as the common medium of expression. The struggle for the common sacred goal and a few years of political union will weld the Slavs into a powerful unit which will protect Russia from hostile Europe and allow the free development of Slavic civilization for the benefit of mankind. Danilevsky, like most of the Russian nationalists, insisted on cloaking his violent and unrestrained call for conquest in the language of peace and love, qualities peculiar, according to him, to the Slavs.[10]

III

In 1871 Dostoevsky returned to Russia, this time to a life of relative affluence and secure fame. The atmosphere of his native land had changed again. The great hopes aroused by the first reforms of Alexander II had been disappointed. A younger generation, impatient with the lawlessness and backwardness of Russia, exasperated by the obstinacy of the court and the inertia of the masses, confronted with the eagerly sought but in its social reality so distant example of Europe, had resolved to overthrow the autocracy by revolutionary means. Dostoevsky came to the defense of the native autocracy and orthodoxy against the revolution, behind which he saw the destructive influence of the West. Two of his greatest novels, *The Possessed* and *The Brothers Karamazov*, the journals he edited,[11] and his famous lecture on Pushkin were devoted to what he regarded as the task of his life, to bring the Russian intellectuals back to the true traditions of the Russian folk and soil, and thus to save Russia and mankind. In the works of this period Dostoevsky's power as a novelist and psychologist is without equal in his generation and perhaps in the whole century. Out of the struggle of his own heart, out of the dark depth of his human frailty and titanic revolt, out of his own conflict of reason and faith which he could not resolve, he created unforgettable human characters and situations. The great artist's humanity sometimes contradicted the dogmas which the national prophet pro-claimed. For the human heart is richer than any national idea can comprise, and the individual—this passing and yet unique incident, unaccountable and unfathomable—demands his rights from the artist against the claims of blood and soil. Though Dostoevsky could not help being a great artist, he considered himself above all a national prophet.

When he dealt with human beings, they were almost always true to life. They were "broad" and full of mystery and sur-prise. There was much evil in them, but also great force, suffer-ing and joy. In dealing with politics and nations, however, both in his novels and in his articles, Dostoevsky's vision narrowed down to a simple contrast of black and white, of irreconcilable opposition, and thus destroyed his faculties of understanding. The man who felt such a deep regard and pity for sinners showed not the slightest tolerance for political adversaries. There no accusations seemed violent and vile enough to him, no treatment but extermination seemed suitable, a treatment de-manded with medieval fanaticism in the name of human salva-tion, and therefore justified. He explained the revolutionary movement of the Westernized intellectuals as the fruit of Euro-pean civilization and rational liberalism. Liberalism and nation-alism appeared to him as the mortal danger: they set the individual free from his dependence upon God and the moral order, they led to doubt and to immorality; if man and his con-science became independent judges on their own responsibility, soon anything seemed permissible. Westernized liberals might not be criminals themselves, they might be even honest seekers; their liberalism by necessity corrupted and produced criminal nihilism. In *The Possessed* Stepan Trofimovich Verkhovenski, a moderate and kind liberal, is the father of Pyotr, the nihilist, whose second spiritual father, Karmazinov, was intended as a caricature of Turgenev's liberalism. Ivan Karamazov, the noble rationalist, is unwittingly the spiritual guide of his half-brother, the repulsive criminal Smerdyakov.

So truthful is the great artist in Dostoevsky that Ivan and Stepan Trofimovich, and not Alyosha or Shatov, hold our—and the author's—love and attention throughout the novel. But the national prophet found only words of bitter hatred and distorting scorn for rational liberty and for everything un-Russian. Rarely has a man of great stature spoken of foreign nations and religions with similar contempt and without the slightest effort at understanding. In his glorification of Russia there was no trace of humility. Yet he ascribed Russia's claim to world leadership to the very humility and all-embracing understanding which according to him distinguished the Russians from all other nations on earth. He claimed that the Russians were destined to be the mediators, pacifiers and rulers of mankind, that they did understand all other peoples, while these could not understand the Russians and therefore could not appreciate their intentions. Russian was not a nation like other nations, but a world for itself, which, Dostoevsky taught, could be understood only by loving intuition, not by rational thought.

Only through this intuition (the "idea-feeling" as Dostoevsky named it, or "life-knowledge" as Ivan Kireevsky called it), could man arrive at true understanding. He was then no longer confined to rational analysis, which reaches only the surface, but he penetrated into the center and conceived the object as a whole; he was "living life." This deep understanding which transcends all reason was according to Dostoevsky peculiar to the Russian people. It was rooted in their deep feeling of community, the *sobornost* which characterized the whole of Russian life; and it was fundamentally opposed to the rationalism and individualism which disfigure all manifestations of the West, be it the Church or the bourgeois society or modern socialism—which to Dostoevsky spring all from the same root. The idea of a self-contained individual's sphere of personality has never taken deep root in Russian thought. The West has taken the "I" as the starting point, the Russians the "We"; the West, the thinking individual, Russia the concrete and immediate experience of community.[12] This attitude added to the difficulties of developing in Russia a free society of free individuals under law. The autocracy of the past had assured order among people of great strength yet little voluntary self-restraint. Would the proclamation of liberty not unleash anarchy?

Dostoevsky and the Russians, thinking in extremes and absolutes, found themselves faced by the social and moral dilemma of either complete freedom or total order. Freedom seemed to carry in it the danger of an excessive pride and a titanic *hybris*, of the individual, emancipated from all ties, asserting himself as a superman, a law unto himself. Order in its extreme meant excessive submissiveness and self-humiliation, the individual degraded to "a worm like every one else." The unreality of this dilemma was not realized.[13] The only way out which was found was the total separation of ideal and reality. In theory, absolute freedom was proclaimed, a vision of an unobtainable brotherhood of love without force or constraint, the ideal of primitive Christianity and of communist anarchism. In actuality, the total order was realized, an unlimited autocracy with its brutal force and its denial of all individual liberty. Dostoevsky envisaged as the essence of Russian life the spiritual church of free brotherhood and the withering away of the state and all its apparatus of force; but actually he defended and praised the Russian autocracy, the most backward tyranny of nineteenth-century Europe, and the Orthodox Church with its deadening subservience to the autocracy, as necessary for Russian power and therefore for human salvation. In a dangerous and confusing anticipation of an ideal aim, Dostoevsky often spoke of the vision as if it actually existed, and thus hallowed the degrading Russian tyranny.

He carried the confusion even farther in his insistence on religion as the true life-force. To realize the national idea and mission Dostoevsky demanded a return to God. He saw the root of all evil in the lack of religion. But the God of whom he spoke was the Russian God, the religion which he meant was nationalism. Dostoevsky himself was not a religious man, he never knew the bliss of true religious certainty. Like Ivan Karamazov he was a God-seeker, assailed by all the doubts. His only certainty was the reality of the Russian people. He was a prophet not of a universal God but of the Russian God in Whom he saw "the way, and the truth, and the life": no man and no people could come to salvation but by Him. In *The Possessed*, Shatov, who voices Dostoevsky's own opinions in his extreme nationalism, a man of the people who has found his way back to them, asks: "Do you know who are the only god-bearing people on earth, destined to regenerate and save the world in the name of a new God, and to whom are given the keys of life and of the new world?" The answer is obvious: the Russian nation and its God form an inseparable unit. Dostoevsky asserts that an atheist can not be a Russian; he means that no one can be a Russian who does not believe in the Russian God—which is none else than the Russian nation.

"Not a single nation," Shatov continues, "has ever been founded on principles of science or reason. Nations are built up and moved by another force which sways and dominates them, the force of an insatiable desire to go on to the end, though at the same time it denies that end. It is the force of the persistent assertion of one's own existence, and the denial of death. The object of every national movement is only the seeking for its god, who must be its own god, and the faith in him as the only true one. God is the synthetic personality of the whole people, taken from its beginning to its end. It's a sign of the decay of nations when they begin to have gods in common. Every people has its own conception of good and evil." And to Stavrogin's objection that God is thus reduced to a simple attribute of nationality, Shatov replies: "On the contrary, I raise the people to God. Every people is a people only so long as it has its own god and excludes all other gods irreconcilably; so long as it believes that by its god it will conquer and drive out of the world all other gods. Such, from the beginning of time, has been the belief of all great nations, all who have been leaders of humanity. If a great people did not believe that the truth is only to be found in itself alone; if it did not believe that it alone is destined to save all the rest by its truth, it would at once sink into being ethnographical material, and not a great people. But there is only one truth, and therefore only a single one out of the nations can have the true God. That's the Russian people." Rarely has there been in the literature of any people such a rejection of all universalism and rationalism as in this profession of faith. Never has nationalism—and this in the name of God—been driven to greater extremes, or raised to more blasphemous heights. Each nation creates its God, Dostoevsky tells us, and yet one nation claims universality for its God, not for the universal God of Christianity, but for the tribe and its own creation. The exclusive fanaticism of a racial God is proclaimed here, as in most primitive antiquity, without any trace of the ethical sublimation into the God of universal justice demanded by the Hebrew prophets.

Shatov believed with a burning faith in the Russian people. Yet he was not certain whether he believed in God. Asked by Stavrogin about it, he began trembling all over. Struggling for expression, wrestling with his deepest convictions, he finally stammered: "I believe in Russia. . . . I believe in her orthodoxy. . . . I believe in the body of Christ. . . . I believe that the new advent will take place in Russia. . . ."—"And in God? In God?"—"I, I will believe in God." Shatov's God is the Russian people; to him, not universal standards but Russia alone was the criterion for knowing what is good and evil. Therefore he could say that whoever loses touch with his people loses the distinction between good and evil. There was no way to attain God but by the people's work, the work and way of the masses. In deep humility Dostoevsky bowed to the Russian masses as the bearers of the God on Whom the salvation of mankind depended. Russia was destined to save, and to rule, the world. Her sense of community, her wide-open understanding, her humility and her boundless ability of suffering singled Russia out for her mission as the chosen people.[14]

IV

Dostoevsky found two forces opposing Russia's mission: the liberalism of Western society and the universalism of the Western Church. He pursued both in his writings with relentless hatred. He saw Russia and her Church [15] rejecting dominion and aggression in a truly universal spirit of service, while the Roman Church seemed to him to aspire to egoistic world domination by force. Yet in the West Christianity had opposed, or at least limited, by its universal claims the power of Caesar and the state, while in the East Christianity had served them, recognizing their unquestioned supremacy. By its attitude the Western church had preserved and strengthened the seeds of spiritual liberty inherited from antiquity and had laid the foundation of the modern world. Dostoevsky scented the danger which Western liberalism harbored for the traditional ways of Russia; hence the vehemence of his reaction against the Western Church and Western society. He saw nothing but force and violence in the West; he did not notice that there were few states in history as warlike and oppressive as the Russian autocracy. He himself glorified war, when it was Russia's, in glowing terms which so strangely contrasted with his philosophy of love, humility and compassion. Wars by other nations seemed to him acts of imperialism which he bitterly condemned; he never applied the same yardstick to Russia. He found harsh words for the misery and oppression encountered in bourgeois Europe; he never seemed to notice the incomparably greater oppression and misery of the masses in Russia. His two entirely different worlds were not held together by any common moral standards: without apparently being aware of it, Dostoevsky called black white and white black, depending upon the circumstances of the inevitable struggle between the Russian and the alien gods.

In the years 1876 and 1877 the Balkan crisis and Russia's war against Turkey held Dostoevsky's breathless attention. The great moment seemed to have arrived in which the Slav world under Russia's leadership would fulfill its destiny. He enthusiastically welcomed the approach of the war. "The present peace is always and everywhere much worse than war, so incomparably worse that it finally becomes downright immoral to maintain it. . . . Man inclines by nature to cowardice and dishonesty. Therefore he longs so much for war and loves it so much; he detects in it the panacea. War develops in him love for his fellow men and brings nations together by teaching them esteem for each other. War rejuvenates men. It raises the spirit of the people and the recognition of their own worth. War is indispensable in our time; without it the world would perish or transform itself into dirty mud with festering wounds." [16]

One year later, he praised the Russians for their readiness for war. "It was a wonderful time," he wrote; "the spirit and the heart of the whole Russia rose and the people marched out voluntarily, to defend Christ and the faithful, to fight for those who are our brethren by religion and by blood." But it was not only a war for brethren: "We need the war for ourselves; we are rising not only for our Slav brothers tortured by the Turks, but for our own salvation. War will clear the air which we breathe, the air in which we stifle in helpless rottenness and spiritual narrowness. We need war and victories. With them the new word will come and the new life will begin." To the objections of a pacifist Dostoevsky answered that pacifism cannot at present be applied to Russia: "In the present historical period Russia represents an exception," though Europe, which judges Russia after its own image, does not yet realize it. Russia will emerge from the war immensely strengthened; by this very fact she will spread love and brotherhood and will assure peace, because a strong Russia will finally be able to desist from war and to give the example of true peace, international harmony and disinterestedness. In her wars and conquests Russia has only one aim: to promote the liberty and brotherly union of all other nations. Therefore Russia's war is not a selfish war but a war for a sacred idea, the first step for the realization of eternal peace.[17]

For Russia's mission of world reconciliation cannot be fulfilled without war. First Russia must unite under her leadership all the Slav peoples, not for the sake of expansion or empire, as other nations would do, but to insure their peace and freedom. The next step must be the conquest of Constantinople, acquired not for profit but for the realization of that truth which is preserved only in Russia. That cannot be understood by the Europeans, who do not believe in the brotherhood and regeneration of man. But that is the very thing which Russia will bring them; for that purpose the Russians must become more Russian and must have faith in their national idea, so that Russia can reveal to Europe the new humanity, the new social order which she alone represents and can bring forth.[18] The great war between Russia and the West seemed to Dostoevsky inevitable, though it might be postponed for some time. But he hoped that the war against the Turks would spread to a general war which would decide all the great problems with one stroke and so save the world many future wars. Dostoevsky was convinced that the war would end with a Russian victory, and that the face of Europe would be completely changed. "So much that is new and progressive will begin in human relations that it would be useless to mourn and to hesitate on the eve of the last great struggle, which will bring about the great regeneration of all Europe." [19] A catastrophe was approaching, but out of it salvation would come.

With it a new epoch (he held) will commence for the whole of mankind. In place of Roman Catholicism a revived Eastern Christianity will arise. Europe, Dostoevsky felt certain, was on the eve of a transformation of such magnitude that human reason refuses to believe it. Bourgeois free society will be unable to survive the great war: the fate of Poland awaits France; and perhaps "not we, but our children, will see the end of England." In this terrible time of troubles only one mighty refuge will remain for mankind, one holy altar for truth, Russia. She will have to take over from Europe its science and technical appliances, but not its bourgeois civilization nor its rotting and inefficient forms of government. Then, in this new world order, true civic liberty may develop in Russia to a greater degree than anywhere in Europe and even in the United States. [20]

Occasionally Dostoevsky seemed ready to share Russia's world salvation and world rule with other nations. In November 1877 he wrote in his *Journal of an Author* on German-Russian relations: "In any case, one thing is clear: Germany needs us even more than we think, and not for a momentary political alliance, but for an eternal union. The idea of a united Germany is great and dignified, and reaches back into the depths of centuries. But what will Germany share with us? Her object is all Western humanity, she has ordained for herself the European Western world; she will bring to it her own ideas in place of the Roman and Romanic principles, and will become its leader. To us Russians she will leave the East. Thus our two great nations are destined to change the face of the whole world. This is no fantasy, no proposal of human ambition; this is the course of the world. New and strange facts are emerging and confirm it more and more. Russia's friendship with Germany is sincere and firm, it will spread and grow more and more in the national consciousness of both nations." [21] A few days before his death, in what may be regarded as his last word on the future of Russia and the world, Dostoevsky spoke once more of a possible division of the world; this time, retrospectively, with Napoleon. He regretted that the Russians in 1812, after driving out Napoleon, had not stopped at Russia's frontiers and left the West, at least temporarily, to Napoleon. In both cases Dostoevsky envisioned the future in the same way: Russia should turn her back on Europe and should carry her banners and her civilization to Asia.[22]

In this political testament, Dostoevsky expressed his hope of seeing Russia's domination established over all Asia. He demanded that the name of the Russian autocrat be raised above that of all the princes of the East, including the Caliph of all the Mohammedans and the Empress of India. This increased attention to Asia was necessary for Russia's future because the Russian was as much Asiatic as European. Dostoevsky even believed that "our hopes lie perhaps more in Asia than in Europe: in our future Asia will be our salvation." [23] He reiterated his usual complaint that Europe despises the Russians as Asiatic and will never treat them as equals or regard them as Europeans. He found the explanation and justification for it in those deep differences between Russia and Europe in which Dostoevsky believed and which, so he thought, the Western world instinctively recognized. But in Asia the Russians will not come as inferiors and imitators, but as masters and civilizers. Yet Dostoevsky was not satisfied with Russia's civilizing mission in the Orient; he thought of it, above all, as a means to the end which was always before his mind, Russia's world domination. The march across Asia was for Russia only a detour on the way to the West. If Russia in 1812 had divided the world with Napoleon and conquered Asia, he thought, then Napoleon's dynasty might have been overthrown in the West, but the Orient would have remained Russian, "and we would at present have controlled the oceans and could have opposed England at sea, as well as on land." Dostoevsky had a truly prophetic vision of Asia becoming Russia's America, where the Russians would produce immense wealth and, with the help of science, exploit the resources, increase the population, build mighty industries, and by so doing acquire a new sense of power, dignity and creative joy. A new Russia would grow up in Asia which would regenerate old Russia and make her masses understand her destiny. With the productive power and the population of her Asiatic empire, Russia would become materially and morally strong enough to fulfill her world mission.

V

This was the last great political vision which occupied Dostoevsky's mind in January 1881, a few days before his death. By then he had become the recognized national prophet. The year 1880 brought the publication of *The Brothers Karamazov*, a novel of such vital force and originality that it immediately impressed his readers as it impresses us, as one of the immortal creations of the human spirit, certainly as the greatest monument erected to the Russian man. Compared with this work the lecture on Pushkin which he delivered in Moscow before a meeting of the "Friends of Russian Letters" on June 8 might seem insignificant to us. It did not appear so to his Russian contemporaries. It was received by the large and representative audience, which included most of the great names of Russia, with an unprecedented enthusiasm. The session turned into a spontaneous national demonstration in which Slavophiles and Westernizers equally participated, hailing Dostoevsky as the national prophet. In that lecture Dostoevsky tried to harmonize the seeming opposites, the Slavophiles and the Westernizers,

Russia and Europe, by a synthesis which Russia achieved by turning to herself and yet embracing and understanding Europe and the whole world and saving them in that very act. Pushkin was hailed as the first to have accomplished such a synthesis, a truly great national Russian poet with a world-wide understanding and with a universal mission.

In Dostoevsky's interpretation, Pushkin was the first to create and understand the type of the Russian "wanderer," the *skitalets*, the unhappy intellectual who has lost touch with his people and who errs on the surface of the earth without any roots. Aleko in Pushkin's poem "The Gypsies," and the hero of the novel "Eugene Onegin" were the ancestors, the first representatives of that long line of "superfluous" men who were ever-present in nineteenth-century Russian literature, the truly lost generations of intellectuals for whom life had no meaning and society no place. Dostoevsky found that Pushkin had done much more than to present and understand the Russian intellectual and his problem; he had also pointed the way out. He had called upon Aleko, as Dostoevsky was now calling upon all the Russian intellectuals who had drifted away from their people and their soil and looked down with contempt or pity upon the peasant masses: "Humble yourself, proud man, and break above all your pride. Humble yourself, idle man, and above all labor in your native field." [24] Thus Pushkin, in Dostoevsky's interpretation, pointed the road back to blood and soil. He did more: he also created, as a contrast to the Europeanized youth of wanderers, exemplary types of Russian moral beauty which moved and captivated the hearts of Russian readers and which he as a truly national poet derived from his deep intuitive knowledge of the real Russian people. He seemed to tell the Russian intellectuals: "Believe in the people and the folk-mind, in them alone is truth and beauty, from them alone expect your salvation and you will be saved."

Yet Pushkin, the greatest national poet and nationalist, was not a narrow or self-centered Russian. He was a true Westerner, a world-open mind, for the very reason that he was a true Russian; he had a unique ability, according to Dostoevsky, to understand all other nations, to feel with them, to probe their depths and to represent them in his work. Naturally Dostoevsky claimed this universality of understanding as typically and uniquely Russian,[25] for the Russian people surpass all other nations in the gift of identifying themselves with them, to understand them, to love them, and to harmonize their contradictions and conflicts. From that point of view Dostoevsky, the Slavophile, could justify and even glorify the Westernizing tendencies in Russia, the efforts to know and assimilate Europe; for do they not derive from the deepest nature of the Russian national spirit? Where the Russian is most deeply and most consciously Russian, where he is truly nationalist, there, by his unique nature, he is at the same time most deeply and most truly human; in fact the nationalist Russian—and he alone—is all-man, Russian nationalism is all-human, striving for and representing the universal unity of mankind, or at least—for even here Dostoevsky remains a racialist—of all the peoples of "the great Aryan race." "To become a true and whole Russian means, ultimately, only to become brother to all men, an all-man. To a true Russian, Europe and the fate of the whole great Aryan race are as dear as Russia herself, because our mission is the embodiment of the universal idea on earth." Out of the moral and intellectual chaos of the West, out of its class struggles and national conflicts, all-comprehending Russia will point the way to the brotherly harmony and the perfect society of all nations. Though it may seem absurd to the West and to the Westernized Russian intellectuals, it will be Russia, this poor and backward land, that will speak the new word to humanity.

The harmony of Russia and Europe which Dostoevsky claimed to have achieved in his lecture will appear to less intuitive readers full of unresolved contradictions. Fittingly he concluded his lecture by saying that when Pushkin died young he unquestionably took with him a great secret which we must now try to comprehend without him. Though Dostoevsky died full of years and achievements he too took a great secret with him, the complexity and irreconcilability of so many of his views. His last lecture in no way resolved them. It but stated them anew.[26] He expressed, almost simultaneously, the gospel of peace and humility and the ruthless imposition of the sword; brotherly love and intolerant hatred, the spiritual anarchy of free men and the rigid regimentation of autocracy.[27] But all his contradictions were held together and made meaningful by the one principle to which he remained unerringly faithful—Russia and her future. He foresaw tremendous world events of which Russia would be the center. Shortly before his death he wrote: "The future genuine Russian idea has not yet appeared among us, but the earth is portentously pregnant with it and is making ready to deliver it amid agonizing pain."

Dostoevsky died on January 28th. His funeral on the 31st became an unprecedented manifestation of the love of the nation for its greatest writer. Not a despised and unheeded prophet, but an uncrowned king was buried that day in St. Petersburg. Sixty-three official deputations with wreaths and fifteen singing societies attended. Like a last call to his people, the last issue of his *Journal* appeared fittingly on the day of his burial. It contained what had been nearest and dearest to the dead man's heart: his appeal for the conquest of Asia and a discussion on the relation of the Russian intelligentsia to the Russian people.

Dostoevsky's excessive nationalism was in no way shared by the majority of the Russian intellectuals of his time. The liberal intelligentsia did not regard Russia as a unique and peculiar case which could not be understood by reason nor measured by a common yardstick. They wished Russia to follow the general progressive development of Europe, to combat the lawlessness

and primitivity of the Russian tradition and masses and to educate the nation to liberty under law after the model of Western
civil society. They labored faithfully for the education of the
Russian people, for the improvement of its living conditions, for
a greater freedom and dignity of life. It was a slow and bitter
struggle. A few weeks after Dostoevsky's death the revolutionary movement claimed its foremost victim, Alexander II. For
the next twenty-five years Russia was ruled by Dostoevsky's
friend, Konstantin Pyotrovich Pobyedonostsev who regarded
the fight against reform, progress and revolution as the main task
of the Russian government. He realized the conservative side
of Dostoevsky's program: the relentless struggle against Europe
and against the nineteenth century. He shared Dostoevsky's vision of Europe and modern civilization sinking into darkness,
death and night and of Holy Russia rising toward her day, light
and life. Parliamentarism and constitutions appeared to him as
"the great lie of our age"; he put in their place an autocracy
supported by church and police, and an exclusive and racial nationalism.

Pobyedonostsev's regime ended in 1905. For a brief span Russia lived in the expectation of liberty and the rule of law. The
events of March 1917 seemed to realize these hopes: the traditional autocracy and isolation of Russia appeared suddenly a
matter of the past. But this dream of the Russian intelligentsia
proved short-lived. As Dostoevsky had foreseen, the intellectuals lacked contact with the masses for whom the dignity of the
individual and the free state of the West had little meaning. In
November 1917 the masses swept away the fragile defenses of
liberty and law. Through men and means unforeseen by Dostoevsky, without the narrowness of his racial views, in a far more
universal spirit than he could conceive of, the revolutionary side
of his program was carried forward, and the masses were raised
from their depth of unselfconsciousness to national selfcon-
sciousness. A new generation of intellectuals—ignorant of, and

unattracted by, the lure of Western liberty—and the masses met in the fulfillment of a destiny which Dostoevsky had prophesied: for without the intellectuals, the masses could not perceive their mission of renewing humanity; without the masses, the intellectuals could not utter the new word to the world.[28] In its awakened masses the great Eurasian empire found the strength for the mission which Dostoevsky had envisaged for Russia.

Notes

NOTES TO THE INTRODUCTION

1. Quoted in H. C. F. Bell, *Woodrow Wilson and the People* (New York: Doubleday, Doran, 1945) p. 101.
2. See on the origins of English and American nationalism Hans Kohn, *The Idea of Nationalism* (New York: Macmillan, 1944), chs. IV and VI.
3. The sixth great power of the nineteenth century, the Habsburg monarchy, never adapted itself to the age of nationalism. At the end of the century she represented the only example of a pre-nationalist power in Europe. See Hans Kohn, *Not by Arms Alone* (Cambridge, Mass.: Harvard University Press, 1940) pp. 43–64. There were no "national prophets" for the Habsburg monarchy, though some of its great writers, Franz Grillparzer or Hugo von Hofmannsthal, tried to elaborate an "Austrian idea." But there seemed no future for Austria in the age of nationalism, especially after the unfortunate settlement with Hungary in 1867.
4. Guido de Ruggiero, who set out in *The History of European Liberalism* "to study the liberalism of the nineteenth century in the diversity of its national forms and the unity of its historical organism," saw the unity of Europe in all the differences and even oppositions of movements and emphasis. He considered only four nations, omitting Russia.
5. The faith in the progress of history (at least in modern times) was expressed by Renan to Romain Rolland in 1887: "Vous verrez venir encore une grande réaction. Tout paraîtra détruit de ce que nous défendons. Mais il ne faut pas s'inquiéter. Le chemin de l'humanité est une route de montagne: elle monte en lacets, et il semble par moments qu'on revienne en arrière. Mais on monte toujours."
6. Anatole France has described the impression produced by the news of this defeat in 1898 in an aristocratic French family which at the height of the Dreyfus Affair sympathized deeply with the Spanish Catholic monarchy and its past glories as against the young democratic forces from across the sea. The news of the destruction of the Spanish Fleet produced a deep and sorrowful silence. "Cette vision soudaine avait attristé les âmes, une flotte bénie par le pape, battant le pavillon du roi Catholique, portant à l'avant de ses navires les noms de la vierge et des saints, disemparée, fracassée, coulée par les canons de ces marchands de cochons et de ces fabriquants de machines à coudre, hérétiques, sans rois, sans princes, sans passé, sans patrie, sans armée." ("That sudden vision had saddened the souls, of a fleet blessed by the Pope, flying the flag of the Catholic King, carrying at the prow of its ships the name of the Virgin and of the Saints —and this fleet disabled, battered, sunk by the guns of these merchants of hogs and manufacturers of sewing machines, heretics without Kings, without an aristocracy, without a past, without a fatherland, without an army.")
7. "Un jour prochain, l'union des nations d'Occident formera la nouvelle

patrie. Elle même ne sera qu'une étape sur la route qui mène à la patrie plus large: l'Europe." Romain Rolland, *Les Précurseurs* (Paris: Éditions de L'Humanité, 1920) p. 17. Michelet wrote: "In this marvellous transformation the spirit has triumphed over matter, the general over the particular and the idea over reality. The barbarian periods represent almost nothing but the local, the particular, the material. Man still clings to the soil, he seems to be part of it. . . . Slowly the strength which is the real essence of man will detach him, will uproot him from the soil. . . . He will need, instead of his native village, instead of his town or his province, a great fatherland. The idea of this fatherland, an abstract idea which owes little to the senses, will carry him through a new effort to the idea of a universal fatherland, of the City of Providence."

One of the most promising steps toward Europe was suggested in June 1940 when the British government proposed to France the formation of a Franco-British Union. This unprecedented step brushed away with daring vision all the accumulated distrust of many centuries. It set the path to a rebuilding of mankind as no other single step has done. It was the official offer of a government in power, not the wishful dream of prophets or private individuals. Its ultimate effect, if or wherever accepted, upon the liberties and peace of mankind would be incalculable. The proposed declaration of the British government, showing Churchill's spirit, read in part: "The two governments declare that France and Great Britain shall no longer be two nations but one Franco-British Union. The constitution of the Union will provide for joint organs of defence, foreign, financial, and economic policies."

Albert Guérard, *Europe Free and United* (Stanford University Press, 1945) p. 181 f., makes the excellent suggestion of Basic Latin as the lingua franca of the European community. It has very deep roots there and is in no way an "artificial" language.

8. Euripides, "Bakchai," 1388–1391:

πολλαὶ μορφαὶ τῶν δαιμονίων,
πολλὰ δ'ἀέλπτως κραίνουσι θεοί·
καὶ τὰ δοκηθέντ' οὐκ ἐτελέσθη,
τῶν δ' ἀδοκήτων πόρον ηὗρε θεός.

NOTES TO CHAPTER ONE

1. See on the Puritan Revolution Hans Kohn, *The Idea of Nationalism* (New York: Macmillan, 1944) pp. 165–183; on the Glorious Revolution two recent writings by the Professors of Modern History at Cambridge University, George Macaulay Trevelyan, *The English Revolution 1688–1689* (Home University Library, London: Thornton Butterworth, 1939) and H. Butterfield, *The Englishman and his History* (Cambridge: University Press, 1944). "The settlement of 1689 was in its essence the chaining up of fanaticism alike in politics and in religion." Trevelyan, p. 241 f. "This is the logic of political compromise and of government by discussion; and without it democracy can only destroy itself in a conflict of divine right versus diabolical wrong—which in politics can only be regarded as an end to all discussion, a euphemism for a resort to force. The system that we have inherited replaces a doctrinaire quest for the highest good by the more difficult search—that demands so much more austere self-discipline—that pursuit of the highest practicable good. It implies even a reluctance to bring things to a decision until something like the general sense of the nation makes itself clear." Butterfield, p. 98.

2. Thomas B. Macaulay, *The History of England from the Accession of James II*, vol. I, ch. 3 (New York: J. W. Lovell, n.d.) p. 371.

3. G. M. Young, *Victorian England: Portrait of an Age* (London: Oxford University Press, 1936) p. 19. "The greatest Liberal of all times (Gladstone) was penetrated to his innermost fiber with the veneration for all established things: Church, Universities, Crown." *Ibidem*, p. 140 f.

4. Guido de Ruggiero, *The History of European Liberalism* (London: Oxford University Press, 1927) p. 163 f., has some pertinent remarks on the similarity of sects and parties.

5. "The literature of France has been to ours what Aaron was to Moses, the expositor of great truths which would else have perished for want of a voice to utter them with distinctness. The great discoveries in physics, metaphysics, in political science are ours. But scarcely any foreign nation except France has received them from us by direct communication. Isolated by our situation, isolated by our manners, we found truth but we did not impart it. France has been the interpreter between England and mankind." T. B. Macaulay in his essay on Horace Walpole. *Critical, Historical, and Miscellaneous Essays* (New York: Armstrong & Son, 1860) vol. III, p. 153.

   Professor Roger Soltau in his excellent *French Political Thought in the Nineteenth Century* (New Haven: Yale University Press, 1931) p. 54 points out that for the development of free states on the European continent the United States might be a better model than England, the root and source of American democracy, for the very reason that liberty in England was a slow deep-rooted growth which cannot be easily transplanted, while in the United States it is a recent ready-made institution grown from English roots in a new, different, less historical and more rational soil.

6. See Elmer Louis Kayser, *The Grand Social Enterprise, A Study of Jeremy Bentham in His Relation to Liberal Nationalism* (New York: Columbia University Press, 1932). On October 24, 1831, in his 84th year, Bentham sent an autograph to Lady Hannah Ellice in which he wrote: "The way to be comfortable is to make others comfortable; the way to make others comfortable is to appear to love them; the way to appear to love them is to love them in reality. Probatur ex experientia per Jeremy Bentham."

7. John Morley, *Critical Miscellanies* (London: Macmillan, 1892) p. 42. See also in Morley, *Recollections* (New York: Macmillan, 1917) vol. I, pp. 52–57.

8. The best estimate of Mill was given by Prof. Harold J. Laski in the Preface to the World's Classics edition of the *Autobiography* (1924): "In the fifty years that have passed since Mill's death, no teacher has arisen whose influence upon the mind of his generation has been so beneficent or so far reaching. . . . Accessibility to new ideas, indignation against injustice, catholicity of temper, and an infinite patience—these were the qualities that made him the mirror of all that was best in his age" (and we might rather add: his nation). "He was a democrat, but no one was more critical of the evils of democracy. He was an individualist, but no one was more hostile to the excesses of laissez-faire. The ultimate thing for which he was concerned was the elevation of the mind of man. . . . The thing for which Mill was concerned was that the citizen should be given the full chance to be himself at his best. That, at bottom, is the meaning alike of his emphasis upon the importance of diversity and upon the fact that there are reserves within the human mind into which organization cannot, and ought not to, enter. No one, on any final estimate, can doubt that Mill, as no other figure of his time, raised the moral stature of his generation." See also Robert H. Murray, *Studies in the English Social and Political Thinkers of the Nineteenth Century*, vol. I (Cambridge: W. Heffer & Sons, 1929); Emery Neff, *Carlyle and Mill, Mystic and Utilitarian* (New York: Columbia University Press, 1924); George Morlan, *America's Heritage from John Stuart Mill* (New York: Columbia University Press, 1936); Helen M. Lynd, *England in the Eighteen-Eighties* (New York: Oxford University Press, 1945) pp. 99 ff.; on Bentham see Graham Wallas, *Men and Ideas* (London: Allen & Unwin, 1940) pp. 19–48.

9. Mill quoted from the Report of the English Commissioner to the New York Exhibition (of 1853) some remarks which illustrated to his mind the value of democracy with its sense of initiative and free enterprise for the education of the common man: "We have a few great engineers and mechanics and a large body of fellow workmen; but the Americans seem likely to become a whole nation of such people. Already, their rivers swarm with steamboats; their valleys are becoming crowded with factories; their towns are the abodes of all the skill which now distinguishes a town population; and there is scarcely an art in Europe not carried on in America with equal or greater skill than in Europe. A whole nation of

Franklins, Stephensons, and Watts in prospect, is something wonderful for other nations to contemplate. In contrast with the comparative inertness and ignorance of the bulk of the people of Europe, the great intelligence of the whole people of America is the circumstance most worthy of public attention."

10. He did not shrink back in case of extreme necessity from war or revolution though he never praised them and knew their horrors and tragedies. He wrote in *Dissertations and Discussions*, vol. I (Boston: Spencer, 1864), p. 84: "Men are not to make it the sole object of their political lives to avoid a revolution, no more than of their natural lives to avoid death. They are to take reasonable care to avert both those contingencies when there is a present danger, but not to forbear the pursuit of any worthy object for fear of a mere possibility. Unquestionably it is possible to do mischief by striving for a larger measure of political reform than the national mind is ripe for; and so forcing on prematurely a struggle between elements, which, by a more gradual progress, might have been brought to harmonize. And every honest and considerate person, before he engages in the career of a political reformer will inquire whether the moral state and intellectual culture of the people are such as to render any great improvement in the management of public affairs possible. But he will inquire, too, whether the people are likely ever to be made better, morally and intellectually, without a previous change in the government. If not, it may still be his duty to strive for such a change, at whatever risk."

Letter to John Austin April 13, 1847: "After all, what country in Europe can be compared with France in the adaptation of its social state to the benefit of the great mass of its people, freed as they are from any tyranny which comes home to the greater number, with justice easily accessible and the strongest inducements to personal prudence and forethought. And would this have been the case without the great changes in the state of property which, even supposing good intentions in the government, could hardly have been produced by anything less than a revolution?" *The Letters of John Stuart Mill* ed. by Hugh S. R. Elliot (London: Longmans, Green, 1910) vol. I, p. 131.

Mill's position was similar, in very many respects, to that of T. G. Masaryk, who in a talk with Čapek said: "Revolution or dictatorship can sometimes abolish bad things, but they can never create good and lasting ones. Impatience is fatal in politics."

11. "To suppose that the same international customs, and the same rules of international morality, can obtain between one civilized nation and another, and between civilized nations and barbarians, is a grave error, and one which no statesman can fall into, however it may be with those who, from a safe and unresponsible position criticize statesmen. . . . The criticisms, therefore, which are so often made upon the conduct of the French in Algeria, or of the English in India, proceed, it would seem, mostly upon a wrong principle. The true standard by which to judge their proceedings never having been laid down, they escape such comment and censure as might really have an improving effect, while they are tried by a standard which can have no influence on those practically engaged in

such transactions, knowing as they do that it cannot, and if it could, ought not to be observed, because no human being would be the better, and many much the worse, for its observance." *Dissertations and Discussions* (London: Longmans, Green, 1867) vol. III, p. 167 f.

12. Published in December, 1859, reprinted *ibidem*, pp. 153–178.

13. It is generally believed on the continent "that the very existence of England depends upon the incessant acquisition of new markets for our manufactures; and that we are at all times ready to trample on every obligation of public or international morality, when the alternative would be, pausing for a moment in that race." Yet "of all countries which are sufficiently powerful to be capable of being dangerous to their neighbors, we are perhaps the only one whom mere scruples of conscience would suffice to deter from it. We are the only people who regards with jealousy and suspicion, and a proneness to hostile criticism, precisely those acts of its government which in other countries are sure to be hailed with applause." *Ibidem*, p. 160 f.

14. Mill's article "The Contest in America" was published in February 1862 and was reprinted *ibidem*, pp. 179–205. He wrote it at a moment when the clouds of war which hung over England and America as a result of the North's high-handed action in arresting the Southern emissaries on a British ship had passed. He was happy that "the fear has not been realized that the only two first-rate powers who are also free nations would take to tearing each other in pieces." He objected to any sympathy with the South. "We, the emancipators of the slave, who for the last half century have spent annual sums equal to the revenue of a small kingdom in blockading the African coast, for a cause in which we not only had no interest, but which was contrary to our pecuniary interest,—we should have lent a hand to setting up a powerful republic, devoted not only to slavery, but to pro-slavery propagandism . . ."

15. "I am far from saying that the present struggle, on the part of the Northern Americans, is wholly of this exalted nature; that it has arrived at the stage of being altogether a war for justice. But there was from the beginning, and now is, a large infusion of that element in it; and this is increasing, and if the war lasts, will in the end predominate."

In a letter of December 30, 1847, Mill wrote: "I regard war as an infinitely lesser evil than systematic submission to injustice." *Letters, op. cit.*, vol. I, p. 133.

16. Lord Acton, "Nationality," published in July 1862, reprinted in his *The History of Freedom and Other Essays* (London: Macmillan, 1907) pp. 270–300.

Similar ideas on state and nationality were expressed at about the same time by Charles Renouvier, the French philosopher, whose science of morals and history with its guiding principles of liberty, reason and peace is of lasting value. In his *Science de la Morale* (Paris: Ladrange, 1869), vol. II, pp. 416–430, he compared the ideas of nationality and of the state. He regards the ideas of "national mission," propagated by Michelet, Mazzini and others, as a new form of the "divine rights" theory transferred from kings to peoples. To quote some of his conclusions: "L'idée de la nationalité naturelle se rapporte éminemment au système des faits sociaux involontaires, et je dirais presque aux fonctions instinctives de l'humanité. Mais la notion de l'État est le fruit de la réflexion et du vouloir. Elle soumet tous les faits de diversités légitimes entre hommes, à plus forte raison les faits irrationnels et illégitimes, au principe de l'identité de la nature morale. Elle est donc moralement supérieure, tout comme l'association volontaire est préférable aux coopérations spontanées, une république d'agents libres à une ruche d'abeilles. . . . Nous devons répondre négativement à la question de savoir si le but d'une politique générale rationnelle est d'arriver à la constitution des nations naturelles en autant d'États distincts. Le vrai but est d'améliorer les États en les amenant au respect de l'autonomie de leurs sujets et de leurs autonomies réciproques, de les considérer comme des produits de la raison et de la volonté encore plus que des affections, et, par suite, de faire dépendre leurs lois de formation ou de division, premièrement de la volonté délibérée de leurs membres, secondement des affinités et convenances diverses qu'il est permis à ceux-ci de consulter, troisièmement des conditions historiques imposées par le présent et par le passé. Il n'est pas facile, il n'est généralement pas possible de mettre d'accord des éléments nombreux et variables comme ils sont, sans sacrifices. Mais la poursuite intérieure de la liberté dans chaque État répond à toutes les difficultés surmontables, et doit se conseiller dans tous les cas comme la fin morale essentielle et le grand moyen légitime des autres fins. . . . On imagine que chaque peuple anciennement distinct est un élément naturel et providentiel des relations générales de l'humanité; on veut donc faire à chacun sa place·dans le concert de la paix. Mais si la nature est dirigée dans des voies providentielles quand elle produit les races, les langues et les aptitudes nationales, comment l'histoire est-elle à son tour si peu providentielle, et pourquoi vient-elle troubler, broyer ces éléments au point de les rendre méconnaissables? La vraie providence, en ce qui concerne la direction des affaires humaines, est dans la raison même, ou doit avoir la raison pour organe, et se manifester dans la fondation des États justes, sans acception ni exception de races, non dans l'agglomération de telles ou telles similitudes. C'est donc toujours la raison qu'on subordonne; c'est la nature physique ou morale qui reçoit la suprématie selon la doctrine des nationalitiés."

17. Mill published in 1868 a pamphlet "England and Ireland" showing the undesirableness, for Ireland as well as for England, of separation between the countries, and discussing a proposal for settling the land question.

18. The nationality problem in Spain for instance does not demand the independence of the Catalans and the Basques, but the transformation of Spain into a liberal state based on rational tolerance, individual freedom and broadest self-government for all its component nationalities. The peace of Europe might have been better preserved by the transformation of the Habsburg Empire into a "monarchical Switzerland" as suggested by T. G. Masaryk on the eve of World War I. (See R. W. Seton-Watson, *Masaryk in England*, Cambridge: University Press, 1943, p. 20.) Such a democratic federation would have formed a protection of all the nationalities against German or Russian power and a safeguard for their liberties. (See also Hans Kohn, *Not By Arms Alone*, Cambridge: Harvard University Press, 1940, pp. 43–64.) The regard for peace and liberty does not

demand the dissolution of the Russian empire and the proclamation of the national independence of Ukraine and Lithuania, Armenia and Uzbekistan, but the introduction of individual liberties and legal guaranties for the whole empire with tolerant regard for differences and the true development of self-government.

19. One of Mill's observations deserves special attention today. He stressed the important role played by imperial home governments in protecting the natives against the European settlers to whom it often seems "monstrous that any right of the natives should stand in the way of their smallest pretensions." The government in London, and later the government in Washington, tried in North America to protect the Indians against the lawlessness and greed of the white settlers and local officials; in Africa the rights of the natives are better protected in dependent colonies than in independent lands like the Union of South Africa where the London government cannot interfere to protect the natives; the position of the Negro is better in the French colonies of Martinique or Guadeloupe than in the southern states of the Union; in India the British government protected tens of millions of Untouchables from the utmost degradation into which human beings ever sunk in any part of the world. Mill rightly pointed out that the home governments are generally more concerned with native rights and welfare than are the settlers or private adventurers subject to them. "As it is with the English in India, so, according to trustworthy testimony, it is with the French in Algiers; so with the Americans in the countries conquered from Mexico; so it seems to be with Europeans in China: there is no necessity to record how it was with the Spaniards in South America."

In a letter to Sir Charles Dilke, after having read his book *Greater Britain,* Mill wrote on Feb. 9, 1869: "I most cordially sympathize with all you say about the insolence of the English, even in India, to the native population, which has now become not only a disgrace, but, as you have so usefully shown, a danger to our dominion there. . . . I observe that your preferences seem to be, as mine are, for the systems which give permanent right of property to the actual cultivator. But have you not, on the questions which concern the English planters, leant too much to their side?" (*Letters, op. cit.* vol. II, pp. 187 ff.) Mill stressed the difficulty of granting self-government to white settlers and at the same time safeguarding the natives against the settlers, in a letter about the Maoris in New Zealand to Judge Chapman of Jan. 7, 1866 (*Letters, op. cit.,* vol. II, pp. 53 ff.).

Mill also pointed out that oppression is in no way confined to the relations between the conquering and the subject peoples; the worst cases of oppression exist generally among the subject people itself. In fact, civilized government everywhere tends in the colonies to put an end to the savagery of traditional oppression. Yet public opinion in the ruling countries is generally agitated by the interests not of the most oppressed part of the dependent people, but of that part which has the financial and educational means of making itself heard. "What makes matters worse is, that when the public mind is invoked (as, to its credit, the English mind is extremely open to be) in the name of justice and philanthropy, in behalf of the subject community or race, there is the same probability of its missing the mark. For in the subject community also there are oppressors and oppressed; and it is the former, not the latter, who have the means of access to the English public. They have no difficulty in procuring interested or sentimental advocacy in the British Parliament and press. The silent myriads obtain none."

20. Letter to Judge Chapman, Jan. 14, 1870 (*Letters, op. cit.*, vol. II, p. 237 f.). Mill's doctrine of empire was that of the liberal party. It was brought nearer to realization in the administration of Campbell-Bannerman. Mill's disciple, John Morley, was a staunch adherent of home rule for Ireland and throughout the empire, and denounced the wave of British imperial feeling after 1878. He called manifest destiny "moonshine." As secretary for India he became responsible for the reforms which started India on her fast march toward self-government. But he was always aware of the fact that advancing India from the early Oriental middle ages to the twentieth century was in view of the complex nature and the vastness of the problem "a stupendous process," which could be solved only by the gradual and even growth of India "to a modern utilization of her incalculable capacities." See Warren Staebler, *The Liberal Mind of John Morley* (Princeton: University Press, 1943).

21. *Letters, op. cit.*, vol. II, pp. 46 ff. What the foremost German scholarly interpreter and critic of Britain, Wilhelm Dibelius, said in his *England* (2nd ed., Stuttgart: Deutsche Verlags-Anstalt, 1923, vol. I, p. 58 f.) about Britain is to a very large extent true also of the United States: In the expansion of these two countries "doubtless the desire for political power and economic influence was the actual motive. And yet there is an idealistic impulse in these wars which gives a sanction to England's struggle for power in the name of civilization: England felt that she stood for freedom. She had found a universal watchword in which every Englishman believed honestly and fanatically and which possessed the power of every gospel, not only to influence all mankind but gradually to purge its devotees of the dross which still hampered its power. It is not pertinent for England's place in world history whether the conception of English liberty was truth or legend. What is pertinent is that at a time when diplomats were haggling with all their arts over territory and alliances, England, in addition to all these arts which she mastered, had a watchword for mankind in which every Englishman believed. She conferred upon the world a vital principle which at that time it needed and which has not yet lost its vigor. . . . England is the only state in the whole world which, even while pursuing its own interests, has something to give to other peoples, the only state in which patriotism is not synonymous with an attitude of defensive pugnacity toward all the rest of the world, the only state which always invites the cooperation of some part of the progressive, able and idealistic elements in every nation."

NOTES TO CHAPTER TWO

1. Ernest Renan, *L'Avenir de la Science, Pensées de 1848* (Paris: Calmann-Lévy, 1890) p. 25. On p. 494 Renan wrote: "The year 1789 will be a holy year in the history of mankind. This place where humanity proclaimed itself, the Tennis Court, will one day be a temple; people will go there as they go to Jerusalem when the intervening time will have sanctified the particular facts into general symbols. Golgotha became sacred only two or three centuries after Jesus." And on p. 35 f.: "In the Orient thousands of men die of hunger or misery without ever thinking of revolt against the established order. In modern Europe a man, rather than dying of hunger, finds it simpler to seize a rifle and to attack society, instinctively feeling that society has obligations to him which it has not fulfilled. That is a totally new idea. Man has ceased to regard evils as ordained by fate."

2. On Michelet see especially the works of his foremost disciple, Gabriel Monod, *Les Maîtres de l'Histoire: Renan, Taine, Michelet* (Paris: Calmann-Lévy, 1894); *Jules Michelet; Études sur sa vie et ses oeuvres* (Paris: Hachette, 1905); *La Vie et la Pensée de Jules Michelet 1798–1822*, 2 vols. (Paris: Champion, 1923); and Jean-Marie Carré, *Michelet et son Temps* (Paris: Perrin, 1926). See also Albert L. Guérard, *French Prophets of Yesterday* (London: T. Fisher Unwin, 1913); Roger Soltau, *French Political Thought in the Nineteenth Century* (New Haven: Yale University Press, 1931); Edmund Wilson, *To the Finland Station* (New York: Harcourt Brace, 1940). On Quinet see Mme. Edgar Quinet, *Cinquante ans d'Amitié; Michelet-Quinet, 1825–1875* (Paris: Colin, 1899).

3. After 1870 Michelet wrote: "J'espérais mieux de l'Allemagne et je suis frappé de la voir morte en la victoire même, au sepulchre de fer où un État slave, la Prusse, l'a inhumée." Monod, *La Vie, op. cit.*, vol. I, p. 169. When Renan printed in 1890 his *Avenir de la Science*, he added in a footnote on p. xi of the Preface: "I left all the passages where I presented the German culture as synonymous with the aspiration toward the ideal. They were true when I wrote them. Not I have changed. Treitschke had not yet taught us that these are only outmoded dreams." See on Renan's attitudes to Germany and England Henri Tronchon, *Ernest Renan et l'étranger* (Paris: Les Belles Lettres, 1928).

4. The word "chauvinisme" was introduced into the European languages from the figure of a veteran, Chauvin, whose memories of the glories of the armies of the Revolution and of Napoleon made him the exponent of fanatical patriotism in a vaudeville "La cocarde tricolore" by Thiand Hippolyte Coigniard in 1831.

5. This criticism is very well made by Monod, *La Vie, op. cit.*, vol. I, p. 197 f.

6. Monod, *op. cit.*, vol. I, p. 268, testified to the power of Michelet's historical writing: "I have just reread the first two volumes of *The History of*

France. I have been as stirred and full of wonder as the first time when I read them at the age of eleven and said to myself: I shall become a historian. Sometimes I hear people say that these volumes are dated. Those who speak so either have not read them or have forgotten them or don't wish to recognize what they owe to these books which were the first to make the history of France alive. They have changed something in our way of understanding history and that forever."

7. Albert Thibaudet, *Histoire de la Littérature Française de 1789 à nos jours* (Paris: Stock, 1936), p. 273.

8. Jean Reynaud, *Terre et Ciel*, 4th ed. (Paris: Furne, 1864) p. 106.—Daniel Stern, *Histoire de la Révolution de 1848* new ed. (Paris: Calmann-Lévy, 1878) vol. I, p. XLVIII. On Lamennais see Waldemar Gurian, *Die politischen und sozialen Ideen des französischen Katholizismus 1789–1914* (M. Gladbach: Volksvereins-Verlag, 1929) pp. 101–184. The poem of Victor Hugo is the last verse from "Ce que dit la bouche d'ombre" in "Les Contemplations" Bk. VI, written in exile after 1848. The mood of the July days 1830 was also well expressed by Victor Hugo in the first poem "Dicté après juillet 1830" of his "Les chants du crépuscule," in which he addressed the young men of July as the heirs of the wars of the Revolution and of Napoleon, of the glories of Austerlitz, Moscow, Cadiz, Rome and Cairo:

> Vous êtes bien leurs fils! c'est leur sang, c'est leur âme
> Qui fait vos bras d'airain et vos regards de flamme.
> Ils ont tout commencé; vous avez votre tour.
> Votre mère, c'est bien cette France féconde
> Qui fait, quand il lui plaît, pour l'exemple du monde,
> Tenir un siècle dans un jour.

>   .   .   .

> Oh! L'avenir est magnifique!
> Jeunes Français, jeunes amis,
> Un siècle pur et pacifique
> S'ouvre à vos pas mieux affermis.
> Chaque jour aura sa conquête.
> Depuis la base jusqu'au faite,
> Nous verrons avec majesté,
> Comme une mer sur ses rivages,
> Monter d'étages en étages
> L'irrésistible liberté!

> Vos pères, hauts de cent coudées,
> Ont été forts et généreux.
> Les nations intimidées
> Se faisaient adopter par eux.
> Ils ont fait une telle guerre
> Que tous les peuples de la terre
> De la France prenaient le nom,

Quittaient leur passé qui s'écroule,
Et venaient s'abriter en foule
À l'ombre de Napoléon!

Vous n'avez pas l'âme embrasée
D'une moins haute ambition.
Faites libre toute pensée
Et reine toute nation;
Montrez la liberté dans l'ombre
À ceux qui sont dans la nuit sombre;
Allez, éclairez le chemin.
Guidez notre marche unanime,
Et faites, vers le but sublime,
Doubler le pas au genre humain.

9. Michelet characterized his teaching at the Collège de France in its activism and its glorification of the people: "Ce qui a caractérisé le nouvel enseignement tel qu'il parut au Collège de France, 1840–1850, c'est la force de sa foi, l'effort pour tirer de l'histoire, non une doctrine seulement, mais un principe d'action, pour créer plus que des esprits, mais des âmes et des volontés. . . . Ces cours qu'on pourrait nommer de physiologie sociale dirent comment la plante humaine, l'arbre de vie part d'en bas, de l'obscure, mais toute puissante inspiration populaire. Ils posèrent le droit du peuple. De là mon livre de ce nom. De là ma Révolution; et je dirai, tous mes écrits. Cette ardente recherche du droit m'imposait de pénétrer dans l'intelligence de l'esprit des masses, plus qu'on n'avait fait encore, bien plus, m'obligeait à refaire, à ressusciter ces vieux âges. Berthelot a dit en chemie, cette parole féconde: On ne sait que ce qu'on refait. Ces mots, c'est ma méthode même. Voilà pourquoi j'ai nommé l'histoire: Resurrection." Of one of his lectures on the Jesuits, on May 11, 1843, he wrote: "On vit auprès de moi Quinet and Mickiewicz, l'un à droite, l'autre à gauche, proclamant notre concorde et donnant à cette jeunesse le plus beau spectacle du monde, celui de la grande amitié. Saint nom de l'harmonie des coeurs, sous lequel si heureusement nos pères mêlaient deux choses: la fraternité d'hommes, la fraternité de patrie! Entre la Pologne et la France, ayant près de moi, devant moi, tant d'illustres étrangers, Italiens, Hongrois, Allemands, je me sentis dans la poitrine une âme, celle de l'Europe."

10. See Monod, op. cit., vol. II, pp. 105 ff. All important books of Quinet dealt with the religious problem, Génie des religions (1841); Ultramontanisme (1844); Christianisme et la Révolution française (1845); Enseignement du peuple (1850). In a letter to Eugène Sue Quinet proposed in 1856 Unitarianism as the ideal form of Christianity. "Who would not wish that the voice of a French Emerson, of a Channing, would be heard in the midst of our French society, in our provinces, in our workshops?" In his La Révolution Française (1865) he wrote: "Robespierre et les jacobins qui ont eu l'audace de décimer une nation n'ont pas eu l'audace de fermer avec éclat le moyen âge. Leurs violences sont ainsi sans proportions avec l'idée; elles n'en sont que plus intolerables. Les massacres de Moise n'ont

point nui au judaisme, ni ceux de Mahomet au Coran, ni ceux du duc d'Albe au catholicisme, ni ceux de Ziska et d'Henri VIII à la Réforme . . . Les hommes même sans foi, pris en masse, se sont toujours montrés clements pour ceux qui ont versé le sang au nom du ciel. Ils ne gardent leurs sévérités que pour ceux qui, en versant le sang humain, n'ont su y interesser que la terre." (XVI, 7) "Ce qui est rare, c'est de persévérer dans la première ardeur, de ne pas se laisser abattre par sa propre victoire; or, c'est ce qui a manqué le plus aux hommes de la Révolution. Une si grande fureur s'est devorée elle-même. . . . Après cet immense fracas, le silence universel; un éclat formidable, et presque aussitôt un oubli complet de soi-même et des autres. Il semble d'après cela que les révolutions soutenues d'un esprit religieux soient les seules qui n'usent pas les forces humaines." (VI, 14)

11. Monod, *op. cit.*, vol. II, p. 242 f. rightly criticizes these thoughts from Michelet's Foreword to his *History of the Revolution* which are more important to an understanding of Michelet than to that of the history of the past. "All that is no longer history. It is a preface, the appeal to a new revolution, it is the natural preface of that Revolution of 1848 which, born out of the vehement emotions of the people, nourished by enthusiasm, hopes and mirages, led up quite naturally to the days of June, the presidency of Louis Napoleon and the second of December."

12. Quinet dedicated to Michelet his book *Christianisme et Révolution,* stressing that without even talking it over they had so often thought and felt alike. "Cet accord de l'âme a toujours été pour nous la confirmation du vrai: depuis vingt ans ce combat nous réussit; c'est le combat éternel qui ne finira qu'en Dieu."

13. England appeared to him as the land of the status quo, France as the land of movement. He accused the capitalist interests in France—among them the Jews—of being eager for peace and the preservation of the status quo and therefore supporting the government of Louis Philippe and siding with England. *Le Peuple* (*Œuvres Complètes de Michelet. Histoire Sociale* vol. VI, Paris: Calmann-Lévy, n.d.) p. 159. "La France n'a pas l'âme marchande, sauf ses moments anglais, comme celui de Law et celui-ci, qui sont des accès rares." p. 145.

14. Michelet's *Le Peuple* is an important source book for the understanding of modern nationalism, which he dates from the French Revolution. "Loin que les nationalités s'effacent, je les vois chaque jour se caractériser moralement, et, de collections d'hommes qu'elles étaient, devenir des personnes." pp. 295 f.—"Les nations dureront encore s'ils n'ont l'attention de supprimer les villes, les grands centres de civilisation, où les nationalités ont resumé leur génie." p. 297.—"La patrie (la matrie, comme disaient si bien les Doriens) est l'amour des amours. Elle nous apparaît dans nos songes comme une jeune mère adorée, ou comme une puissante nourrice qui nous allaite par millions . . . Faible image! non-seulement elle nous allaite, mais nous contient en soi: In ea movemur et sumus." p. 298.—"Pour nous, quoi qu'il advienne de nous, pauvre ou riche, heureux, malheureux, vivant, et par delà la mort, nous remercierons toujours Dieu, de nous avoir donné cette grande patrie, la France. Et cela, non pas seulement à cause de tant de choses glorieuses qu'elle a faites, mais surtout parce qu'en elle, nous

trouvons à la fois le représentant des libertés du monde et le pays sympathique entre tous, l'initiation à l'amour universel." p. 302.

On France's mission: "Si l'on voulait entasser ce que chaque nation a dépensé de sang, et d'or, et d'efforts de toute sorte, pour les choses desinteressées qui ne devaient profiter qu'au monde, la pyramide de la France irait montant jusqu'au ciel." p. 311—"Et l'armée de la France? c'est la défense du monde, la réserve qu'il lui garde, le jour où les Barbares arriveront, où l'Allemagne, cherchant toujours son unité qu'elle cherche depuis Charlemagne, sera bien obligée ou de nous mettre devant elle ou de se faire contre la liberté l'avant-garde de la Russie." p. 311.

On the education of the child by his father: "Un autre jour, plus tard, quand l'homme s'est un peu fait en lui, son père le prend; grande fête publique, grande foule dans Paris. Il le mène de Notre Dame au Louvre, aux Tuileries, vers l'Arc de Triomphe. D'un toit, d'une terrasse, il lui montre le peuple, l'armée qui passe, les baionnettes frémissantes, le drapeau tricolore . . . Dans les moments d'attente surtout, avant la fête, aux reflets fantastiques de l'illumination, dans ces formidables silences qui se font tout à coup sur le sombre océan du peuple, il se penche, il lui dit: Tiens, mon enfant, regarde; voilà la France, voilà la Patrie! Tout ceci, c'est comme un seul homme. Même âme et même cœur. Tous mourraient pour un seul; et chacun doit aussi vivre et mourir pour tous . . . Ceux qui passent là-bas, qui sont armés, qui partent, ils s'en vont combattre pour nous. Ils laissent là leur père, leur vieille mère, qui auraient besoin d'eux . . . Tu en feras autant, tu n'oublieras jamais que ta mère est la France." p. 317 f.

On the education in the schools: "La patrie d'abord, comme dogme et principe. Puis, la patrie comme légende: nos deux redemptions, par la sainte Pucelle d'Orléans, par la Révolution, l'élan de 92, le miracle du jeune drapeau, nos jeunes généraux admirés, pleurés de l'ennemi, la pureté de Marceau, la magnanimité de Hoche . . . Plus haute encore la gloire de nos assemblés souveraines, le génie pacifique et vraiment humain de 89, quand la France offrit à tous de si bon cœur la liberté, la paix . . . Enfin, par dessus tout, pour suprême leçon, l'immense faculté de dévouement, de sacrifice, que nos pères ont montrée, et comme tant de fois la France a donné sa vie pour le monde." p. 343.

15. The influence of Michelet is very clear in Romain Rolland and his plays of the French Revolution. In his *Le Théâtre du Peuple* (*Cahiers de la Quinzaine*, 5th ser., IV, pp. 123, 128), Rolland wrote entirely in the intention and even the style of Michelet: "L'Épopée nationale est toute neuve pour nous. Nos dramaturges ont negligé le drame du peuple de France. Il y a là un trésor de pensées et de passions, dont il faut ouvrir l'accès aux artistes et à la foule, qui ne le connaissent point ou qui le connaissent mal. Notre peuple a peut-être la plus héroïque histoire du monde, depuis Rome. Rien d'humain ne lui est étranger. D'Attila à Napoléon, des champs Catalauniques à Waterloo, des Croisades à la Convention, les destinées du monde se sont jouées sur son sol. Le cœur de l'Europe a battu dans ses rois, ses penseurs, ses révolutionnaires. Et si grand qu'ait été ce peuple dans tous les domaines de l'esprit, il le fut par-dessus tout dans l'action. L'action fut sa création la plus sublime, sa poésie, son théâtre, son épopée.

Il accomplit ce que d'autres révèrent. . . . Ramenons les Français à leur histoire nationale, comme à une source d'art populaire; mais gardons-nous bien d'exclure la légende historique des autres nations. Sans doute, la nôtre nous est plus immédiatement sensible, et notre premier devoir est de faire valoir le trésor que nous avons reçu de nos pères. Mais que . . . les héros du monde soient aussi les nôtres. Surtout, qu'ils aient chez nous une seconde patrie, ceux qui furent les héros du peuple, dans les autres siècles et les autres pays. Que le Théâtre du Peuple recherche par tout l'univers les lettres de noblesse du Peuple. Elevons à Paris l'Épopée du Peuple européen!"

16. In his course on nationalities he remembered Poland, where in 1846 the uprising of Cracow occurred: "I pray God for the victory of a people of whom we all think. For where is our soul? On the Seine? No. On the Vistula. This great people of the East, awake while all sleep in the West, this people who acts, of whom we have no news, if this people should not be victorious as we all pray, we nevertheless would believe that its cause is legitimate and saintly, and therefore eternal, and must one day in the future triumph." By then Mickiewicz had been recalled from his chair, not through the fault of the highly patient and considerate government of Louis Philippe but because he turned the classroom into a revivalist meeting of messianic expectations.

This great poet, ranking with Pushkin as the greatest poet in any Slav language, who was born in the same year as Michelet, ceased all creative writing at the age of 35, at the very moment that he had finished the greatest masterpiece of Polish literature *Pan Tadeusz*. For the remaining twenty years he devoted himself entirely to religious national propaganda. As a student he had been influenced by Joachim Lelewel, a man who through his work as a historian, a patriot, a radical democrat, occupied a position in Polish cultural life similar to that of Michelet in France. Mickiewicz, after the uprising of 1831, in which he did not participate, became one of the leaders of Polish messianic nationalism. Poland was the Christ among the nations; innocently crucified, but it will rise again and its liberation will become the liberation of mankind. Poland became a symbol of the road to liberty through suffering. Its martyrdom received a meaning. In the pamphlet *Books of the Polish Nation and of the Polish Pilgrims* Mickiewicz was acting as a prophet of a new faith. The *Books of the Polish Nation* are comparable to the historical narrative and the prophecies of the Old Testament. The last sentence reads: "And as after the resurrection of Christ blood sacrifices ceased in all the world, so after the resurrection of the Polish Nation wars shall cease in all Christendom." The *Books of the Polish Pilgrims* were intended to serve as a New Testament of parables and teachings for the Polish pilgrims, "who are the soul of the Polish nation." Poland appeared as the Lazarus among nations. The Poles in exile must be messengers of freedom and preserve their national character.

Mickiewicz later came under the influence of a Polish mystic Andrzej Towianski who regarded himself as the Messiah. Mickiewicz and Towianski shared the worship of Napoleon. In his lectures in the Collège de France Mickiewicz propagated the new faith. In his lecture on January

16, 1844, he said: "Can one deny that the bulletins of the Grand Army are more like the words of Jesus Christ and His apostles than are the discussions that we now hear in churches and schools?" In 1849 Mickiewicz published for a short time a paper *La Tribune des Peuples* which propagated the idea of a holy war for the freedom of the peoples of Europe. See George R. Noyes (ed.), *Poems by Adam Mickiewicz* (New York: Polish Institute of Arts and Sciences, 1944); Waclaw Lednicki, *Life and Culture of Poland* (New York: Roy, 1944); idem, "Mickiewicz at the Collège de France, 1840–1940," *The Slavonic Review*, vol. XX (1941), pp. 149–172; Manfred Kridl in Stephen P. Mizwa (ed.) *Great Men and Women of Poland* (New York: Macmillan, 1942), pp. 190–204.

17. Michelet's problem was to find a way to make Frenchmen love each other even after the June days. "Dans ce cadre j'enseignais le lendemain de la guerre civile, à aimer encore, finissant les discordes de religions, de races." —"J'entreprends une chose difficile, insensée, le lendemain d'un pareil déchirement, de vouloir que les hommes aiment encore. Le Moyen-Âge dure encore, et empêche de comprendre la vraie nature de l'amour. Il veut l'imposer. Mais le désir d'amour, c'est le respect de la liberté." Monod, *op. cit.*, vol. II, pp. 250 ff.

18. "Ce qu'on peut appeller l'anti-France, l'Angleterre." *Le Peuple, op. cit.*, p. 307.

19. Michelet visited England in 1834. Of his impressions Monod, *op. cit.*, vol. I, pp. 330 ff. writes: "Michelet sentait bien, d'ailleurs, que cette ruine de l'Angleterre, qu'il prévoyait et desirait peut-être (Talleyrand, plus judicieux, disait déjà en 1834 que la prosperité de la France était liée à celle de l'Angleterre), n'était pas près de se produire, et, rentré en France, il éprouve un sentiment d'humiliation en comparant notre indigence à l'opulence britannique. . . . Dans les notes qu'il consacre à l'Angleterre, de 1834 à 1839, Michelet revient constamment sur ces pensées: 'Nous sommes, dit-il, pour l'alliance anglaise plutôt que russe, car c'est la cause de la civilisation.' Il sent la grandeur de l'Angleterre et concède que le niveau moral moyen de la population y est plus élevé qu'ailleurs; . . . Malgré les efforts qu'il fait pour rendre justice aux Anglais, malgré son admiration pour 'cette grandeur orientale dans les brumes du Nord' . . . il éprouve une insurmontable aversion à son égard. Il lui faut la vue d'Oxford pour calmer en lui la revolte du souvenir que tous les monuments de Londres reveillent: 'Waterloo, Waterloo, partout!' . . . Les évenements de 1840, la dure humiliation infligée à la France par l'Angleterre, reveillèrent toute l'animosité de Michelet. Surtout il fut indigné quand, aussitôt après, il vit, sous l'influence de Guizot, l'Entente cordiale devenir le pivot même de notre politique étrangère, et l'anglomanie sévir à la cour, dans la politique, la societé mondaine et la littérature."

Lamartine wrote in 1836 to Michelet: "J'ai pensé et j'ai dit que l'alliance anglaise, pour la communauté de principes, était normale et nécéssaire à nous comme à l'equilibre européen, mais qu'un jour viendrait où, si cette alliance était trop exigeante, nous pourrions appuyer le levier de notre diplomatie sur la Russie et être les arbitres du monde et compléter notre territoire en concédant en Orient ce que la fatalité concède." Jean-Marie Carré, *Michelet et son temps*, p. 10. In his later days Lamartine insisted on

Anglo-French collaboration. He asked that all old quarrels be forgotten and declared an Anglo-French hostility in the 19th century as meaningless as massacres between Armagnacs and Bourguinons. He demanded "le culte constant et avoué de cette paix plus glorieuse pour les deux pays que leurs plus belles victoires." See A. de Lamartine, *Lettres des années sombres 1853–1867.* (Fribourg: Librairie de l'Université, 1942).

20. *Histoire du XIX siècle* vol. II, Preface (*Oeuvres Complètes* vol. XXV, p. 9). On November 16, 1872 Michelet wrote a letter to Darwin regarding the tunnel under the Channel: "Un pont se fait entre les deux nations. Les deux grands génies nationaux se reconnaissent enfin."

21. Jean-Marie Carré, *op. cit.,* pp. 197–205.

22. See Jean-Marie Carré, *op. cit.,* pp. 227 ff. The appeal contains the following sentences: "Si la victoire favorise l'unité allemande sous le militarisme prussien, l'Allemagne sera, selon la pensée d'un de ses grands publicistes, un danger permanent pour les nations voisines, et nous nous trouverons au commencement d'une periode de guerre qui menace de nous rejeter aux plus tristes époques du Moyen Âge.

"Que si c'est la France qui est victorieuse sous le césarisme napoléonien, elle n'échappera jamais, quoi qu'elle fasse, au soupçon de vouloir recommencer l'ère de Louis XIV ou de Napoléon Ier.

"Cette guerre, engendrée elle-même par celle de 1866, engendrera donc la guerre encore et conduira nécessairement à l'apogée du despotisme militaire. . . ."

23. In 1832 Quinet analyzed the situation in the following words: "Si nous nous representons l'Allemagne, c'est encore l'Allemagne de Mme. de Staël, l'Allemagne d'il y a cinquante ans, un pays d'extase, un rêve continuel, une science qui se cherche toujours, un envirement de théorie, tout le génie d'un peuple noyé dans l'infini, voilà pour les classes éclairées; puis des sympathies romanesques, un enthousiasme toujours prêt, un donquichottisme cosmopolite, voilà pour les generations nouvelles; puis l'abnégation du piétisme, le renoncement à l'influence sociale, la satisfaction d'un bien-être mystique, le travail des sectes religieuses, du bonheur et des fêtes à vil prix, une vie de patriarche, des destinées qui coulent sans bruit, comme les flots du Rhin et du Danube, mais point de centre nulle part, point de lien, point de désir, point d'esprit public, point de force nationale, voilà pour le fond du pays. Par malheur tout cela est changé. Comme la Révolution française a constitué dans l'Etat les theories flottantes du dix-huitième siècle, ainsi les nations germaniques marchent aujourd'hui à grands pas vers la réalisation des principes abstraits qu'elles ont mis près de cinquante ans à etablir chez elles.

"Ces considérations, qui s'étendent à toute l'Allemagne, sont surtout vraies de la Prusse. C'est là que l'ancienne impartialité et le cosmopolitisme politique ont fait place à une nationalité irritable et colère, et que l'empressement a été grand à se défaire de l'admiration que la Révolution de 1830 avait reconquise à la France. C'est là que le parti démagogique a fait d'abord sa paix avec le pouvoir, à la condition de reprendre les provinces d'Alsace et de Lorraine. C'est qu'en effet, ce gouvernement donne aujourd'hui à l'Allemagne ce dont elle est le plus avide, l'action, la vie réelle, l'initiative sociale. Il satisfait outre mesure son engouement subit pour la puissance et la force matérielle, et elle lui sait gré de montrer que, sous ce nuage idéal où on se l'était toujours figurée, elle sait au besoin forger comme un autre des armes et des trophées de bronze. Au premier aspect, il est étonnant que le seul gouvernement populaire, au delà du Rhin, soit presque le seul despotique dans sa forme; mais ce despotisme n'est pas le despotisme hébété de l'Autriche; c'est un despotisme intelligent, remuant, entreprenant, auquel il ne manque encore qu'un homme qui regarde et connait son étoile en plein jour; il vit de science autant qu'un autre d'ignorance. Entre le peuple et lui, il y a une entente secrète pour ajourner la liberté et mettre en commun leurs ambitions à la poursuite de la fortune de Frédéric. Pour le reste de l'Allemagne, ce despotisme est plus menacant que celui de l'Autriche; car il n'est pas seulement dans le gouvernement, il est dans le pays, il est dans le peuple, dans les moeurs et le ton parvenu de l'esprit national; et puis il ne veut pas seulement durer et s'accroupir, comme sur les bords du Danube.

"Au contraire, le despotisme prussien ne perd pas des yeux les destinées intérieures des nations germaniques; c'est sur elles qu'il veut peser sciemment; il faut qu'il les envahisse de haute lutte par l'intelligence, et puis plus tard par la force, s'il le peut. Autant on aime le silence à Vienne, autant lui a besoin de fracas; il veut faire du bruit et il en fait, car il est vain, vif, prêt à tout; de plus, il a des idées à lui, il a des systèmes à lui, une philosophie, une science et des sectes à lui; il réunit, on ne peut le nier, ce qu'il y a au monde de plus pratique et de plus idéal, de mieux ordonné et de plus devergonde, et prouve à merveille que le soin des intérêts les plus matériels peut trouver des accommodements avec cet éclat de théorie et cette préoccupation de l'infini, dont ce pays, pour son honneur, ne se defera jamais."

He understood the strength and the justification of the demand for unity. "Cette pensée est l'unité du territoire de la patrie allemande, ce cri est l'abolition des frontières artificielles, le renversement des limites arbitraires, derrière lesquelles ils sont parqués, eux et leurs produits; sans échange, sans lien, sans industrie possible, chacun obligé de se suffire à lui-même et d'enfouir sa misère dans un coin, comme après la guerre de Trente ans. . . . Il faut bien savoir que la plaie du traité de Westphalie et la cession des provinces d'Alsace et de Lorraine saignent encore au cœur de l'Allemagne, autant qu'à nous nos traités de 1815, et que, dans ce peuple qui rumine si longtemps ses souvenirs, on la trouve, cette plaie, au fond de tous ses projets et de toutes ses rancunes d'hier."

In 1836 he wrote: "Les Allemands, révélés par leurs poètes, ont été, dans ces derniers temps, l'objet d'une idolatrie qui tend à les corrompre. Qu'est devenue l'humilité qu'ils avaient conservée jusqu'au dix-huitième siècle? Une susceptibilité ombrageuse et hargneuse tourmente incessamment ces nouveaux rois de l'opinion. Leur prétention, comme celle de tous les heros de romans, soit qu'on les loue, soit qu'on les blame, est de n'être jamais compris de leurs adorateurs; et personne ne nie qu'ils ne s'arrangent parfaitement pour cela. S'il se trouvait même à la fin, quelque part, un jugement sur eux vrai et impartial, je doute fort qu'ils s'en montrassent satisfaits; car ce jugement, supposé qu'il fut exact, serait une limite à l'idolatrie; quand on a été Dieu un jour, on tient à son nuage. . . . Le docteur Faust a quitté sa cellule, il a quitté ses livres et son creuset; il a réjeté loin de lui la tête de mort qui ajoutait à ses pensées enthousiastes le serieux du tombeau. Le docteur s'est fait vif; il court au bal en chapeau brodé; il est galant, leste, musqué. Seulement avec son manteau de philosophe, il a oublié au logis son âme et son imagination. Quel magicien pourrait les lui rendre?"

24. Paul Gautier, *Un Prophète: Edgar Quinet* (Paris: Plon, 1917), p. 30 f. The book is a careful re-edition of Quinet's remarkable articles on Germany.

25. One of the soundest analyses of the consequences of the Franco-Prussian War was written by Frederic Harrison, the English humanitarian and radical, who consistently advocated the rights of small peoples and subject races. In *The Fortnightly Review* he wrote in December, 1870, an article "Bismarckism." Many of its sentences, written when the German armies besieged Paris, sound strangely prophetic today: "It is pitiful to hear the grounds on which the issues at stake are so often decided. . . . To besiege Paris is what it would be to besiege Berlin, if it were fortified. . . . The annexation of two provinces is not to be counted as a crime merely since it is done at the expense of a republic. . . . The familiar picture of the German soldier, with the inevitable three children at home, writing letters to his wife between the pauses of each battle, and studying his pocket copy of the Vedas on the outposts, is striking; but it is not decisive on a question of boundaries. . . . These fathers of families and model husbands can burn down villages on system, set fire to farmhouses with petroleum, massacre a village in cold blood by superior order. . . . There is not the smallest reason to suppose that either the French or the German people would deliberately have chosen a war of conquest. It is this which makes the war peculiarly the crime of Napoleon and his civil and military abettors. . . . Even the Government never pretended to make, and never dreamed of making, this a war for the Rhine frontier. A victory, the shadow of a success, and a plausible ground for peace, was all that they dreamt of. . . . In this state of things the war began and no one desired more earnestly than the present writer that the Germans might repel the iniquitous invasion, and destroy the military power and prestige of the Empire. . . . The gain to civilisation in the extinction of Napoleonism, and of the wretched impostor in whom it has ended forever, in the disgrace which has covered the corrupt army he had created, is almost a sufficient compensation to France and to Europe for all the sufferings of this war. . . . What does all this portend to Europe? It is of little use to weigh out the relative measure of guilt in either Government, or the degree in which their people participated in it. . . . We have protested so fiercely against the military ambition of France, that we have come to forget there is such a thing as military ambition outside France at all. But what is Prussia? The Prussian monarchy is the creation of war. Its history, its traditions, its ideal are simply those of war. It is the sole European kingdom which has been built up, province by province, on the battle-field, cemented stone by stone in blood. Its kings have been soldiers: sometimes generals, sometimes, as now, drill sergeants; but ever soldiers. The whole state organisation from top to bottom is military. Its people are

a drilled nation of soldiers on furlough: its sovereign is simply com-
mander-in-chief; its aristocracy are simply officers of the staff; its capital
is a camp. . . . Unhappily this gospel of the sword has sunk deeper into
the entire Prussian people than any other in Europe. . . . It is entirely
forgotten that individual is a very different thing from national character.
And the quiet or jovial Hans of his own fireside, under a complex set of
national institutions, becomes, as the unit of a nation, one of a conquering
people. . . . I say it most deliberately that Germany is now carrying on
war with inhuman cruelty. War so savage, torture so steadily inflicted on
a civil community, has never been seen within two generations in Europe
—save once. That once was the Russian war of extermination in Poland.
It rests on the German race, with their pretended culture, to have carried
into the heart of Western Europe the horrible traditions of Eastern barbarism. . . . The Germans, though they do not love cruelty, are perfectly
capable of it to meet their ends; and indeed take to it with a calm inward
satisfaction, and a businesslike completeness, which is more horrible even
than the excesses of passion. . . . On them, and on their children, will
remain the curse of reviving in modern Europe the most bloody and
barbarous traditions of the past—the wholesale wasting of an enemy's
country, and the systematic massacre of civilians. . . . Now it is not necessary to suppose that Prussia is about to overrun Europe with her troops
as she is overrunning France. That is not the danger. . . . But what is to
be feared is the passing of the undisputed supremacy of force to such a
power as Prussia—organised exclusively for war, retrograde, feudal,
despotic—more unscrupulous and ambitious than Napoleonism itself."

In the February 1871 issue of *The Fortnightly Review*, Harrison published another article "The Effacement of England" where he wrote:
"Condemn, as we may, the national faults of France, denounce, as we
please, their pretension to supremacy in Europe (a pretension exactly
equivalent to that which England makes to maritime supremacy), we must
still feel that in no other nation does there exist a public opinion so akin to
our own, and at the same time so completely in the ascendant. . . . The
new Empire of Germany is thus, in its origin, a menace to Europe. The
house of Hohenzollern, with its traditions of aggrandisement, with its
consummate bureaucratic machinery and its bodyguard of a warlike caste,
can never be the titular chief of peaceful industrial German kingdoms. It
is no case of chance personal despotism, or mushroom revolutionary ad-
venture. It is a great power, whose roots go deep into every pore of the
two upper-classes of German society. It is arbitrary, military, fanatical.
In one word, it is the enemy of modern progress. Though not representing
the German people, it has debauched and mastered the German people.
Six months of this gigantic war have turned the flower of the German
citizens into professional troopers. The very fact that they have as a
nation submitted to the military yoke, the fact that every German is a
soldier, is itself a proof of a lower type of civilisation, and marks them as
a nation capable of becoming a curse to their neighbours."

26. Ernest Renan, *La Réforme Intellectuelle et Morale* (Paris: Michel Lévy,
1872), p. 119 f.
27. Charles Renouvier wrote: "Neither in politics nor in religion, neither at

home nor abroad, has France, taking her national life as a whole, been the initiator or even the chief factor of modern civilization. Her sole claim to honor is the universalist and liberally human character of the eighteenth-century philosophy, and her repeated, though ineffectual, attempts to raise her practice to the level of that ideal." Quoted in Roger Soltau, *op. cit.*, p. 317.

NOTES TO CHAPTER THREE

1. Mazzini wrote to his mother on September 25, 1838: "I did not find the world as I would have wanted it to be; this is common to many men; but what is not common to all is that I cannot accommodate myself to the world as it is." Thirty years later, on July 6, 1869, he wrote to Mrs. Hamilton King: "I do believe—could you doubt it for one moment?—in Eternal Life. The belief is the very soul of all my political, social and religious ideas. The earnestness with which I have endeavored to look at our own terrestrial phase of existence, and the feeling of duty which has accompanied me through it, have their root in that belief. . . . Without that belief, I would have despaired and fled to suicide long ago."

2. Vincenzo Gioberti's *Del primato morale e civile degli Italiani* was published in two volumes in Brussels in 1843. When Mazzini read the book he wrote to his mother on June 16, 1843, that the subject of the book was *il più bel tema che io conosca*, but he rejected utterly its pro-papal and federalist tendency. See on Gioberti, A. Anzilotti, *Vincenzo Gioberti* (Florence: Vallecchi, 1923); Giuliano Balbino, *Il primato d'un popolo: Fichte e Gioberti* (Catania: Battiato, 1916); Giovanni Faldella, *Profeti massimi* (Torino: Lattes, 1910) on Gioberti and Mazzini. Gioberti later, as a result of his experiences in 1848, developed into a liberal and published in 1851 his second great book *Del rinnovamento civile d'Italia.*

3. "Nella nazionalità italiana si fondano adunque gl'interessi della religione a le speranze civili e universali del mondo, l'Italia è il popolo eletto, il popolo tipico, il popolo creatore, l'Israele dell' età moderna." In *Il Gesuita moderno* (Lausanne, 1846-47), vol. V, p. 461, quoted in Robert Michels, *Der Patriotismus* (Munich: Duncker & Humblot, 1929), p. 14.

4. The best studies on Mazzini are Gaetano Salvemini, *Mazzini* (Catania: Battiato, 1915) and Alessandro Levi, *La filosofia politica di Giuseppe Mazzini* (Bologna: Zanichelli, 1917). Both books are written by Mazzinians, heirs to his democratic aspirations; Salvemini's volume, however, not without the critical judgment of a rational humanist. The book was published in a collection of writings called *La Giovine Europa*, dedicated to discussing the oppressed peoples striving towards their regeneration. It has been reissued since (4th ed. Florence, 1925). From the fascist point of view see Giovanni Gentile, *I Profeti del Risorgimento* (Florence: Vallecchi, 1923), two articles on Mazzini and Gioberti, published in 1919 and issued as a book dedicated "a Benito Mussolini, Italiano di razza, degno di ascoltare le voci dei profeti della nuova Italia." Excellent critical appraisals of Mazzini are found in Luigi Salvatorelli, *Il pensiero politico Italiano dal 1700 al 1870* (Turin: Einaudi, 1935) and Guido de Ruggiero, *The History of European Liberalism* (London: Oxford University Press, 1927). Bolton King, *The Life of Mazzini* (Everyman's) and Gwilym O. Griffith, *Mazzini: Prophet of Modern Europe* (London: Hodder and Stoughton,

1932) are the best biographies in English. In German see Otto Vossler, *Mazzinis politisches Denken und Wollen in den geistigen Strömungen seiner Zeit* (Munich: Oldenbourg, 1927).

Mazzini's writings were published as *Scritti editi ed inediti* in 18 vols., the first 8 vols. (Milano 1861–1871) with Mazzini's participation, the last 10 vols. (Rome 1877–1891) after his death. The first 7 vols. were translated into English (somewhat abbreviated) as *Life and Writings of Joseph Mazzini*, 6 vols., new ed. (London: Smith, Elder & Co. 1890–91). A very useful collection of his most important writings appeared under the title *The Duties of Man and other Essays* in Everyman's Library. The most complete edition of his writings and letters is the *Edizione Nazionale* (Nuola 1905 ff.)

Mazzini was an active though not successful editor and publisher of newspapers. Their names were programs: *La Giovine Italia* (Marseilles and Switzerland, 1832–1836); *La Jeune Suisse* (Bienne 1835–1836); *L'Apostolato Popolaro* (London 1840–1843); *L'Italia del Popolo* (Milan 1848, Rome 1849; Lausanne and Lugano 1849–1850); *Pensiero ed Azione* (London 1858–1860); *La Roma del Popolo* (1870–1872)—they all mark decisive stages in his life.

5. The General Instructions for the Members of Young Italy and the Manifesto of Young Italy can be found in *Life and Writings*, vol. I, pp. 96–113, 117–128, 234–245.

6. Before 1830 Mazzini was a cosmopolitan liberal. He wrote in an article "Of an European Literature" in 1829: "A community of desires and wants does exist in Europe; a common thought, a universal mind, is leading the nations through different paths to one and the same goal. Literature, therefore—if it is not to sink into triviality—must identify itself with this general tendency; must express, assist and direct it, must become European." He maintained that Italy has long ceased to possess a literature of her own, and that she must reform her laws of taste in order to create a literature which shall express the one universal principle. Poetry had to unite the different nations, awaken the spirit of international love, break down every barrier to human brotherhood and sing the passions that are universal. The source of inspiration has to be the universal and the human, beauty and joy. *Life and Writings*, vol. II, pp. 4–48.

7. As Mazzini opposed art for its own sake, so he also opposed philosophy for its own sake. In a letter to Daniel Stern on January 1, 1865, he wrote that philosophy will never be able to fill the religious void, because it lacks "ce souffle de vie qui, renouvelant, agrandissant la Morale, décrète le devoir et pousse les hommes à l'action." Art and philosophy have to serve the same purpose: prepare men for moral action.

Mazzini treated history and economics as he treated art. In 1861, when he republished the article "On the Unity of Italy," he tried to reinterpret Italian history from the point of view that "unity ever was the destiny of Italy." He saw the whole history of the peninsula for the last 2,500 years as leading up to a united Italian nation. He wished to write such a history of Italy, to sustain the unity of the country "upon the firm basis of history and tradition." Like art and philosophy, history had to serve the nationalist purpose. In the economic field Mazzini rejected socialism as internationalist and materialist. He demanded the harmony of the classes in national union and proposed a far-reaching program of social betterment for the Italian workers.

8. This was written in 1861. In the Preface to *Life and Writings*, vol. I, Mazzini declared that all individual biography appeared insignificant "in the face of the re-awakening of that people to whom alone God has as yet granted the privilege, in each great epoch of its own existence, of transforming Europe." In the Roman Assembly in 1849 Mazzini declared: "For what little of good I may have accomplished, or attempted, has owed its inspiration to my life's talisman, Rome. In my heart I have said, It is not possible that the City that has already lived two lives should not rise to see a third. After the Rome of conquering soldiers, after the Rome of the triumphant Word, so I kept saying to myself, there shall come the Rome of virtue and example; after the City of the Emperors, after that of the Popes, shall come that of the People." In "The Duties of Man" he wrote in 1858, addressing the Italian workingmen and speaking of the time when they will advance in beautiful and holy concord toward the fulfillment of the Italian mission, which is the moral unity of Europe: "Italy is the only land that has twice uttered the great word of unification to the disjoined nations. Twice Rome has been the metropolis, the temple of the European world; the first time when our conquering eagles traversed the known world from end to end and prepared it for union by introducing civilized institutions; the second time when, after the Northern conquerors had themselves been subdued by the potency of Nature, of great memories and of religious inspiration, the genius of Italy incarnated itself in the Papacy and undertook the solemn mission—abandoned four centuries ago—of preaching the union of souls to the peoples of the Christian world. To-day a third mission is dawning for our Italy; as much vaster than those of old as the Italian People, the free and united Country which you are going to found, will be greater and more powerful than Caesars or Popes. The presentiment of this mission agitates Europe and keeps the eye and the thought of the nations chained to Italy."

9. *Life and Writings*, vol. III, pp. 26–34. See also Hans Gustav Keller, *Das Junge Europa 1834–1836. Eine Studie zur Geschichte der Völkerbundsidee und des nationalen Gedankens* (Zurich: Max Niehans, 1938).

10. Mazzini confined his vision to Europe. He never thought of demanding national rights for the peoples of Asia or Africa. They were to him the field of the colonizing and civilizing mission of the European nations, especially of Britain and Russia. He saw as England's mission "industry and colonies," as Russia's mission "colonization of Asia." He wished to turn Russia away from Europe. He expected the liberation of all the Slav peoples under the "yoke" of Russia, Turkey and Austria, and he assigned the initiative for the liberation of the Slavs not to the Russian "oppressor" nation but to Poland, which would take the initiative of liberating herself and all the other "oppressed" Slavs. Mazzini opposed Ireland's separation from England and the constitution of an Irish nationality.

11. The map of Europe was to be reconstructed "in accordance with the special mission assigned to each people by its geographical, ethnographi-

cal, and historical conditions," an extremely arbitrary and indefinite criterion. Mazzini, who talked so much about the "mission" of each nationality, never was able to define that mission or to say clearly in what it consisted. But he can say dogmatically that the "incapacity of the French to advance appears to be a historical necessity" (!), that the "historic law (!) forbade (!) the onward march of France." (*Life and Works*, vol. I, p. 191 f.)

12. "The People! The People! It is a cry of the age, a cry of the millions eager to advance—the cry of the new epoch that gains upon us apace. All hail to the people! for they are the elect of God, chosen by Him to fulfill His law of universal love, association, and emancipation." To the poets of the nineteenth century he declaimed: "This yearning of the human mind toward an indefinite progress; this force that urges the generations onward toward the future; this impulse of universal association; this banner of young Europe waving on every side; this varied, multiform, endless warfare everywhere going on against tyranny; this cry of the nations arising from the dust to reclaim their rights, and call their rulers to account for the injustice and oppression of ages; this crumbling of ancient dynasties at the breath of the people; this anathema upon old creeds, this restless search after new; this youthful Europe springing from the old, like the moth from the chrysalis; this glowing life arising in the midst of death, this world in resurrection;—is not this poetry?"

13. Otto Vossler, *op. cit.*, p. 81 f., points out the similarity between Mazzini's and Fichte's concepts.

14. Mazzini always attacked England's policy of isolation and not intervening in Europe's affairs. In 1845 he published a letter to the British Home Secretary, Sir James Graham, in which he demanded English intervention for the Italians, the Poles, etc., to help to redraw the map of Europe, otherwise the new nationalities will be born without any "homogeneity of tendencies, recollections of gratitude, no germs of sympathy" for England. On the European continent a life and death struggle between the forces of evil and those of good was going on; how could England remain a neutral spectator? *Life and Writings*, vol. III, pp. 197–262. In an address in London to the Council of the People's International League he declared a policy of isolation morally wrong and politically imprudent. *Ibidem*, vol. VI, p. 287. In an article written in England in 1851 he said: "The principle of non-intervention in the affairs of other nations is a product of the negative and purely critical (egoistic) spirit of the last century." *Ibidem*, p. 300. An article on Europe in the *Westminster Review* in 1852 ended with a plea for Anglo-American cooperation in the cause of liberty in Europe. He reported a voice from America declaring that America will not tolerate the triumph of evil on the continent of Europe. "We will no longer give Cain's answer to God, who has made us free." And Mazzini continued: "Let England accept it and rebaptize her alliance with America by a policy worthy of both. The laying of the first stone of the religious temple of humanity which we all foresee, is a labor well worthy the cooperation of the two worlds." *Ibidem*,

p. 264 f. See also his article of 1871 printed in *The Fortnightly Review*, April 1877, p. 570 f.
15. Mazzini wrote as early as December 25, 1838, to Mme. Lisette Mandrot (*Ed. Naz.* XV, p. 323): "Je sympathise plus que je ne saurais l'exprimer avec l'Allemagne; j'ai foi en elle; mais je ne puis voir, sans une sorte d'irritation, cet esprit exclusif, monopoliste, et fanfaron que nous avons tous attaqué en France se montrer aujourd'hui dans les écrivains patriotes allemands. Quand on a assisté, les bras croisés, aux efforts de l'Italie, aux luttes de la Pologne, et au martyre de toute une jeunesse en Europe qui se poursuit en detail depuis cinquante ans, sans protester autrement que par l'émeute de Francfort, il ne faut pas venir nous dire, que l'Allemagne porte les destinées du monde en son sein: qu'à elle seule est donné de sauver l'Europe, et que ce sera en renversant une troisième fois Rome que cela se fera. Il n'y aurait pas beaucoup de gloire à s'ébranler pour renverser un fantôme; et quant à avoir renversé deux fois Rome pour sauver le monde, il nous est permis, à nous Italiens, de remarquer que le Nord est bien plutôt venu chez nous prendre son étincelle de vie, puisqu'il a vécu pendant seize siècles de la parole d'unité sortie de Rome. N'allez pas croire, Madame, que je deviens réactionnaire et nationaliste à mon tour; non; mais je sens que l'Italie a plus souffert que l'Allemagne pendant ce tiers de siècle, et je n'aime pas qu'on l'oublie, quand ce n'est pas pour faire mieux."
16. In the "Program" of 1871 Mazzini explained the title of his organ by repeating sentences he had written as long ago as 1844: "This Unity all pray for can come, Italians, whatever men may do, from your country alone, and you can only write it on the flag, which is destined to shine on high above those two military columns that mark the course of thirty centuries and more in the world's life—the Capitol and the Vatican. ROME OF THE CAESARS gave the Unity of civilization that force imposed on Europe. ROME OF THE POPES gave a Unity of civilization that authority imposed on a great part of the human race. ROME OF THE PEOPLE will give, when you Italians are nobler than you are now, a Unity of civilization accepted by the free consent of the nations for Humanity."
17. "Suprema su tutti i calcoli, su tutte le tattiche umane, viva una legge morale que i Popoli non violano impunamente," *Scritti*, vol. X, p. 303.
18. Mazzini published in the *Foreign Quarterly Review* of 1844 a long article "On the Minor Works of Dante," *Life and Writings*, vol. IV, pp: 145–203. Unhistorically he made Italian nationalism the central idea and moving force of Dante's life. He read Mazzini into Dante. And he spoke really about himself when he wrote: "He who bore within himself the soul of Italy was misunderstood by the whole nation, but he did not yield; he wrestled nobly against the external world and ended by conquering it. . . . He concerned himself not about the length or the shortness of life, but about the end for which life was given; for he felt God in life, and knew the creative virtue there is in action. He wrote as he would have acted, and the pen in his hand became like a sword." The article concludes with the expectation that the country will inscribe on the base of his statue: "The Italian Nation To The Memory Of Its Prophet."

Dante was more of an imperialist than a nationalist, glorifying Rome as chosen by God for empire, distinguishing races apt to govern and apt for subjection and praising empire as fulfilling the common good by subjecting the world.

See also on Mazzini and Dante Sydney M. Brown, "Mazzini and Dante," *Political Science Quarterly*, vol. XLII (1927) pp. 77–98.

From his spiritualist point of view, Mazzini rejected all racial or biological interpretations of nationality. "Le razze, per Mazzini, non avrebbero nessun valore per la costituzione della nazionalità, se non intervenisse la coscienza e la volontà degli uomini. Il principio della nazionalità, come forma morale dell' esistenza del popolo, non è nella nature, ma nello spirito." *Enciclopedia Italiana*, vol. XXII, p. 654.

19. Published in English translation in *The Fortnightly Review*, April 1877, p. 569.

20. *Ibidem*, pp. 573–577. Mazzini demanded that Italy take the initiative, addressing the small Slav nations as follows: "We who have ourselves arisen in the name of our national right, believe in your right, and offer to help you to win it. But the purpose of our mission is the permanent and peaceful organization of Europe. We cannot allow Russian Tzarism—a perennial menace to Europe—to step into the place now occupied by your masters, and no partial movement executed by a single element amongst you can be victorious; nor, even were victory possible, could it constitute a strong barrier against the avidity of the Tzar: it would simply further his plans of aggrandizement. Unite, therefore; forget past rancor, and unite in one confederation; let Constantinople be your Amphictyonic city, the center of your federative power, free to all and servant to none." Such a Slav confederation would play an important role in the balance of Europe and preserve its peace. It would protect Germany from Russia and Russia from Germany. But it would also protect France "from the dangerous predominance of the Teutons. And Italy allied with the Slavs, who are unfriendly to Germany, would, if necessary, threaten the invader in the rear."

21. *Ibidem*, p. 579.

22. "La religione di patria è santissima; ma dove il sentimento della dignità individuale, e la coscienza di diretti inerenti alla natura d'uomo non la governino—dove il cittadino non si convinca che egli deve dar lustro alla patria, non ritrarlo da essa,—è religione che può far la patria potente, non felice; bella di gloria davanti allo straniero, non libera." (*Ed. Naz.*, vol. II, p. 191.)

23. To Thomas Mann, Mazzini appeared as the typical Western liberal with his emphasis on political virtue, democracy, equality, republicanism, completely alien to the German mind. See *Betrachtungen eines Unpolitischen* (Berlin: Fischer, 1920), pp. 392–394, 570. At the end of October 1917 Mann greeted the Italian defeat at Caporetto as a great liberating act. It was to him "the defeat of Mazzini and of d'Annunzio, of the democratic-republican rabble-rouser and rhetor and of the literary-political dandy and clown, both of whom I hate out of the depths of my heart." (*Ibidem*, p. 544 f.) In *The Magic Mountain* Mann is infinitely more sym-

pathetic to the representative of Western democracy, Settembrini, who is a spiritual descendant of Mazzini.

24. Mazzini discussed the problem of the French Revolution repeatedly, so in his "Faith in the Future" in 1835 and in his "Thoughts on the French Revolution of 1789" in the *Roma del Popolo* in 1871. The French Revolution appeared to him as the consummation of the age of Christianity. Mazzini thought this age concluded. In 1835 he wrote: "All our hearts and intellects have the presentiment of a great Age." In 1871: "If I am right, the Christian Age is concluded. We have another conception of Life, and travel in search of a new earth and a new heaven." He shared the feeling of Heine and Ibsen that the Christian Age was terminated and a Third Age approaching, an expectation going back to the Italian mystic of the twelfth century, Joachim of Flora.

25. See the criticism by Guido de Ruggiero, *op. cit.*, p. 314 f. "The social, political and religious problems in which Mazzini was generally interested, really concerned England and France more than Italy. His political and religious mysticism . . . forms as it were a secondary branch of the Reformation and is foreign to Italy, the country in which the outlook of the Catholic Counter-Reformation finds almost its only complement in the religious scepticism of humanistic origin." Mazzini was thinking of the industrial society of early nineteenth-century England with its ruthless individualism, while Italian society was still in a stage of feudalism which did not need an attack on the exaggeration of individualism.

Ruggiero criticizes also the "primacy" idea. The memories of humanism and Renaissance created "an inveterate national pride" among the Italian writers and made them less able to thrive in the climate of general European culture and too willing to belittle the importance of foreign influences. The Italian *risorgimento* represents an attempt "to raise Italy to the level of the other European nations by a rapid assimilation of the most vital elements in their cultural and political institutions; yet the goal appears distorted and disfigured by a literary fiction which treats a reproduction as if it were an original creation, and fills the gaps in the present with rhetorical references to the past." A false patriotic shame deprived a nation of the courage to look within itself and to recognize its defects and limitations. *Ibidem*, p. 298 f.

26. Alfieri understood much better the meaning of liberty and of English representative institutions. In his *Della Tirannide* he wrote: "If in some things the English republic seems more firmly based than the Roman, this is because there is in England a permanent and vitalizing disagreement, not, as in Rome, between the nobles and the people, but between the people and the people: that is between the ministry and the opposition. Thus, because this disagreement is generated not by disparity of hereditary interests, but by disparity of changing opinion, it does perhaps more good than harm; for no one so completely belongs to one party that he might not often pass over to the opposite; neither of the two parties having interests permanently opposed to and incompatible with the good of the whole." And of fatherland and liberty he wrote: "The land in which a man is born is under a tyranny called only in mockery by the name of

fatherland; for the only true fatherland is the land in which man enjoys freely, and under the security of invariable laws, those most precious rights which nature has given him." See on him Hans Kohn, *The Idea of Nationalism* (New York: Macmillan, 1944) pp. 505–509.

27. In 1871 Mazzini refused to participate in rendering homage to Carlo Bini, a friend of his youth with whom he had published in 1829 *L'indicatore Livornese*, because "we all represent today whether pleased or mournful, only a lie of Italy." Even if all her natural frontiers were achieved, "noi avremmo il contorno materiale, l'organismo inerte d'Italia; manca l'alito fecondatore di Dio, l'anima della nazione. I popoli che s'erano levati attoniti e presaghi di grandi cose a contemplare il risorgere dell' antica padrona del mondo, guardano delusi altrove, e dicono a se stesse: non è se non il fantasma d'Italia." *Scritti*, vol. XVIII, p. 239 f.

28. See Luigi Salvatorelli, *op. cit.*, p. 284 f., 303, 317. Cavour wrote in a letter on December 28, 1860, in answer to a proposal to assume dictatorial powers for the period of the unification of Italy: "Pour ma part je n'ai nulle confiance dans les dictatures et surtout dans les dictatures civiles. Je crois qu'on peut faire avec un Parlement bien des choses qui seraient impossibles au pouvoir absolu. Une expérience de treize années m'a convaincu qu'un ministère honnête et énergique, qui n'a rien à redouter des révélations de la tribune, et qui n'est pas d'humeur à se laisser intimider par la violence des partis, a tout à gagner des luttes parlementaires. Je ne me suis jamais senti faible que lorsque les Chambres étaient fermées. D'ailleurs je ne pourrais trahir mon origine, renier les principes de toute ma vie. Je suis fils de la liberté, c'est à elle que je dois tout ce que je suis. S'il fallait mettre un voile sur sa statue, ce ne serait pas à moi à le faire. Si l'on parvenait à persuader aux Italiens qu'il leur faut un dictateur, ils choisiraient Garibaldi et pas moi. Et ils auraient raison. La route parlementaire est plus longue, mais elle est plus sûre."

In a speech on April 9, 1861, he revealed his faith in the principle of liberty, in the free development of man's moral and intellectual nature, in orderly progress through all the dangers and inconveniences of liberty: "Noi non possiamo immaginare uno stato di cose fondato sulla libertà dove non siano partiti e lotte. La pace completa, assoluta, non e compatibile con la libertà. Bisogna saper accettare la libertà coi suoi benefizi e forse anche co'suoi inconvenienti." ("We cannot imagine a state of affairs founded on liberty where there would not be parties or conflicts. Complete and absolute peace is not compatible with liberty. We must know how to accept liberty with all its benefits and perhaps also with all its inconveniences.") Cesare Balbo also stressed in his *Della monarchia rappresentativa in Italia* (Florence, 1857) the need and importance of parties: "As if it would be possible that the good of the fatherland could be understood in the same way by twenty-three million people! As if parties were anything else than different opinions about the good of the fatherland! As if it would be possible to hinder such a diversity; as if it were good! As if the free expression of this diversity were not among the first and most useful results of all national freedom!"

29. In his *Sommario della storia d'Italia*, quoted by Salvatorelli, *op. cit.*, p. 255.

30. Salvatorelli, *op. cit.*, pp. 338–341, 346–354. It is worthy of note that Salva-

torelli concluded his book printed in Italy in 1935 with the following sentences: "So Carlo Cattaneo concluded the cycle of Italian political thought in the *Risorgimento*. He concluded it by reaffirming thoughtfully and consciously the humanitarian and progressive values which had been exalted in the thought of the Italian and European eighteenth century enlightenment."

31. *Lettere di Giosuè Carducci* (Bologna: Zanichelli, 1911) vol. I, p. 169 f.

32. Letter of October 24, 1864. *Lettres de Joseph Mazzini à Daniel Stern* (Paris: Baillière, 1873) p. 40. Mazzini wrote an excellent eulogy of his friend Jakopo Riffini which could be applied also to himself. (*Life and Writings*, vol. I, p. 333.)

NOTES TO CHAPTER FOUR

1. The best appreciations of Treitschke by leading German historians can be found in Erich Marcks, *Heinrich von Treitschke, ein Gedenkblatt zu seinem zehnjährigen Todestag* (Heidelberg, 1906) and his "Heinrich von Treitschke, eine Erinnerung," *Preussische Jahrbücher*, vol. 237, Sept. 1934, pp. 193 ff. and in Friedrich Meinecke, *Die Idee der Staatsräson in der Neueren Geschichte*, 3rd ed. (Munich: Oldenbourg, 1929), pp. 488–510. Of the most recent German literature on Treitschke the book by Ernst Leipprand, *Heinrich von Treitschke im Deutschen Geistesleben des Neunzehnten Jahrhunderts* (Stuttgart: Kohlhammer, 1935) deserves attention.
2. In the preface to the fifth volume of the *Deutsche Geschichte im Neunzehnten Jahrhundert* (1894).
3. Friedrich Meinecke, "Kultur, Machtpolitik und Militarismus" in Otto Hintze, Friedrich Meinecke, Hermann Oncken and Hermann Schumacher, *Deutschland und der Weltkrieg* (Leipzig: Teubner, 1915), p. 628 wrote: "Wir müssen also feststellen, dass die Lehre von den Two Germanies nicht ganz richtig ist. Es ist falsch, dass das 'zahme' Deutschland von 1800 von dem 'wilden' Deutschland Bismarcks verschlungen worden sei, sondern das 'zahme' Deutschland hat schon sehr früh bedenkliche Neigungen zum 'wilden' Deutschland verspürt und mit ihm eine freiwillige und herzliche Ehe geschlossen. Es ist andererseits richtig, dass gewisse Reste und Ueberlebsel des kosmopolitischen Idealismus des 18. Jahrhunderts in der Kultur und politischen Denkweise der gebildeten Schichten Deutschlands sich noch lange erhalten haben, aber weggefegt worden sind durch die Taten und Lehren Bismarcks." Carl Wittke, *Against the Current, The Life of Karl Heinzen* (Chicago: University of Chicago Press, 1945), pp. 273–281, shows how even in America the famous German liberals of 1848, Carl Schurz and others, vied in emotional servility to the new Reich and Bismarck. Only Heinzen remained faithful to the liberal ideal.
4. Theodor Schiemann, *Heinrich von Treitschkes Lehr- und Wanderjahre 1834–1866* (Munich: Oldenbourg, 1896), p. 50. "Der Geist des Alldeutschen Verbandes [of the beginning of the twentieth century] war hundert Jahre früher schon unter uns, nur im Gewand einer älteren Zeit; wen erinnert diese neue Bewegung für deutsche Macht und deutsche Art nicht an Ernst Moritz Arndt und sonst an Patrioten von 1813? Die Alldeutschen hatten ein Recht, sich auf sie zu berufen." Adolf Rapp, *Der Deutsche Gedanke, seine Entwicklung im politischen und geistigen Leben seit dem 18. Jahrhundert* (Bonn: Kurt Schroeder, 1920), p. 334. See also Alfred G. Pundt, *Arndt and the Nationalist Awakening in Germany* (New York: Columbia University Press, 1935).
5. "Dennoch wird von einer baldigen Heilung Deutschlands die Entscheidung über die Frage abhängen, ob unser Weltteil seinen hohen Stand

Amerika gegenüber, welches ganz andere Wege geht, länger wird verteidigen können." Schiemann, *op. cit.*, p. 55 f.

6. Letter from Göttingen, March 4, 1856. *Heinrich von Treitschkes Briefe,* ed. by Max Cornicelius, vol. I (Leipzig: Hirzel, 1913), p. 352.

7. Letter to his father from Bonn, Jan. 18, 1854. *Briefe, op. cit.*, p. 209 f.

8. *Historische und Politische Aufsätze*, Neue Folge (Leipzig: Hirzel, 1870), vol. I, p. 648.

9. *Ibid.*, p. 152. Fichte assumed, though only temporarily, in an article published in 1807 the same positive attitude toward Machiavelli as Treitschke did.

10. *Ibid.*, vol. II, p. 693.

11. In 1853 A. L. von Rochau, whom Treitschke calls "one of the best German publicists" (*Deutsche Geschichte*, vol. IV, p. 301), published his "Grundsätze der Realpolitik, angewendet auf die staatlichen Zustände Deutschlands," in which he wrote: "The immediate connection of power and dominion (Macht und Herrschaft) forms the fundamental truth of all political life and the key of all history."

12. See in his "Bundesstaat und Einheitsstaat" in *Aufsätze*, vol. I, pp. 559 ff.

13. *Deutsche Geschichte*, vol. IV, p. 407.

14. *Aufsätze*, vol. I, p. 590. See also his "Cavour," *ibid.*, vol. II, pp. 349 ff.

15. He wrote in the Preussische Jahrbücher on July 10, 1866: "Seit langem sehnen sich die Patrioten der Halbinsel, die anmassende Vormundschaft Frankreichs abzuschütteln. . . . Die Allianz der beiden Mächte, auf deren Kraft und Blute die Zukunft Mitteleuropas beruht, ist nicht das Werk vorübergehender diplomatischer Kombinationen; sie soll dauern und dem Weltteile ein wirkliches Gleichgewicht der Macht, einen gesicherten Friedenszustand schaffen."

16. Gustav Freytag, *Politische Aufsätze*, Leipzig, 1888, p. 86.

17. Letter to Ferdinand Frensdorff, Leipzig, November 25, 1860. *Briefe*, vol. II, p. 114.

18. *Preussische Jahrbücher*, June 1866. See also Hans Goldschmidt, "Treitschke, Bismarck und die Deutsche Geschichte im Neunzehnten Jahrhundert," *Preussische Jahrbücher*, Sept. 1934, pp. 227 ff.

19. Letter of December 10, 1865. *Briefe*, vol. II, p. 447.

20. Letter to Julius Jolly, Heidelberg, Jan. 26, 1870. In Willy Andreas "Briefe Treitschkes an Historiker und Politiker des Oberrheins," *Preussische Jahrbücher*, Sept. 1934, p. 222.

21. G. G. Gervinus, *Hinterlassene Schriften* (Vienna: W. Braumüller, 1872), pp. 21–23, see also pp. 73, 92, 95, 97. In 1832 Karl Rotteck declared: "Ich will die Einheit nicht anders als mit Freiheit, und will lieber Freiheit ohne Einheit als Einheit ohne Freiheit." (*Nachgelassene Schriften*, Pforzheim 1843, vol. IV, p. 400.) Georg Herwegh wrote in the spring of 1871 a poem "Den Siegestrunkenen":

> Vorüber ist der harte Strauss,
> Der welsche Drache liegt bezwungen,
> Und Bismarck-Siegfried kehrt nach Haus
> Mit seinem Schatz der Nibelungen. . . .
> Ihr habt ein neues deutsches Reich
> Von Junkerhänden aufgerichtet. . . .

Ihr wähnt euch einig, weil die Pest
Der Knechtschaft sich verallgemeinert,
Weil täglich noch der kleine Rest
Lebend'ger Seelen sich verkleinert;
Ihr wähnt euch einig, weil ein Mann
Darf über Krieg und Frieden schalten
Und euch zur Schlachtbank führen kann
Mit der Parol: das Maul gehalten!

And Gervinus addressed to himself the following poem foreseeing clearly the future of Bismarck's Reich under Bismarck's successors:

Im ungeheuren Abfall dieser Tage
Bist du dem echten Glauben treu geblieben,
Dem ew'gen A und O der Weltgeschichte:
Wer nicht an's Mass sich bindet, wird zunichte.

22. *Politics* (London: Constable, 1916), vol. I, p. 31.
23. Hegel's *Philosophy of Right*, No. 258, note. Translation by S. W. Dyde (London: Bell, 1906), p. 240. See also Christopher Dowson, "The Politics of Hegel," *The Dublin Review*, October 1943, pp. 97–107. Treitschke's praise of Hegel in *Deutsche Geschichte*, vol. III, p. 718 f.
24. *Politik*, 5th edition (Leipzig: Hirzel, 1922), vol. I, pp. 89 ff., vol. II, p. 544.
25. The Pan-German mission had been expressed long before 1870 by leading German writers. Jakob Grimm, one of the most violent Pan-Germans, expressed his confidence that the peace and salvation of the whole continent will rest upon Germany's strength and freedom. Emanuel Geibel, who wrote tender and delicate poems which enjoyed a tremendous popularity, wrote in 1861 "Deutschlands Beruf," a poem on Germany's mission which became famous though it was one of the mildest of its kind.

Macht und Freiheit, Recht und Sitte,
Klarer Geist und scharfer Hieb
Zügeln dann aus starker Mitte
Jeder Selbstsucht wilden Trieb,
Und es mag am deutschen Wesen
Einmal noch die Welt genesen!

Karl Simrock, Professor of Old Germanic Literature in Bonn, who translated and popularized all the main works of old German literature, prefaced his "Lieder vom Deutschen Vaterland" (1863) with the following prophecy:

Wenn die Deutschen Deutsche werden,
Gründen sie das Reich auf Erden,
Das die Völker all' umschlingt
Und der Welt den Frieden bringt.

One of the most widely read authors of Treitschke's period was Felix Dahn, Professor of German Law and a scholar in the field of earliest German history. His innumerable novels from early German history, especially the four volumes of "Ein Kampf um Rom" (1876), formed the intellectual food of the German middle classes before the turn of the century. His poems were favored for recitations in the German Reich. One of the best reads:

> Thor stand am Mitternachtende der Welt.
> Die Streitaxt warf er, die schwere:
> Soweit der sausende Hammer fällt,
> Sind mein das Land und die Meere!
>
> Und es flog der Hammer aus seiner Hand,
> Flog über die ganze Erde,
> Fiel nieder an fernsten Südens Rand,
> Dass alles sein eigen werde.
>
> Seitdem ist freudig Germanenrecht,
> Mit dem Hammer Land zu erwerben:
> Wir sind von des Hammergottes Geschlecht
> Und wollen sein Weltreich erben.

26. John Emerich Edward Dalberg-Acton, *Historical Essays and Studies* (London: Macmillan, 1919), p. 378.
27. *Deutsche Geschichte*, vol. IV, p. 350.
28. *Deutsche Geschichte*, vol. I, p. 25.
29. Max Weber, *Gesammelte Politische Schriften* (Munich: Drei Masken Verlag, 1921), pp. 19 ff. See J. P. Meyer, *Max Weber in German Politics* (London: Faber, 1944) and Guido de Ruggiero, *The History of European Liberalism* (London: Oxford University Press, 1927), pp. 271 ff.
30. "When we examine more closely . . . society we find that under all its forms it tends naturally toward aristocracy. The Social Democrats imply in their very title the absurdity of their aspirations. . . . All social life is built upon class organization." *Politics*, vol. I, p. 41 f.
31. See Evalyn A. Clark, "Adolf Wagner: from National Economist to National Socialist," *Political Science Quarterly*, Sept. 1940, pp. 378–411. Schmoller wrote in a collection of essays *Handels- und Machtpolitik* (ed. by Schmoller, Wagner and Max Sering, Stuttgart, 1900, vol. I, p. 35 f.): "I cannot dwell on the details of the commercial and colonial tasks for which we need the navy. Only some points may be mentioned briefly. We are bound to wish at all costs that in the coming century a German country of twenty or thirty million Germans be established in southern Brazil. . . . Without communications continually safeguarded by battleships, without Germany's standing ready for vigorous interference in these countries, this evolution would be exposed to peril."
32. *Encyclopaedia Judaica* (Berlin 1928), vol. II, p. 1010.
33. Anti-Semitism became officially represented in 1887 in the German Parliament. In 1907 the officially anti-Semitic parties which made anti-Semitism their main program had 17 deputies. By that time anti-Semitism in Germany had received a powerful stimulus through the writings of Houston Stewart Chamberlain, Richard Wagner's apostle and son-in-law. More direct was Treitschke's influence on anti-Semitism in Austria, especially on Georg Schönerer, who like Treitschke was violently pan-German, anti-Habsburg, anti-Catholic and a fervent admirer of Bismarck and the Hohen-

zollern. See *Georg Schönerer, der Vorkämpfer Grossdeutschlands,* ed. by Eduard Pichl, 2nd. ed., six vols. (Oldenburg: Georg Stalling, 1938) and Erwin Mayer-Löwenschwerdt, *Schönerer der Vorkämpfer* (Vienna: Braumüller, 1938). Under Schönerer's influence the German students of Austria declared in 1897 in Waidhofen a.d. Ybbs, not to give satisfaction to Jewish students because Jews were without honor ("der Ehre bar"). Different was the Catholic anti-Semitic movement organized by Dr. Karl Lueger in Vienna, where he was elected Mayor in 1895. It was a pro-Habsburg movement, addressed to the lower middle-class, anti-capitalist and anti-proletarian. Treitschke himself had several Jewish friends, among them Alphons Oppenheim; see Theodor Schiemann, *op. cit.,* p. 59, 147. Ernest Renan wrote in his *Souvenirs d'Enfance et de Jeunesse* (Paris 1883, vol. I, p. 190): "L'Allemagne depuis qu'elle s'est donnée toute entière à la vie militaire, n'aurait plus de talent si elle n'avait les juifs, envers qui elle est si ingrate."

34. See also H. W. C. Davis, *The Political Thought of Heinrich von Treitschke* (New York: Scribner, 1915), pp. 227–288.

35. When Bismarck acquired the Cameroons, Treitschke told his friend Adolf Hausrath: "Cameroons? What are we to do with this sand box? Let us take Holland, then we shall have colonies." (*Treitschke, His Doctrine of German Destiny and of International Relations,* New York: Putnam, 1914, p. 110). "Our existence as a state of the first rank is vitally affected by the question whether we can become a power beyond the seas." *Politics,* vol. I, p. 33, 36, 118 f. For his racial views see on pp. 275 ff. Even for territories inhabited by white races and falling under German control like Latvia he demanded that "the subject race be kept in as uncivilized a condition as possible, and thus prevented from becoming a danger to the handful of conquerors," p. 122.

36. *Deutsche Geschichte,* vol. III, p. 685, vol. IV, p. 409; *Politics,* vol. I, p. 87, vol. II, p. 68.

37. *Politics,* vol. II, pp. 390 ff.

38. *Politics,* vol. I, p. 24, 29, vol. II, p. 395 f., 597 ff.

39. *Politics,* vol. I, p. 34 f., vol. II, pp. 593 ff.

40. "Zum Gedächtnis des grossen Krieges," delivered July 19, 1895, reprinted in *Deutsche Kämpfe* (Leipzig: Kroner, 1935), pp. 374 ff. Even in this last speech he remarked gratefully that among the many millions abroad there was only one person, "our loyal friend Thomas Carlyle who recognized lovingly the nobility of our national soul." On "Thomas Carlyle, Prophet of Fascism," see J. Selwyn Schapiro in *The Journal of Modern History,* June 1945, pp. 97–115.

41. John Morley, who had no understanding for the danger of German militarism, was reported to have dismissed Treitschke in a lecture on democracy at the University of Manchester on June 28, 1912, by saying, "No professor in this university could keep a class for a month upon Politik of that stamp." Treitschke's *Politics* had a great influence on Pan-Germanism. Ernst Hasse, professor in Leipzig from 1888 to 1908, a disciple of Treitschke, was president of the Alldeutscher Verband. In his *Deutsche Politik,* vol. II, part 1 (1908) he demanded the disappearance of small nations which he considered no longer capable of existence, at-

tacked violently British imperialism but demanded cooperation with Russian imperialism, fought against free trade and open door policy for a closed economy and desired the creation of a federation which would include Germany, Austria-Hungary, the Netherlands and its colonies, Belgium and the Congo, Switzerland, the Balkans, Rumania and Turkey. See on other literature of this kind Friedrich Hertz, *Nationalgeist und Politik* (Zurich: Europa Verlag, 1937), vol. I, pp. 464-479.

42. "Government so understood is the intellectual guide of the nation, the promoter of wealth, the teacher of knowledge, the guardian of morality, the mainspring of the ascending movement of man. That is the tremendous power, supported by millions of bayonets, which grew up in the days of which I have been speaking at Petersburg, and was developed, by much abler minds, chiefly at Berlin; and it is the greatest danger that remains to be encountered by the Anglo-Saxon race." Lord Acton, *Lectures on Modern History* (London: Macmillan, 1906), p. 289.

NOTES TO CHAPTER FIVE

1. The best study on modern Russia is T. G. Masaryk's *Russland und Europa. Studien über die geistigen Strömungen in Russland,* 2 vols. (Jena: Diederichs, 1913). The English translation changes the characteristic title into *The Spirit of Russia.* A second corrected edition was published in Czech, *Rusko a Evropa,* 2 vols. (Prague: Laichter, 1930, 1933). The work was only a preparatory study to an analysis of Dostoevsky as a central figure and the key to an understanding of modern Russia. Masaryk himself rejected completely Dostoevsky's world outlook and interpretation of history. Masaryk was a "Westerner," a rational humanist whose philosophy was shaped by Locke and Hume. Dostoevsky's central position is also emphasized in V. V. Zenkovsky, *Russkie mysliteli i Evropa.* (Paris: YMCA Press, 1926). The book discusses the crtical attitudes of Russian thinkers toward Europe. It is written in Slavophile spirit.

   In addition to Masaryk, see on modern Russia Sir John Maynard, *Russia in Flux, Before October* (London: Gollancz, 1941) and Karl Nötzel, *Die Grundlagen des geistigen Russland* (Jena: Diederichs, 1917). On Dostoevsky himself, the English reader has three recent good biographies: Edward H. Carr, *Dostoevsky, A New Biography* (Boston: Houghton, Mifflin, 1931); Avrahm Yarmolinsky, *Dostoevsky, a Life* (New York: Harcourt, Brace, 1934); Ernest J. Simmons, *Dostoevsky, The Making of a Novelist* (New York: Oxford University Press, 1940). Of German biographies the pioneer venture by N. Hoffmann (Berlin: Ernst Hofmann, 1899) and especially Karl Nötzel's book (Leipzig: Haessel, 1925) deserve mention. Merezhkovsky's important study on Tolstoy and Dostoevsky can be found also in a German translation, 3rd edition, (Berlin, 1924).
2. The poem "Klevetnikam Rossii" (To the Slanderers of Russia) was written on August 2, 1831. See A. S. Pushkin, *Sobranie Sochinenii* (Berlin: Ladyzhnikov, 1921) vol. II, p. 43.
3. See Hans Kohn, *World Order in Historical Perspective* (Cambridge: Harvard University Press, 1942), p. 126.
4. N. N. Strakhov, Dostoevsky's friend and biographer, gives a good description of his attitude: "A boundless patriotism—that was the emotional atmosphere in which I grew up and was educated in the provinces. Russia appeared to me as a country of immense strength, covered with incomparable glory, the first country of the world, so that I literally thanked God for having been born a Russian. For a long time I could not conceive that there could be men who felt and thought differently in that respect. It was equally difficult for me to understand opinions which ran counter to this my feeling. When I finally became convinced that Europe despises us, that it regards us as semi-barbarians, and that it is for us not only difficult but impossible to convert the European peoples to a different opinion, the discovery was for me unbelievably painful,

and I still feel this pain. But I never thought, even for a moment, of abandoning my patriotism or of preferring the spirit of any other land to that of my land. Though I often believed that Russia, as the poet Tyuchev says, 'can not be understood by reason' and that one must have 'faith' in Russia, I began more and more to understand how it happened, that 'the haughty glance of other peoples will not recognize nor understand what glows within Russia's humble nakedness and shines forth full of secrecy.' The contempt of the Europeans served only as a continuous goad which strengthened my loyalty to the spirit of my people and promoted my understanding of it." In F. M. Dostojewsky, *Literarische Schriften* (Munich: Piper, 1920) p. 65 f.

5. See Hans Kohn, *The Idea of Nationalism* (New York: Macmillan, 1944), p. 437 f.

6. The similarity with Barrès' "Déracinés" is evident.

7. Theoretically Dostoevsky expressed sometimes an admiration for Europe, but it was always for a Europe gravely diseased or already dead. That Europe presented a problem to the Russians which they alone could solve. "We Russians have two problems—Russia and Europe." Ivan Karamazov told his brother Alyosha: "I want to make a journey to Europe. I know that perhaps I shall only find there a graveyard—but every stone cries out with such warm by-gone life, such faith in her achievements, in her truth, in her struggles and in her science that I know in advance—I shall fall to the ground and kiss these stones and weep over them." Russians of Dostoevsky's type pity Europe. "You can not know how much we love and honor Europe and everything great and beautiful that arises from her; how tormented we are about the fate of that near and dear land, how oppressed by the dark clouds that overcast its sky."

This pity was mitigated by the hard necessity of fighting Europe and by the deep revulsion produced by the contact with Europe. Dostoevsky wrote from Geneva to A. N. Maikov on January 12, 1868: "If you only knew, what a stupid, dull, insignificant, savage people it is. . . . Bourgeois life in this vile republic has reached the ne plus ultra. . . . There are parties and continuous squabbles, pauperism, terrible mediocrity in everything. A workman here is not worth the little finger of a workman of ours. The customs are savage . . . their inferiority of development: the drunkenness, the thieving, the paltry swindling, that have become the rule in their commerce! Yet they have some good traits which after all place them immeasurably above the Germans." To these Europeans he compared the Russians. While Europe developed her rotting civilization, "we were forming ourselves into a great nation, we checked Asia forever, we bore an infinity of sufferings, we did not lose our Russian idea, which will renew the world, but strengthened it; finally we endured the Germans, and yet after all our people is immeasurably higher, nobler, more honest, more naïve, abler; full of a different idea, the highest Christian idea, which is not even understood by Europe with her moribund Catholicism and her stupidly self-contradictory Lutheranism." Dostoevsky, *Letters and Reminiscences,* tr. by S. S. Koteliansky and J. Middleton Murry (New York: Knopf, 1923), p. 29. In his letter of March 1,

1868 (*ibidem*, p. 40), Dostoevsky promised a great renewal for the whole world through Russian thought in less than one hundred years. But in order that this great object may be achieved, the incontestable supremacy of the Great Russian race over the whole Slav world must be established.

8. In Florence he conceived the idea of writing a great national epic, a cycle of legends written "with love for Russia streaming forth as from a living spring." In a letter to A. N. Maikov of May 27, 1869, he described how Ivan III of Moscow by marrying the heiress of the emperors of Constantinople, "laid the first stone of the future hegemony of the East, . . . the idea not only of a great state, but of a whole new world, which is destined to renew Christianity by the Pan-Slav, Pan-Orthodox idea and to introduce a new idea to mankind." The following centuries bring the disintegration of the West, "which will occur when the Pope distorts Christ finally and thereby begets atheism in the defiled humanity of the West." For the final vision of the twentieth century Dostoevsky envisaged Russia, and beside her Europe and her civilization eclipsed, lacerated, and brutalized. "Here I would not stop at any imagination." *Ibidem*, pp. 72–76.

9. Letter to A. N. Maikov from Dresden, October 21, 1870, *ibidem*, pp. 92–95.

10. The federation which Danilevsky foresaw with uncanny prophetic gifts, will consist of Russia with Galicia and the Ukrainian part of Bukovina added; even the Ukrainian part of Hungary, the present Carpatho-Ukraine, will be added to Russia; then there will be Yugoslavia which will practically consist of all the lands she had in 1920, and in addition Trieste, Gorizia, Istria and the major part of Carinthia; then Czechoslovakia as constituted in 1919 but without the Carpatho-Ukraine; Rumania without Bessarabia, northern Bukovina and Dobruja, but with a large part of Transylvania; Hungary without the parts ceded to Czechoslovakia and Rumania; Bulgaria and Greece, more or less in their present size; and Constantinople with the adjoining provinces in Europe and Asia.

Similar plans were proposed by Professor Michael Pogodin and by General Rostislav Fadeev. His *Opinion on the Eastern Question* was translated into English (London: E. Stanford, 1871); two other works into German, *General Fadejew über Russlands Kriegsmacht und Kriegspolitik* (Leipzig: Brockhaus, 1870) and *Briefe über die gegenwärtige Lage Russlands, April 1879–1880* (Leipzig: Brockhaus, 1881). The first of the two books was occasioned by Prussia's victories in 1866, an event of which the German editor, the well known journalist and diplomat Julius Eckardt, wrote in his introduction that "the year 1866 has transformed our continent into an armed camp unparalleled for many centuries." Fadeev started from the premise that the whole of Europe was hostile to Russia and regardless of internal dissensions was ready to fight Russia. "This hostility has its cause not in this or that political system of Russian government, but in the distrust against a new, alien, all too numerous nation which has suddenly emerged on the borders of Europe, an immense empire with traditions different from those of the West, where so many fundamental social questions are differently handled, where the whole mass of people possessed land, and where a religion is professed which is one hundred times more dangerous to papacy than Protestantism, a religion which rejects both. . . . Whatever we shall do, we shall never destroy Europe's fear of us, for the simple reason that we are growing more powerful every day, and we do not yet know ourselves how we shall feel in a few years about Slavism and Orthodoxy, for we can not speak for ourselves, and even less for our children." (p. 34 f.)

Danilevsky's work does not exist in an English translation, but there is a German translation by Karl Nötzel, *Russland und Europa; eine Untersuchung über die kulturellen und politischen Beziehungen der slawischen zur germanisch-romanischen Welt* (Stuttgart: Deutsche Verlagsanstalt, 1920). Dostoevsky heartily agreed with Danilevsky. He read his articles as they appeared in *Zarya* in 1869 with enthusiastic approval and impatient expectation for the succeeding installments. He wrote to Strakhov from Florence on March 18, 1869, that Danilevsky's ideas coincided so much with his own ideas and convictions that they both arrived at identical conclusions. See on Pan-Slavism: Alfred Fischel, *Der Panslawismus bis zum Weltkrieg* (Stuttgart: Cotta, 1919); Karl Stählin, "Die Entstehung des Panslavismus," *Germanoslavica*, vol. IV (Brünn, 1936), pp. 1–25, 237–262; Jerzy Braun, "Die slavische messianistische Philosophie als Entwicklung und Vollendung der deutschen philosophischen Systeme Kants und seiner Nachfolger," *ibidem*, vol. III (1935), pp. 291–315. A different interpretation of Russia and the Slavs, without any racial idea, was presented by the Polish messianists like Adam Mickiewicz, who believed that in Europe only two parties existed, that of freedom led by Poland and that of slavery led by Russia. Poland stood through self-sacrifice for universal liberty and equality; Russia stood for domestic despotism and through Tsarism which was a new, active and propagandizing force, for universal despotism. *Poems by Adam Mickiewicz*, edited by George R. Noyes (New York: Polish Institute of Arts and Sciences, 1944), p. 484.

11. Dostoevsky edited in 1873 a weekly *Grazhdanin* (*The Citizen*). In his last years he wrote, edited and published a one-man journal, the famous *Dnevnik Pisatela* (Journal of an Author). It was published as a monthly in 1876 and 1877. In August 1880 one issue was published, containing the lecture on Pushkin; shortly after the author's death in 1881, the last issue appeared. The *Dnevnik Pisatela* was published first in book form as vol. V of the Complete Works (*Polnoe Sobranie Sochinenii*), published by his widow, St. Petersburg, 1886. Unfortunately no English translation exists. S. Koteliansky and J. Middleton Murry translated the Pushkin speech and "The Dream of a Queer Fellow" in *Pages from The Journal of an Author* (Edinburgh, 1916?). There is a complete French translation by Jean Chuzeville, *Le journal d'un écrivain*, 3 vols. (Paris: Bossard, 1927). Chuzeville also wrote *Rome et l'internationale: une prediction de Dostoievski* (Paris: Bossard, 1927). There is an almost complete German translation, but arranged topically rather than chronologically, in F. M. Dostojewski, *Politische Schriften* (Munich: Piper, 1917) and *Literarische Schriften* (Munich: Piper, 1920).

12. "Die Vorstellung einer in sich abgeschlossenen individuellen Persönlichkeitssphäre ist dem russischen Denken ganz fremd." Simon Frank, *Die*

Russische Weltanschauung, Philosophische Vorträge der Kant-Gesellschaft 29 (Charlottenburg: Rolf Heise, 1926), p. 21. Frank points out that the Russians can imagine life only as a communal life; with them all political questions tend to become problems of personal salvation; for that reason they are unable to compromise. He warns that "in these days of Russian collapse and political weakness it should not be forgotten that the Russian people founded the greatest and most powerful empire in Europe and consolidated it in the course of several centuries." *Ibidem,* p. 25 f.

13. Shigalov in *The Possessed* (Part II, ch. VII, 2, The Modern Library ed., p. 410) suggests as a final solution of the social question the division of mankind into two unequal parts. "One-tenth enjoys absolute liberty and unbounded power over the other nine-tenths. The others have to give up all individuality and become, so to speak, a herd, and, through boundless submission, will by a series of regenerations attain primeval innocence, something like the Garden of Eden. They will have to work, however." This paternalistic order assuring the happiness and peace of the masses through the unlimited autocracy of a small elite, recalls the famous story of the Grand Inquisitor in *The Brothers Karamazov.*

14. Part II, ch. I, 7 (The Modern Library Edition, pp. 250–260). See also the interesting notes for *The Possessed* quoted by Ernest Simmons, *op. cit.,* p. 296 f. and Dostoevsky's letter to A. F. Blagonravov of December 19, 1880.

15. Anatole Leroy-Beaulieu has pointed out that the use of the national language in the Russian Church liturgy from the beginning has helped to "nationalize" the Russian Church and to isolate Russia from the life-giving forces of antiquity, including the Greek past. "This intimate connection between church and state has inoculated Russia with the disease peculiar to the East—stagnation, and aggravated the evil peculiar to Russia—isolation. The two united powers put a stop to the inroads of ideas from abroad. Old-time Russians used to flee from contact with Europe as from contagion; a trip to foreign countries was all but a sin, endangering the soul. . . . One of the things which during the Middle Ages favored most the blossoming of modern civilization was having a scholarly clerical language for international use; the East had no such language. The Greek Church, more than any other, seemed entitled to impose her language upon her spiritual colonies, for was it not that of the New Testament and the Septuagint? She did not do so. Ever since their conversion, the Russians celebrated divine service in old Slavic." By using the Slavic language Russia became separated from both classical civilizations. The Slavic language could not open to the Russians the treasures of antiquity and had no literature of its own. Its use had political advantages for the Russian empire, but it divided Russia from Europe and limited its cultural life. *The Empire of the Tsars* (New York: Putnam's, 1898), vol. III, p. 73 ff.

16. *Journal of an Author* for April 1876. *Dnevnik,* pp. 345–348; *Politische Schriften,* pp. 173–176. Dostoevsky wrote in the *Grazhdanin* in September 1873: "There is a political law, even a law of nature, according to which one of two strong and close neighbors, whatever their friendship may be, wishes to destroy the other and sooner or later will realize that wish."

17. *Journal of an Author,* March 1877 and April 1877. *Dnevnik,* pp. 552 ff. and

573 ff. *Politische Schriften*, pp. 383, 401–418. In spite of all his theoretical praising of peace, Dostoevsky wrote: "Peace much more than war brutalizes man, especially the long peace, and makes him cruel. A long peace always produces meanness, cowardice, a brutal egoism, above all spiritual stagnation. . . . War for an idea heals the soul and strengthens the spirit of the whole nation by the feeling of solidarity and the consciousness of duty well done. Schools are important, nobody will deny that; but schools need an idea and a direction—we go out to war for the idea and for a sound direction."

18. That is the ever-recurring thesis of the *Journal*. See the issues for June, 1876, p. 379 f., January 1877, pp. 522 ff., March 1877, pp. 552 ff., May–June 1877, pp. 604 ff., September 1877, pp. 682 ff. *Politische Schriften*, pp. 193 f., 198 ff., 215 ff., 222 f., 399, 474 ff.

19. *Journal of an Author*, September 1877. *Dnevnik*, pp. 679–682; *Politische Schriften*, pp. 137–143. Professor Simmons remarks of Dostoevsky's ideas: "The curious fact is if one substituted communism for his conception of the mission of the Orthodox faith, and world revolution for his notion of a Pan-Slavic war against Europe, the identity of his whole position with that of modern Soviet Russia would be striking." (*Op. cit.*, p. 327). This was written in 1940. Since then Russia has produced a synthesis of communism and world revolution with Orthodoxy and Pan-Slavism. She conducts her policy with the same double meanings of imperialism, liberation, brotherhood and peace, as Dostoevsky did.

20. *Journal of an Author*, January 1881; *Dnevnik*, 808–810; *Politische Schriften*, 315 ff.—*Journal of an Author*, April 1877; *Dnevnik*, 539; *Politische Schriften*, 419.—*Journal of an Author*, November 1877; *Dnevnik*, 729; *Politische Schriften*, 481. The United States were outside Dostoevsky's horizon, yet they represented the foremost capitalistic bourgeois society, the leading free state. Shatov in *The Possessed* had gone to America to experience the life of the American working class. Apparently he became convinced that, compared with the life of the American proletariat, laborers in Russia lived in a kind of paradise. Similar opinions were put into the mouth of a pompous bureaucrat by Count Alexei Tolstoy, a Russian poet and contemporary of Dostoevsky, in a satirical poem "Son Popova": "We should not look for ideals/And other social principles/in America: America is backward/Property and capital rule there."

The attitude of the Russian liberals was different. Alexander Herzen admired the United States. On the one hand he recognized that the United States was the continuation and flower of Western and especially of English civilization. "Has not the European ideal in one form, to wit, the Anglo-Saxon, found complete expression on the other side of the Atlantic Ocean?" On the occasion of the laying of the first cable between England and America in 1858, Herzen wrote: "In truth, here are not two states but two different shores, belonging to the Anglo-Saxons." And again: "The grand idea developed by the Northern States (of the U.S.A.) is purely Anglo-Saxon, the idea of self-government, that is, of a strong people with a weak government, the home rule of every tract of land without centralization, without bureaucracy, held together by an inner moral unity." But on the other hand Herzen regarded America as having some affinity with Russia. "Outside Europe there are only two progressive countries, America and Russia." With his growing rejection of Western European society and civilization, he constructed an America in similar opposition to Western Europe as he wished Russia to be. From Western Europe "we expect no legacy and equally are neither bound up by memories or hopes. What we needed—their theoretical thought—we took, we made it ours according to our strength. One barren, peevish, diplomatic and withall German ambition forces Russia to be mixed up in Western European affairs, not perceiving that humanity is sailing away from the European continent; if she will free herself from the Petersburg tradition, she has only one ally—the North American States!" David Hecht, "Two Classic Russian Publicists and the United States," *The American Slavic and East European Review,* vol. IV (August 1945), pp. 23–31.

21. *Dnevnik,* p. 731; *Politische Schriften,* p. 489. Germany and Russia have been close for the last two centuries. The court of St. Petersburg, the Russian bureaucracy and army were organized after the German model. German scholars played a great role in Russia's academies and universities. German romanticism influenced the Slavophiles as German Marxism influenced the Russian socialists.

Dostoevsky regarded Germany as implacably opposed to the Western and Roman traditions. Germany's mission, to him, was to be an eternal protest against Rome and against universalism and rationalism. But Germany could only oppose the West; she was unable to speak the new word. Only Russia could do that. Germany could crush the West but not save it. *Journal of an Author,* May–June 1877; *Dnevnik,* pp. 614 ff.; *Politische Schriften,* pp. 65 ff.

German writers in the last decades emphasized Germany's and Russia's common opposition to the West. In 1917 Thomas Mann wrote: "Has anybody ever understood the human meaning of nationalism in a more German way than the greatest Russian moralist? Are the Russian and German attitudes toward Europe, the West, civilization, politics and democracy, not closely akin? Haven't we Germans also our Slavophiles and Westernizers?" Mann regarded Dostoevsky as the true Russian representative and believed that Russia was unable to become a democratic and socialist republic on the Western pattern. "If spiritual affinity can form the foundation and justification of political alliances, then Russia and Germany belong together: their agreement now, their union for the future, has been since the beginning of this war [the war of 1914] the desire and dream of my heart. It is more than a desirability: it is a political and spiritual necessity should the Anglo-American alliance endure." *Betrachtungen eines Unpolitischen* (Berlin: Fischer, 1920), pp. 444 ff. See also André von Gronicka, "Thomas Mann and Russia," *The Germanic Review* (April 1945), pp. 105–137.

22. *Journal of an Author,* January 1881; *Dnevnik,* pp. 815 ff.; *Politische Schriften,* pp. 493 ff. Written when the news arrived that General Skobelev, in pursuit of Russia's central Asiatic conquests, had stormed Geoktepe, the Turkoman stronghold on the gateway to India.

23. After World War I, Russian intellectuals abroad formed the Eurasian movement. It stressed the Russian empire as an independent link between Europe and Asia, for which the Asiatic borderlands were perhaps more important than the Western borders. See D. S. Mirsky, "The Eurasian Movement," *Slavonic Review*, December 1927, pp. 311–319; Paul Miliukov, "Eurasianism and Europeanism in Russian History," *Festschrift Th. G. Masaryk zum 80. Geburtstage* (Bonn: Friedrich Cohen, 1930), vol. I, pp. 225–236; and Zenkovsky, *op. cit.*, pp. 147 ff. and 162 ff., who links the Eurasians with Konstantin Nikolaevich Leontvev.

24. Pushkin never used these words. In "The Gypsies" the old gypsy only calls upon Aleko, "the proud man," to leave the savages who like Rousseau's and Chateaubriand's noble savages were good-hearted. Pushkin would probably have rejected Dostoevsky's interpretation.

25. It is difficult to understand how Dostoevsky could judge that Pushkin understands and presents foreign nations so perfectly. The Germans claim a similar universality of understanding as typically and uniquely German.

26. The liberals objected to Dostoevsky's statement of Russian superiority as an example of national self-glorification. Gleb Ivanovich Uspensky wrote: "It is difficult to understand one who in himself reconciles such contradictions and it will not be surprising if his speech, when printed and carefully read, produces a quite different impression." Another liberal newspaper declared it unjust and extremely egotistical to arrogate exclusively to the Russians' virtues which were human or European. The most serious criticism was offered by Professor Aleksander Dmitrievich Gradovsky of the law faculty of the university of Petersburg, in an article "Mechty i Deistvitel'nost" (Illusions and Reality), reprinted in his *Sobranie Sochinenii* vi, 375–383. Dostoevsky answered in a lengthy reply in his *Journal*. See *Dostoevsky: Letters and Reminiscences* (*op. cit.*), pp. 164–169 and *Literarische Schriften*, pp. 157–212.

A few years after Dostoevsky's death the Russian philosopher Vladimir Sergeyevich Solovyev (1844–1900), who in his youth had been under Slavophile influence and a close friend of Dostoevsky, turned against nationalism in a series of articles on "The National Question in Russia." "In its extreme form it destroys a nation, for it makes it an enemy of mankind, and mankind is always stronger than any one nation. Christianity saves the nations, for it helps them to transcend nationalism." He turned from any kind of Russian mission to the universalism of Christianity. He demanded the application of the moral laws of Christianity to international relations. He reproached the Slavophiles for not recognizing clearly the dark shades of Russian reality. Instead of realizing in a humble spirit of reform that Russia could be improved only by close union with the West, the Slavophiles did not wish to see the evil of "general lawlessness which existed because the concepts of the honor and dignity of the human individual were still very weakly developed in Russia. The principles of human rights and of the absolute value of the personality were essentially Christian and universal principles, but they had been developed historically in Western Europe and had no connection with any peculiar Russian tradition." They had to be implanted in Russia by her contact with Europe. Solovyev regarded the idealization of the Russian people and

Russia's isolation as the greatest obstacles for the progress of life in Russia and as a misfortune for the nation. See his *Ausgewählte Werke*, tr. by Harry Köhler (Jena and Stuttgart 1921–22) vol. IV; George Sacke: *W. S. Solowjews Geschichtsphilosophie* (Königsberg: Ost-Europa Verlag, 1929).

27. Dostoevsky was a violent anti-Semite, using all the vulgar accusations against the Jews. His anti-Semitism took on Hitlerian dimensions in one of his last "notes," written in 1880: "All the Bismarcks, Beaconsfield, the French Republic and Gambetta etc.—all are for me only a façade. Their master, the master of all and of the whole of Europe, is the Jew and his bank. The Jew and the bank now dominate everything: Europe and enlightenment, the whole civilization and socialism—especially socialism, for with its help the Jew will eradicate Christianity and destroy the Christian civilization. Then when nothing will be left but anarchy, the Jew will command everything. For while he preaches socialism, he and the other members of his race remain outside, and while the whole wealth of Europe will be destroyed, the bank of the Jew will remain. Then the Anti-Christ will come and anarchy will reign." *Literarische Schriften* p. 345 f. He devoted part of the March 1877 issue of his *Journal of an Author* to the "Jewish Question," see *Dnevnik* pp. 559–572; *Politische Schriften* pp. 334–371. A. S. Steinberg, "Dostojewski und das Judentum," *Der Jude*, Sonderheft "Judentum und Christentum" (Berlin, 1927) pp. 66–81 explains Dostoevsky's anti-Semitism, as some explained Hitler's anti-Semitism, by the fact that borrowing his idea of a chosen people from the Bible he regarded the Russians as the legitimate heirs of the Jews and the present Jews as usurpers.

28. See Ernest Simmons, *op. cit.*, p. 323. Leontyev foresaw in 1890 a socialist world revolution under the leadership of an autocrat enthroned in Constantinople with the blessing of the Orthodox Church, a "Russian Tsar" organizing the socialist world movement from Constantinople as Constantine had organized Christianity.

Lenin in his "Left Wing Communism, an Infantile Disease" declared that the Bolsheviks would use as barbaric methods as Peter I to overcome the backwardness of the Russian masses. (*Sobranie Sochinenii*, vol. XV, p. 268.) He forgot Russia's great progress since Peter in the fight for liberty and against lawlessness, a progress which the return to Peter's methods undid. Berdyaev has analyzed Bolshevism as Slavophilism inside out. Dostoevsky envisaged the Russian world mission under the banner of primitive Christianity; Bolshevism under the banner of industrial technology. Dostoevsky aimed at the transformation of man; Bolshevism, like Peter, at reform primarily by institutional changes. Dostoevsky believed, like De Maistre and other conservatives, in the evil in man and the redeeming power of suffering. The Bolsheviks share with the classical economists the faith in man's rational concern with his own well-being. Dostoevsky and the Bolsheviks represent extremes in their respective viewpoints, yet there is a deeper affinity in their goal and methods than is sometimes recognized.

INDEX

DATE DUE
